A PLUME BOOK

THE TRUTH ABOUT TRUST

DAVID DeSTENO, PHD, is a professor of psychology at Northeastern University, where he directs the Social Emotions Group. He is coauthor with Piercarlo Valdesolo of the book *Out of Character* and frequently writes about his work for publications including *The New York Times, The Boston Globe,* and *The Atlantic.* He lives in Massachusetts.

Praise for *The Truth About Trust*

"Smart, fun, and informative, *The Truth About Trust* describes the most frightening, most wonderful, and most human thing we do: putting our fates in someone else's hands. This one's worth reading. Trust me."
—Daniel Gilbert, Edgar Pierce Professor of Psychology at
Harvard University and bestselling author of *Stumbling on Happiness*

"Trusting others puts us at risk. Yet failure to trust entails risk as well. The ability to navigate through this minefield successfully is one of life's most valuable assets. DeSteno provides by far the best account of what science has learned about how we do this. *The Truth About Trust* is also a terrific read."
—Robert H. Frank, Henrietta Johnson Louis Professor of
Management at Cornell University and bestselling author of
The Economic Naturalist and *The Darwin Economy*

"*The Truth About Trust* tackles some of the most important and challenging issues in life. Psychologist David DeSteno takes a fresh look at fundamental questions, from gauging the trustworthiness of others to whether you can trust yourself."
—Adam Grant, professor at the Wharton School of the
University of Pennsylvania and bestselling author of *Give and Take*

"In concise prose backed by engaging stories, the author addresses the pros and cons of common issues such as trusting a business transaction, using trust in learning situations, and the need for trust in personal relationships. . . . Fresh insight into a necessary part of everyday life."
—*Kirkus Reviews*

THE
TRUTH
ABOUT
TRUST

How It Determines Success in
Life, Love, Learning, and More

DAVID DeSTENO, PhD

A PLUME BOOK

PLUME
An imprint of Penguin Random House LLC
375 Hudson Street
New York, New York 10014
penguin.com

First published in the United States of America by Hudson Street Press, an imprint
of Penguin Random House LLC, 2014
First Plume Printing 2015
Plume ISBN: 978-0-14-218166-9

 REGISTERED TRADEMARK—MARCA REGISTRADA

THE LIBRARY OF CONGRESS HAS CATALOGED THE HUDSON STREET PRESS HARDCOVER
EDITION AS FOLLOWS:

DeSteno, David.
   The truth about trust : how it determines success in life, love, learning, and more /
David DeSteno, PhD.
    pages cm
   Includes bibliographical references and index.
   ISBN 978-1-59463-123-8 (alk. paper)
   1. Trust.   2. Trust—Social aspects.   I. Title.
   BF575.T7D47 2014
   302'.14—dc23
   2013045481

Set in Berling Roman
Original hardcover design by Eve L. Kirch

146119709

To my wife and daughters

CONTENTS

PREFACE

C_{an} *I trust you?* This question—this set of four simple words—often occupies our minds to a degree few other concerns can. It's a question on which we exert a lot of mental effort—often without our even knowing it—as its answers have the potential to influence almost everything we do. Unlike many other puzzles we confront, questions of trust don't just involve attempting to grasp and analyze a perplexing concept. They all share another characteristic: risk. So while it's true that we turn our attention to many complex problems throughout our lives, finding the answers to most doesn't usually involve navigating the treacherous landscape of our own and others' competing desires. When we're young, asking why the sky is blue or why pizza can't be for dinner every night, though sometimes seeming of equal cosmic importance, necessitates only the transmission of facts to answer. Wondering what exactly a Higgs boson is or whether anything out of the ordinary really happened at Roswell can, it's true, keep the gears of the mind whirring. For most of us, though, attempts to find answers to these questions won't

keep us up at night. And while asking our financial advisor for the
eighth time how to calculate compound interest might require
stepping up our mental math, in and of itself, finding the answer is
fairly formulaic. Bring the word *trust* into the equation, however,
and it suddenly becomes a whole different story.

Trust implies a seeming unknowable—a bet of sorts, if you will.
At its base is a delicate problem centered on the balance between
two dynamic and often opposing desires—a desire for someone else
to meet your needs and his desire to meet his own. Whether a child
can *trust* her parents' answer to her question about the color of the
sky requires estimating not only their scientific bona fides, but also
their desire to appear smart even if they really don't know the answer. Whether she can *trust* them to make pizza for dinner, rather
than simply ask why she can't have it every night, relies on divining
her parents' willingness to uphold their promise to cook in the face
of sudden needs to work late or to take an extra trip to the grocery
store to refill an empty pantry. Whether you can *trust* scientists to
tell you why searching for the Higgs or related subatomic particles
is worth the huge taxpayer expense, rather than ask them to simply
provide a definition for what the little particle is, means pitting
everyone's desire to acquire knowledge that can lead to a better
world against the scientists' related desires to pad their research
budgets. The same logic even applies to trusting yourself. Think
about it. Whether you can *trust* that you'll invest your next paycheck for the long term as opposed to spending it immediately to
purchase the newest iPad is quite different from figuring out how
much money you'll have in twenty years if you do choose to invest
it. Whether we're talking about money, fidelity, social support, business dealings, or secret-keeping, trust isn't just about the facts. It's
about trying to predict what someone will do based on competing interests and capabilities. In short, it's about gambling on your

ability to read someone's mind, even if that someone is your future self.

Like all gambles, though, assessing trustworthiness is an imperfect endeavor; there's always a chance you're going to come up short. Sure, most of us have theories about what signals whether people can be trusted. Do they stumble over their words or avert their gaze? Do they seem too "smooth"? Did they "come through" last time? The problem, of course, is that most of us have also had the all-too-frequent experience of being surprised when our guesses turned out to be wrong. We're not alone, however; deception "experts" and security professionals haven't proved much better. Until very recently, there's been precious little evidence indicating that anyone can accurately determine if someone else can be trusted, especially if they don't know the individual well.

Scientists have spent decades looking for markers of trustworthiness in the body, face, voice, penmanship, and the like, all to little avail. Forget what you see on television; it's all science fiction. If polygraphs were foolproof, we wouldn't need juries. After all, the list of famous criminals who were found guilty based on polygraphs doesn't include the likes of CIA-spy-turned-traitor Aldrich Ames and "Green River Killer" Gary Ridgway, both of whom "passed" this physiological test. Likewise, there wouldn't be a long list of people who had to endure false accusations based on failed polygraph tests—people like Bill Wegerle of Wichita, Kansas, who was initially suspected of being the BTK killer. Entertaining movies and television shows aside, the same criticisms apply to the use of facial expressions. If a single smile or twitch could accurately predict who could be trusted, all negotiations would occur under a spotlight with video recordings. Science, put simply, doesn't yet have all the answers to unlocking the mysteries of trust. Still, finding the keys is of such importance that the business community and the military spend millions of dollars a year trying to do just that. In fact, current knowledge has been so limited that the Intelligence Advanced Research Projects Activity (IARPA)—one of the central research units under the Director of National Intelligence—published a notice in 2009 specifically soliciting scientific proposals to develop new and more accurate methods to gauge a target's trustworthiness.

This state of affairs raises some questions, however: If the need to trust is so central to humans, why is it so difficult to figure out who is worthy of it? Why after millennia of evolutionary development and decades of scientific inquiry are answers only beginning to emerge? To my mind, there are two good reasons. The first, as I've hinted, is that unlike many forms of communication, issues of trust are often characterized by a competition or battle. As we'll see, it's not always an adaptive strategy to be an open book to others, or even to ourselves. Consequently, trying to discern if someone can be trusted is fundamentally different from trying to assess characteristics like mathematical ability. Aptitude in math can be estimated from answers to specific types of problems. Unless the person is a genius trying to pull the wool over your eyes, there shouldn't be any competing interests pushing her answers one way or another. As a result, her answers should, on average, serve as accurate indicators of her true abilities and be solid predictors of how she'll perform in the future. With trust, neither of these facts is necessarily true. As we'll see throughout this book, deciding to be trustworthy depends on the momentary balance between competing mental forces pushing us in opposite directions, and being able to predict which of those forces is going to prevail in any one instance is a complicated business.

The second reason why assessing trustworthiness remains something of an enigma is that, to put it bluntly, we've been going about it in precisely the wrong way. I don't say this lightly, as many great minds have been focused on this topic for decades. Yet it's also the case that this intense focus has led to a tunnel vision of sorts that often results in dead ends among the research community and simplistic expectations among the public. Everyone is looking for the one golden cue that predicts trustworthiness in all situations. Everyone assumes that trustworthiness is a fairly stable trait. Everyone believes that they know when and how issues of trust will affect them. The problem, though, is that they're mostly wrong; trust just doesn't work the way most people think.

How do I know? I could say, "Trust me," but that would defeat the whole point. I'm a scientist, so my goal is to convince you based on findings—not on opinions or testimonials. I should note that I haven't spent my life as a trust researcher, a security professional, or a science writer. To the contrary, I spend my days running a lab focused on one primary theme: how and why emotional states guide social and moral behavior. It's been an endeavor characterized by both great discoveries and never-ending questions. It's one that has allowed my research group to plumb the depths of the best and worst humanity has to offer. Whether we're uncovering the processes that give rise to dishonesty and hypocrisy or shedding light on the wonders of compassion and virtue, the task at hand always requires a lot of creativity and a willingness to go where the data lead. It's also a job that requires a bit of humility. The longer I do it, the more I realize that the best way to answer perennially difficult questions is not to go it alone, but rather to bring the best minds from many different fields together to look at old problems in new ways. This is exactly the perspective that my group brought to studying trust, and it's one that has allowed us to approach the issue with an entirely new perspective.

Why the interest in trust in the first place? Primarily because the more we examined vacillations in emotions and moral behavior, the more we realized that trust often played a central role. Whether it's wondering if a partner might cheat, needing to show that you recognize a responsibility to repay a debt, or desiring to signal that your abilities are up to the challenge, issues of trust rear their head. Jealousy and anger often stem from distrust of the loyalty of a partner. Showing gratitude stands as an efficient way to let people know you realize you owe them a favor. Quick flashes of pride can signal people that they can trust your competence. In short, much of human social life, and the emotions that revolve around it, invokes issues of trust in one way or another. Given this fact, my research group turned its lens on the dual aspects of trust—both how it works and whether and how people can accurately predict who is worthy of it. In so doing, we began an in-depth and novel investigation that traipsed across many traditionally separate fields of inquiry. In the end, what emerged are not only new insights into how to detect the trustworthiness of others, but also an entirely new way to think about how trust influences our lives, our success, and our interactions with those around us.

Still, of all the things I learned, one of the most profound—and the one I hope you'll take from this book—is that trust isn't only a concern that emerges at big moments in our lives. It's not relevant just to signing a contract, making a large purchase, and exchanging wedding vows. Yes, these events certainly affect our lives in important ways and depend on trust, but they're just the tip of the iceberg. Whether we realize it or not, issues of trust permeate our days from the time we're born to the time we die, and it's often what's below the surface of consciousness that can have the greatest influence on a life well lived. Our minds didn't develop in a social vacuum. Humans evolved living in social groups, and that means the minds of our ancestors were sculpted by the challenges posed by living with others on whom they depended. Chief among those challenges was the need to solve dilemmas of trust correctly. And it's precisely because of this fact that the human mind constantly tries to ascertain the trustworthiness of others while also weighing the need to be trustworthy itself. Your conscious experience may not correspond with this fact, but again that's because much of the relevant computations are automatic and take place outside of awareness.

As you'll see in this book, trust influences more than most of us would have imagined. It affects how we learn, how we love, how we spend, how we take care of our health, and how we maximize our well-being. It not only affects our communication and comfort with others, but as our social worlds change from the physical to the virtual, the role of trust and its impact on our interactions will change as well. I invite you to come on the journey with me to find out exactly what we do and don't know about the role of trust in our lives. Along the way, I'll discuss not only work from my lab that bears on the issue, but also the work, views, and opinions of some of the best thinkers on the topic. From economists and computer scientists, to social media mavens and security officials, to physiologists and psychologists, it'll be a wide-ranging journey designed to put the pieces together.

To accomplish this goal, I've loosely divided the book into four parts. The first two chapters will set the stage by laying out the fundamentals—what trust is, why it matters, how it's physiologically embodied, and how we might profitably correct older ways of thinking about it. The next three chapters will explore the far-ranging ways trust impacts us—from how trust develops and influences children's morality and ability to learn, to the ways trust or lack thereof shapes relationships with those we love, to how and why power and money have the potential to alter loyalties. The sixth chapter turns the tables from an examination of how trust affects behavior to the age-old question of whether and how we can

xvi   Preface

actually detect the trustworthiness of others. Here, I'll flip the old view on its head and open a whole new vista from which to explore trust detection. I'll also point out some bugs in the system, thereby arming you to avoid succumbing to them.

From this base, the final section—chapters 7 and 8—will move in a slightly different though no less important direction. Here, I'll consider what all of the preceding means for two relatively novel realms when it comes to trust—realms where a partner isn't exactly who, or even what, you'd usually expect. Can you trust a virtual avatar? A robot? An unknown person on Facebook? How trust works in a world of rapid technological advancement and virtual interaction—a world where the science of trust can be manipulated and used for good or ill with unprecedented precision—is the first theme I'll explore. Consideration of the second realm, however, will require adopting a different focus. Rather than looking outward to decide whom you can trust, I'll ask you to direct your gaze inward to ask what may be a more unsettling, yet in many ways a more fundamental, question for reaching your goals: Can you trust yourself? Although it's true that cooperation and vulnerability require two parties, no one ever said that the two parties had to be different people. To the contrary, the parties can be the same person at different times. Can the present you trust the future you not to cheat on your diet by bingeing on chocolate cake? Not to cheat on an exam? Not to cheat on your spouse? Not to go gambling again?

These last questions highlight a nuance it's important to remember as you proceed through this book. Each of us is never just an observer trying to ascertain whether someone else is to be trusted; we're also targets of observation ourselves. The same forces that determine whether someone else will be honest or loyal also impinge on our own minds. Assessing the trustworthiness of another and acting trustworthy ourselves, then, are simply two sides of the same coin. Understanding how to predict and control the flip of that coin is what this book is all about. And as we close in chapter 9, we'll see exactly why understanding trust matters as we explore the links between trust and resilience in an unvarnished way—a way that quite literally shows how trust, when used correctly, can be one of the most important tools to raise us all from ruin.

THE
TRUTH
ABOUT
TRUST

CHAPTER 1

FUNDAMENTALS, FOIBLES, AND FIXES

What Is Trust, Anyway?

At the most basic level, the need to trust implies one fundamental fact: you're vulnerable. The ability to satisfy your needs or obtain the outcomes you desire is not entirely under your control. Whether a business partner embezzles profits that doom your corporation, a spouse has an affair that wrecks your marriage, or a supposed confidant tweets a personal factoid that ruins your reputation, your well-being, like it or not, often depends on the cooperation of others. These others, of course, have needs of their own: needs to pay for a new car that might push them to skim profits and fix the books; needs to have a more charged love life that might lead them to acts of infidelity; or needs to be popular that might cause them to supply some juicy gossip to their friends at your expense. It's precisely where your needs and theirs diverge that trust comes into play. If each person's goals were the same—in both nature and priority—there would be no potential conflict and thereby no need to trust. Such alignments of needs and desires only rarely occur, however. The social lives of humans are characterized by a never-ending struggle between different types of desires—desires favoring selfish versus selfless goals, desires focused on immediate gratification versus long-term benefit, desires stemming from the conscious versus unconscious minds. Only an overriding threat or an amazing confluence of random factors—what we'd otherwise call pure luck—can result in an exact mirroring of two people's needs and goals at all levels.

Trust, then, is simply a bet, and like all bets, it contains an element of risk. Yet risk is something most of us could do without. Decades of research have shown time and again that humans are generally risk-averse when it comes to making decisions, and with good reason. Risk, by definition, implies the potential for loss, and who likes to lose? In fact, the aversion to loss is so deeply ingrained that our minds have developed a sort of bias in calculating preferences. Losing X amount of something—whether X is dollars, cars, or cupcakes—hurts more in absolute terms than gaining the same amount of X feels pleasurable. There is no absolute value; it depends on whether we're winning or losing. Given an innate risk aversion, the question of why humans trust in the first place is an intriguing one. Why do we take the risk?

The short answer is that we have to. The potential benefits from trusting others considerably outweigh the potential losses *on average*. The ever-increasing complexity and resources of human society—its technological advancement, interconnected social capital, and burgeoning economic resources—all depend on trust and cooperation. Picture for a moment the familiar scene of a NASA mission control during any shuttle launch or space-probe landing. It's a room filled with individuals, each hunched over a computer screen, working in consort to achieve what no single one of them could do alone. Each person, each link in the chain, has a small but central role to play, and each relies on the trustworthiness of the others to do their jobs. If a single individual fails to notice an important data point—whether it involves the pressure in a tank, atmospheric conditions, or the heart rate of an astronaut—the whole enterprise can be in peril. Everyone has to trust the others to do their jobs and do them well if the joint venture is to succeed.

Of course, it's not just amazing feats like space launches where trust plays a role. Trusting others also affects a majority of the everyday things we do, most of which we take for granted. We deposit our money in banks and let the bankers make decisions about how much and to whom they should lend it to help us earn interest. We let our kids go to school assuming that someone else will educate them so that we are freed to earn an income. We divide the labor in running the household so that we can accomplish much more than any one person could on his or her own. The examples are endless, but they all share a common thread: more can be achieved by working together than by working alone. That's why we trust—plain and simple. The need to increase resources—whether they be financial, physical, or social—often necessitates depending on others to cooperate.

As we know all too well, however, not every instance of trust is always well placed. The financial crisis of 2008 is a case in point. People trusted the banks to invest their money wisely, but risky mortgage lending and credit-default swaps provided another classic reminder of the duality of human nature. The banks were taking incredible risks, even betting against the success of their own deals, with money from depositors—money they were entrusted to manage responsibly. The evening news regularly highlights breaches of trust in our schools ranging from administrators falsifying records to teachers abusing students. But here's where the *on average* part of the reason for trust comes into play. *On average*, more is to be gained by trusting others, as the aggregated benefits in the long term tend to outweigh the potential individual losses that come from misplaced trust. But there's the catch: greater benefits *on average* don't mean much when you're the person who loses money, a spouse, or a solid and wholesome education for your child. Still, statistically speaking, trusting usually pays greater dividends in the long run. It's this dynamic tension between the opposing costs and benefits that has shaped how our minds solve the trust equation at different moments in our lives—with respect to both acting trustworthy ourselves and assessing the trustworthiness of others.

If you truly wanted to avoid the risks inherent in trusting other people while still benefiting from cooperation, there's really only one route: transparency. If you could actually verify the actions of another, the risks, by definition, become lower. In fact, if you think you can't trust a potential partner at all, transparency is the only way to go. Think of the classic image from the last crime drama you saw on television. Two criminals need to complete an exchange. What do they say? Usually it's some variant of, "Open the suitcases and we'll exchange them on the count of three." They each want to see—to know for sure—that the other has the money, drugs, kidnapped person, or similar valuable. They also want to make sure that they don't give up their prize without acquiring their desired object at the same time. In such cases, trust is completely out of the picture.

The problem, of course, is that the ability to verify actions isn't always possible—a limitation that can occur for two main reasons. The first involves effort. Verification is onerous; it takes time and energy. The Transportation Safety Administration (TSA) has to verify that no one is boarding a plane with a weapon, hence long airport lines. The mortgage company has to verify that you can pay your bills, hence the mounds of paperwork. And that's just when we're considering one person at a time. Imagine how difficult and costly it would be to run a business if an employer had to verify every action taken by a subordinate. Imagine how much time you'd have to spend watching hidden Web cams in your home if you wanted to verify that your spouse wasn't cheating on you or your babysitter wasn't stealing from you. One reason, then, that true verification directly constrains resource accumulation is that it limits the time and energy that could be devoted to other endeavors.

The second reason verifiability isn't always feasible is that there can be a time lag—a delay between the exchanges. You invest money now expecting a future return. You help a friend move now expecting that she'll help you move when your lease is up. Needs don't always arise in tandem, which means that if people were only willing to act in a trustworthy manner when that trust was simultaneously repaid, nothing much would get done that required mutual support. Consequently, someone has to be willing to take the risk to be the first to invest money, time, or other resources, hoping that the partner will then keep up her end of the deal at a future point. As my friend and collaborator the economist Robert Frank often puts it, solving this commitment problem is one of the central dilemmas of human life. If no one were willing to trust and subsequently honor commitments, human society, as we know it, would cease to exist.

Frank's focus on the challenges posed by delayed interactions is an important one for understanding how trust works. It clearly shows why complete transparency is often impractical. Without delayed reciprocity—the process by which we reap rewards after initially extending ourselves to help others—cooperation would be hamstrung. We'd only help those who could help us back in the here and now—a situation that wouldn't be very efficient. Every time you needed help you'd have to find someone else who was also in need, to ensure that the mutual problems would be solved simultaneously. As a result, the age-old question of whether you could count on a person when you needed him would go right out the window.

It's precisely because of such substantial, and sometimes impossible, constraints that trust becomes necessary. Without it, productive cooperation would be hard to come by. So, we trust at times; we really don't have much of a choice. But once we leave the world of verifiability, we inevitably come across more selfish behavior and at the same time face greater difficulty in predicting who will show it. It's not the case that honesty and loyalty will forever disappear without transparency. As we'll see, a dynamic equilibrium between trustworthy and untrustworthy behavior will eventually result. Where that equilibrium settles, though, is flexible, and being able to predict it is what much of this book is about.

The Fundamentals: What's a Prisoner to Do?

Whether you're a head of state, CEO, or kid on the playground, situations involving trust share a common structure. Ultimately, your outcomes are intertwined with those of your partner, with success or failure often depending on each person's best guess as to what the other will do. Although it's surely true that the gravity of the objective consequences will vary, the fundamental nature—the underlying mathematics of the situation, if you will—remain the same. Different combinations of trustworthy and/or untrustworthy behavior can lead to different magnitudes of gains or losses in metrics ranging from quantities of nuclear arms to hours of detention at school.

Consider the following situation. Jack and Kate get sent to the principal's office for trying to steal their teacher's answer key. Although Jack and Kate did plot the theft, the evidence—though sufficient to get them in trouble—is still a bit murky with respect to who exactly did what. To get a better picture of culpability, the principal separates them and presents the same deal to each. Let's start with Jack. If he is willing to incriminate Kate by squealing while Kate continues to remain silent, he'll get a lighter detention sentence (one day) than will Kate (four days). If they both remain silent, the ability to decisively convict one or the other will be lessened; consequently, they'll both serve a moderate detention (two days). However, if both Jack and Kate implicate the other (remember, Kate is being offered the same deal), they'll each serve slightly less time than if only one is convicted (three days each), since they at least were willing to assist in the investigation.

What should Jack do? Mathematically, the answer is pretty clear: he should rat on Kate. To see why, take a look at the table below. If Jack implicates Kate (i.e., defects on Kate) and Kate keeps

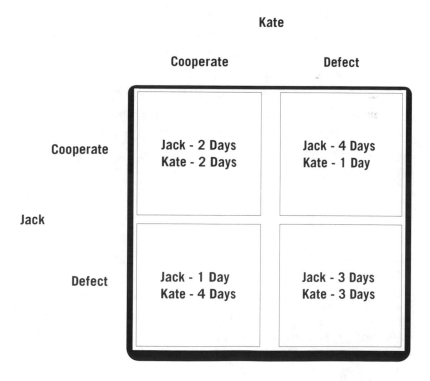

quiet (i.e., cooperates with Jack), he gets one day of detention; he would receive two days if he, too, holds his tongue. Now, if Kate defects, it still makes sense for Jack to rat on her. In this case, Jack would get three days of detention, as opposed to four if he remained loyal to her. Defecting, then, makes perfect sense. It's what game theorists call a dominant strategy—one that always leads to the best results for an individual irrespective of what the other person does.

There's one last aspect to consider, though. Kate is mulling over the same deal at the same time, and Jack knows it. This simple fact alters the whole picture. Although the strategy of defecting is the best one to follow from each individual's perspective, as it maximizes gain regardless of what one's partner decides, it doesn't always lead to the best outcome when fates are joined. If both defect, thereby following the strategy that is in each person's best interest individually, they both end up with a pretty bad outcome: three days in detention. If, however, they both cooperate with each other by remaining silent, they end up only serving two days apiece. And there's the rub. If you can trust a partner—if you know you'll each accept a small sacrifice on the other's behalf—both of you can end up better off than if you each followed a strategy to maximize your own self-interest without regard to the other.

The structure of this problem—referred to as the *prisoner's dilemma* (PD)—was first formalized by game theorists Merrill Flood and Melvin Dresher at RAND Corporation and later formalized by the mathematician Albert Tucker. The interesting aspect of the dilemma—and one that accounts for its long-standing use—is that it captures the essence of the trade-offs inherent in many decisions to cooperate by showing how loyalty can lead to better outcomes than simple self-interest. Its popularity as a tool for scientific investigation also stems from its portability to the lab. Although it reflects the dynamics of decisions that can hold great costs, it can be transformed in a way that allows trust to be studied ethically. For example, the costs and benefits can be made to involve tens of dollars provided by an experimenter instead of thousands of dollars in profit from real business deals. Using variations on this theme, the PD has been utilized to study trust and cooperation in many, many realms.

The fundamental question, of course, is what strategy works best in life? To find out, the political scientist Robert Axelrod decided to compare different strategies for interacting in PDs that were iterative—situations, like real life, where you're given multiple opportunities to defect or cooperate with others who have been trustworthy or selfish in the past. There was a problem with this plan, though. How could he accomplish this goal when he not only needed players that differed in dispositions such as a willingness to forgive past transgressions, be vengeful, and be trustworthy, but also needed them to interact across hundreds of rounds? Finding the best strategy for the long run, after all, would require comparing outcomes across many, many instances. In a stroke of brilliance, Axelrod decided to conduct a tournament where the players would be computer programs designed to behave as different types of people might. He would then run simulations consisting of hundreds of trials each where the programs played against each other in a round-robin, all the while gaining or losing points determined by the structure of the PD.

Axelrod was under no illusion that he had all the answers, so he invited different researchers to submit programs. The "contestants" varied widely in nature. Some programs were vengeful, never cooperating again with a partner who defected. Others showed some level of forgiveness, only defecting on a partner after being cheated twice. Still others possessed even greater levels of complexity. At the end of the tournament, though, one fact became clear. The superior performing strategies all tended to share two properties.

One was an initial willingness to be trustworthy; they never were the first to defect. Another was to be provokable; they were willing to respond to untrustworthy actions in kind. Which instantiation of these guiding principles worked best? The answer, as well as the overall winner, was quite plain. It was an exceedingly simple strategy: tit-for-tat.

As its name suggests, tit-for-tat (TFT) means just that: start out being fair but then copy your partner's actions. If she remains fair, so do you on your next turn. If she defects, then you defect on the next round. While it's true that TFT may not have beaten every other strategy in every round of the round-robin tournament, it fared the best overall; it was a consistent silver medalist in a sea of one-shot wonders. The analogue to human trust and cooperation is clear. If each different strategy represented a different person's tactics (e.g., hostile, cheating, forgiving), TFT provided the best benefits on average against the whole lot. Precisely because TFT allows a willingness to forgive and regain trust, it can avoid entering death spirals when used with partners who employ different strategies. Unlike a strategy that assumes a broken trust should always entail retribution, TFT allows for a partner to be redeemed through her willingness to cooperate again.

Based on Axelrod's simulations, then, playing the game of trust seems pretty simple. Be fair to start, but return favors in kind; in the end, you'll maximize your gains. In truth, though, life's not that simple. Advanced as these simulations were for their time, they differ from true human interaction in an important way. Computers are perfect and rational; humans are not. Sometimes we break a trust when we don't intend to do so, meaning that sometimes we slight others by mistake. We've all been there. We don't complete our part of a team assignment on time because we misremembered the due date, or we don't buy a lottery ticket from the neighbor's kid even though he remembers us saying we would (when actually he's got us confused with the other neighbor). Simply put, human social interaction leaves room for error. Our actions aren't always clear indicators of our intentions; it's a noisy system. And as it turns out, "noise" can cause some real problems.

Consider the following: two well-intentioned people adopt the TFT strategy for deciding whether to be cooperative with each other. All goes well for a while, but then one of these unintended slights occurs. Person A believes that Person B "defected" on her (whether defection here means intentionally revealing a secret, skimming profits, not working hard enough, etc.), when in actuality Person B's behavior was accidental (i.e., she didn't intend to act in an untrustworthy manner). Assuming they both adhere to TFT, the death spiral begins. While tit-for-tat can recover from defections when used against many strategies, this isn't the case when it's used against itself. The result is that noise in the system can doom what otherwise appeared to be the superior strategy.

Among the first to recognize this problem was the physicist Robert May, whose work subsequently led the mathematicians Martin Nowak and Karl Sigmund to explore its significance for comparing cooperative strategies. Nowak and Sigmund, in ingenious fashion, decided to tweak Axelrod's simulation to bring it closer to a model of true human interaction and evolutionary development. They made two fundamental changes. First, they allowed for noise in the system by way of "mutations"; different contestant algorithms would come into being at random and choose to cooperate or defect with others based on probabilities. Second, they allowed these mutants to evolve; their simulation had a generational aspect. Following a basic law of natural selection, contestants that did better in earlier rounds propagated more in successive rounds. In this way, the team could model the dynamics of trust and cooperation in an evolutionary sense. The result forever altered understanding of how trust and fairness flow in a society.

Across Nowak and Sigmund's many simulations, a general pattern typically emerged. One strategy—always defect—initially took the lead. This fact is not entirely surprising, as I already noted that defection is the dominant strategy in an individual game. So, for about the first hundred generations of the simulations, the defectors ruled. They exploited the initial kindness of the more trusting tit-for-tatters and their kin and reaped the benefits of selfishness. Over time, however, the situation changed. While TFTs always performed more poorly against the untrustworthy defectors, as they always ended up getting conned before they learned not to trust, they always performed better when playing other TFTs, where the initial benefits of cooperation were smaller, but the relationship would remain loyal and stable. Over the long run, the TFTs—whose population had at first been driven dangerously low—would regroup and prosper, overtaking the cheating defectors.

What Nowak and Sigmund didn't expect at the outset, however, was that TFT wouldn't end up being the dominant strategy. That prize went to its cousin, a strategy the duo referred to as generous tit-for-tat (GTFT). As its name implies, GTFT was slightly more forgiving than TFT; it would choose to cooperate with some small probability even when facing defection. For example, it might choose to cooperate 25 percent of the time when facing an individual who had previously been untrustworthy. This extra bit of forgiveness functioned to overcome some of the noise mentioned earlier. Sure, sometimes being forgiving led to exploitation, but other times it allowed a loyal relationship to blossom—a relationship where the initial defection was a mistake.

Perhaps the most important point, though, to come from Nowak and Sigmund's simulations was the realization that even GTFT wasn't always best. Winners, at some point, almost always fall, and so did GTFT. The problem was that as GTFT continued to dominate, the population as a whole became more and more trustworthy. Once everyone is a saint, no one expects to be cheated; everyone cooperates. As a result, the situation becomes ripe for the dishonest. It's a con man's paradise; everyone trusts by default. When a random mutation favoring defection again emerges, it's initially unstoppable. The defectors propagate and gain dominance, pushing more cooperative strategies almost to extinction, only then to decline as the trusting and cooperative reemerge. The insight here is to realize that trust isn't about finding the perfect single strategy—there isn't one. It's about realizing that selfishness and cooperation, disloyalty and trustworthiness, exist in an ever-changing equilibrium. It's always been that way; it always will.

Angie Likes Him

Okay, I'll admit it; I hate contractors. When my elderly parents needed to have work done on their house, they asked me to help find someone to do it. Unfortunately for me, though, building and construction are not my forté. That means I was left trying to decide which contractor to hire not only without having dealt with any of them before, but also without a knowledge base with which to evaluate their claims. To this day, I have no idea what the difference is between drywall and blue board. As you can imagine, then, I had no idea which contractor would be the most trustworthy in terms of quoted price and completing the job on schedule. It's a matter of degree, of course, as these elements never go as planned in any construction job. Still, I wanted to help my parents do business with the person I felt was being the most honest. What did I do? Like anyone in the same position, I asked around.

This simple example—one that most of you have no doubt

experienced—shines a light on one of the shortcomings of the models of trust and cooperation we've been discussing. TFT and the like all depend on direct experience with a partner. Yes, it's true that in cases where you don't know what the other person will do, the mathematical models suggest trusting at first. After all, while it's true that trusting someone you don't know can end up in a single loss, it's also true that not being willing to trust can prevent you from finding an honest partner who, over years of cooperation, could provide massive gains—gains that when aggregated often outweigh a single loss. But here again, these models aren't of much assistance when you really don't want to get taken advantage of in the here and now, or, for that matter, when you have several potential partners—or contractors—from which to choose. If I were going to make the best choice for my parents, I needed to resist the opportunity to trust the first contractor who showed up in favor of doing some homework. So, as I just noted, I checked into their reputations. I asked friends; I asked neighbors; I asked Angie's List.

As you might easily guess, the ability to predict if someone you don't know will be trustworthy offers immense benefits. It increases the odds that your decision to work with them will lead to certain gain over certain loss. It completely circumvents the problem posed even by relatively successful strategies like TFT: the possibility of a loss on the first encounter. It also solves the problems posed by complex societies where specialization and wider commerce are the norm. While I may not know whether a contractor is trying to cheat me by using an inferior product, the people whose kitchen and bath he fixed two years ago will. Likewise, while I can use the Internet to get bids from several potential contractors, I can also use the Internet to find reviews of their honesty from people I don't even know.

Reputation, then, is often viewed as a prime method for solving problems of trust. It's a form of what is often termed *indirect reciprocity*—a mechanism by which one person can benefit from another's experiences. If a contractor acted in good faith with one person, this action can be construed as an indicator that he will do so with another. Similarly, if he cut corners once, most believe he's likely to do it again. And if one assumes that accurate reputational information is available, choosing to always trust someone, even on the first encounter, suddenly becomes a less adaptive strategy.

Reputation also possesses a second benefit. It not only provides insight into whether you should trust another person, it increases the odds of trustworthy behavior in general. Everyone becomes subject to what economists call the shadow of the future. If you cheat someone, that reputation will precede you. Word will spread that you are not to be trusted, and your future gains, in terms of both economic and social capital, will rapidly diminish. And in the digital age we now inhabit, access to this information is becoming ever easier.

Foibles and Fixes: What's Right, What's Wrong, and How We Begin to Fix It

As the preceding shows, decades' worth of research on trust has made progress in showing how and why cooperative and cheating strategies can develop, how they can come to dominate and recede in populations over time, and how the use of reputation can solve some of the problems posed by initial decisions to trust people you might not know. This is all well and good at the thirty-four-thousand-foot level—the level at which one might survey different societies on a flyover—but on the ground, where individuals are engaged daily in the battle to succeed, it not only masks much of what's going on, it also fails to conceptualize some of the underlying processes in the right way. In short, the notion of what trust is and how it works needs a bit of revision if we're going to progress in our understanding of it. The view that has long been embraced by scientists and the public alike is based on some principles that, in my opinion, are at best poorly integrated and at worst just plain wrong. Broadly speaking, these problems center on four errors.

Reputation Isn't What It Used to Be

Reputation refers to a person's characteristics, usually involving morality (or lack thereof). A person can, for example, be categorized as an honest broker or a cheat, as being a paragon of virtue or being morally compromised. These labels usually derive from assembling a person's past actions into a composite, although there often tends to be an asymmetry in how this is done. If a supposed good person behaves badly even once, most assume he's morally bereft deep down inside; his good actions simply serve as a façade to hide his otherwise devious nature. Yet, for some reason, it doesn't work the other way. If a supposed bad person does one good thing, most tend to assume it was an aberrant event; it doesn't change the view of his moral bona fides. But this logical inconsistency isn't the problem with reputation; it's merely a symptom.

The primary concern with reputation is that we assume it represents a set of stable traits. If someone is honest, she'll always be honest. If he cheated once, he'll cheat again. In essence, we assume a person's character is etched in stone. Although it intuitively feels right, scientific data from the past two decades, both from my lab and the labs of others, clearly show that human morality is quite variable. Whether we're talking about compassion and altruism, generosity and fairness, infidelity and jealousy, or hypocrisy and gam-

bling, empirical data show time and again that the latitude of everyone's moral behavior is greater than most expect. It's not that human
nature has changed. It's always been this way. It's just that now
we're coming to recognize it.

When I first tell people this hard truth, they often find it difficult to believe. They'll point to the fact that their Uncle Ben or
friend Claire, whom they've known since childhood, has always
been loyal and honest, or, conversely, is someone with whom you
wouldn't trust your money. This may well be true, but not because
Uncle Ben or Claire the friend, possesses some innate deep-seated
character trait that solely dictates moral behavior. To the contrary,
it's because the normal situations in which they usually find themselves haven't changed dramatically in terms of incentives. Consistency in moral behavior results not from an essence or trait engraved
on our minds or souls, but rather from an undisturbed balance between competing sets of mental mechanisms. As long as the general
benefits of situations we encounter in our daily lives don't alter the
relative payoffs for these different mechanisms, our resulting moral
behavior appears pretty much status quo. Change the payoffs, either through altering the objective situation or through altering the
underlying mental computations that determine them, and behavior changes accordingly. Of course, the amount the payoffs need to
change in order to alter trustworthy behavior may vary from person
to person. Yet it's also true that no one's level of trustworthiness is
fixed; everyone, whether they know it or not, has their price. Our
minds are always computing costs and benefits.

As a scientist, I don't expect you to believe this fact just because
I say it; like me, you should demand to see some proof in the form
of data. And while I could readily provide endless examples in many
realms of morality, this is a book about trust, so let's focus there.
Adam Smith, in his rightfully famous tome *The Theory of Moral*

Sentiments, argued that humans possess innate responses, often in the form of intuitions or emotions, that push them to deal kindly and fairly with others. It was an admittedly prescient view, but one that for the longest time had no empirical backing. My students and I reasoned, however, that if feelings like gratitude did function as Smith suggested, momentary fluctuations in them should alter people's trustworthiness without their even being aware of it.

To put this view to the test, we designed an experiment using a variant of the PD known as the Give Some Game (GSG). It works as follows. Each person gets four tokens. Each token is worth $1 to the holder, but $2 to a partner. Like the PD, the GSG pits a goal of maximizing gains for oneself at another's expense against a goal of smaller and equal profit for both partners. Here, the most trustworthy choice would be for each person to exchange all four of her tokens with her partner. In this way, each would convert $4 into $8, thereby doubling their money. Maximizing individual gain, however, requires a different strategy. You give nothing to your partner hoping she'll be cooperative and give you her tokens. If she gives you all of hers, you end up tripling your money to $12 and she ends up with nothing; you've profited by taking advantage of her trust. The big benefit of the GSG over the PD is that it allows for gradations of selfishness as a function of how many coins a player chooses to give; it's not an all-or-nothing decision.

Now that we had a task to measure trustworthy behavior, we needed a way to alter people's emotional states before they played. To accomplish this goal, we constructed a situation that our participants would see as real, but in actuality was designed to evoke in them feelings of gratitude—one of Smith's moral sentiments. To make a long story short, we preprogrammed their computer to crash, thereby appearing to lose all the tedious work they had been completing in the lab. While the experimenter informed them they'd have to start all over, a confederate (an individual who participants believed to be another participant but who actually worked for us) would walk over and miraculously fix the problematic computer through a set of staged steps, thereby relieving true participants from having to complete the onerous work again.

At this point, almost every participant spontaneously expressed feelings of gratitude as well as reported feeling grateful on subsequent measures of emotional states. In the control condition—where we didn't want to induce any feelings of gratitude—the computer didn't crash. Here, confederates simply engaged participants in a short conversation to equate the level of familiarity.

We then moved participants and confederates to different rooms to play the GSG. There was one more catch, though. Half of the participants played the GSG with the confederate with whom they had just interacted; the other half played with a complete stranger. What happened? Let's consider the conditions where people played with the confederate they knew. In the control condition, where people were familiar with the other but didn't have any reason to feel grateful, they chose to give two tokens on average to their partners. In essence, they split the difference between acting completely trustworthy and completely selfish. When they were feeling grateful, however, they became more cooperative, giving significantly more. In so doing, they were not only acting more trustworthy themselves, but also making themselves more vulnerable to loss if their partner didn't cooperate.

Now, you're probably thinking that this experiment doesn't disprove the import of reputation. If anything, it suggests reputation might play a central role, as the partner in the GSG just proved herself to be a compassionate and trustworthy soul; she helped participants out when they needed it. Fair enough, but now let's consider the other two conditions, the ones where people played the GSG with someone they never saw, much less knew. *The results are exactly the same.* If participants were feeling grateful, they offered significantly more tokens to the partner. Remember, they didn't know this person from Adam. They had no reason to expect him to be more trustworthy; yet those who felt grateful behaved more co-operatively with him than did their neutral counterparts. Not only that, but how much they were willing to cooperate—to favor smaller joint gains over asymmetric, selfish profit—exactly tracked the level of gratitude they were experiencing at the moment.

What these data show is that simple, momentary fluctuations in emotional states can alter a person's trustworthiness. The same goes for social stress. Recent work by the psychologist Bernadette von Dawans, the behavioral economist Ernst Fehr, and colleagues examined how experiencing social anxiety and discomfort affects trust. They exposed half of their participants to the Trier Social Stress Test, which requires individuals to engage in public speaking before an audience. Unbeknownst to participants, however, the audience consists of people who have been trained to sit silently and stone-faced. They offer no signs of interest, encouragement, or agreement, leaving the poor speaker to get more and more nervous about his level of social approval. Following completion of the Trier or not (i.e., the control condition), participants played an economic game that, like the GSG, pitted desires to be trustworthy against desires to gain money at a partner's expense. What the researchers found was that experiencing social stress increased trustworthy behavior fairly dramatically; those who were socially anxious increased their rate of cooperation by approximately 50 percent.

It's not just feeling states that alter trustworthiness, either. Work by the behavioral economists and psychologists Francesca Gino, Michael Norton, and Dan Ariely demonstrated that it could be something as simple as what you're wearing. They designed an experiment, which they framed as a product evaluation study, where participants thought they were comparing types of sunglasses. The catch was that the experimenters told some of the people that the ones they liked were true designer brands, while they told others that they preferred knockoffs; the participants couldn't tell on their own, as the labels had been removed. The researchers then had the participants take a timed math test and self-report their scores. The resulting behavior was as surprising as it was unsettling. Seventy-one percent of people who were wearing the knockoffs cheated by inflating their scores (the researchers had a way to access the original worksheets people used to solve the problems); only 30 percent of people wearing the authentic sunglasses did the same. The seeming innocuous act of putting on knockoffs brought to mind the notion of inauthenticity, which, in turn, greatly increased the propensity to lie.

Taken as a whole, what these and numerous experiments like them confirm is that a person's trustworthiness can't be reliably predicted from his past actions. If we're to maximize odds for deciding whom we can trust, reputation clearly isn't the sole answer. Again, this doesn't mean that morality in general, or trust in particular, are random. To the contrary, both follow basic principles. It's just that those principles derive from competing mental mechanisms as opposed to stable patterns stamped into our psyches. A reputation of trustworthiness, then, is an illusion. Yes, stability in how trustworthily people behave can exist, but it derives from fairly unchanging environs where the competing mechanisms remain in détente. When it comes to trust, then, the question we ask shouldn't be: Is he trustworthy? It should be: Is he trustworthy right now?

In the End, It All Comes Down to Me

I've suggested that trustworthiness, or lack thereof, in any given situation results from the current balance between competing mental mechanisms. But what are those mechanisms? When most people think about trust, they conceive of it as a tug-of-war between motives for selfishness (i.e., evil) and selflessness (i.e., good). Cheating on a fiancée or skimming profits can let a person satisfy selfish desires for emotional, physical, or economic gain. At the same time, these behaviors stand in opposition to selfless desires to aid a business partner or remain true to a romantic partner—actions that make others happy. Following this logic, most people tend to view dilemmas of trust as a competition between mental mechanisms personified by the motif of the two shoulder-sitters—an angel on one side and a devil on the other, both whispering intently into your ears.

The problem with this view is fairly clear. Scientists have long recognized that the evolutionary pressures that have sculpted our minds work to maximize our own outcomes, not those of unrelated others. Why, then, should the mind possess mechanisms focused on being nice to strangers? The answer is to be found in the basic fact that humans are a social species; we prosper through cooperation. The upshot of this truism is that our own fitness—our abilities to garner resources and provide for offspring—is increased through "selfless" acts of supporting others. As the evolutionary biologist Robert Trivers argued decades ago, we engage in altruism and trustworthy behavior because it ensures that we will not just be the givers of resources, but also the beneficiaries of others' resources when we need them. Put simply, we scratch others' backs today to get ours scratched tomorrow. Of course, this raises the thorny issue of whether it's really fair to categorize an act as selfless if one is also a beneficiary of it, but that's a long and tortured argument better saved for another day.

If, however, these competing mechanisms can't easily be categorized as selfish or selfless, then what does distinguish them? To my mind, the answer is to be found in two places. If we go back and reconsider the long history of work on the PD and the wonderful mathematical models by scholars like Martin Nowak, what we readily glean is that success is often defined with respect to the *long term*. Successful strategies personified as individuals are the ones that end up with the greatest accumulation of resources over hundreds and hundreds of interactions. Being trustworthy as opposed to defecting by following TFT or GTFT maximizes gains as long as one keeps an eye to the future. These strategies don't maximize gains in the short term. Remember that exploitative strategies such as *always defect* were consistently ahead in resource accumulation at first; in the short run, they maximize your rewards.

In my view, almost all of human morality can be understood to involve trade-offs between short- and long-term gains. Cases of trust are no different; they, too, broadly speaking, involve what scientists term *intertemporal choice*—decisions that hold different consequences as time unfolds. Consider it this way. A decision to be untrustworthy can let you acquire significant resources in the moment. If time stopped now, the money you took at your partner's expense or the satisfaction you gained by cheating on your boyfriend would greatly increase your economic or hedonic capital. However, if the other person finds out, your outcomes in the long run are in jeopardy; what seemed like a sure gain in the moment may lead to less optimal results over time. If you're viewed as untrustworthy, it will be harder to find people who will hire you, marry you, or support you. Why not, then, always favor actions like trustworthiness that maximize long-term outcomes? Simple. Evolutionarily speaking, not everyone makes it to the long term; death can come sooner than most people think. If all your energies go into maximizing benefits that will only pay dividends twenty years from now, an untimely end can wipe away everything. Additionally, it's also the case that not all selfish acts are always discovered. If no one finds out, your long-term prospects aren't diminished; you can have your cake and eat it, too.

This perspective on trust allows us to redefine the competing mental mechanisms that proverbially sit on our shoulders from an angel and devil to an ant and grasshopper. In the old Aesop's fable, the ant signified concerns for the future as it toiled away to store enough food for the winter. The grasshopper signified the opposite; it focused on pleasures in the here and now as it whiled away the summer enjoying itself. It's the same with the mechanisms that shape trustworthiness. Some mechanisms are focused on benefits in the moment; others are focused on benefits in the future. Our minds are continually attempting to find the right balance between these two oppositional forces. Where that balance is at any given instant—leaning more toward one side or the other—will determine how trustworthily we behave. As we saw earlier, feelings of gratitude favor long-term mechanisms; they increase the odds that we'll behave in ways that build relationships. Bringing to mind concepts of anonymity or inauthenticity does the opposite; those concepts increase the dominance of short-term concerns.

Conceptualizing trust as a dilemma of intertemporal choice also solves another problem—one that is not often recognized but, in my view, is exceedingly important to deal with if we're to understand how trust really works: How do you know if you can trust yourself? By this I don't mean divining if you'll abide by an agreement with someone else. To the contrary, I mean figuring out if you'll abide by an agreement with *yourself*. We've all been there. *I promise I won't give in and eat another donut tonight. I promise I'll put money from my next paycheck into my retirement account. I promise this is the last pack of cigarettes I'm going to buy.* Sometimes we honor such promises; sometimes we don't.

Models of trust built on competing drives to be selfish or selfless have virtually nothing to say about trusting ourselves. They can't; by definition, both parties in the transaction are you. However, if we adopt a view of trust based on intertemporal choice, the model applies equally well whether we're talking about trusting someone else or ourselves. In this framework, there are still two parties involved—the present you and the future you. Their outcomes are somewhat joined, of course, but each can also maximize its own desires. Trusting yourself to keep to your diet and not eat the donut later tonight is a bet that the future you will be able to control itself. Trusting yourself to invest the money from your next paycheck is placing faith in the future you to have ample willpower. In each situation, you're counting on the future you to be able to take the long-term view and not give in to short-term temptations when that future time arrives.

One central aspect of trustworthiness, then, becomes the ability to self-regulate—to resist immediate desires in favor of those that possess long-term benefit. In fact, recent research provides an interesting nugget of support for this view. The psychologists Francesca Righetti and Catrin Finkenauer conducted several experiments where they presented individuals with potential partners with whom they would play a trust game. Participants were given a certain sum of money that they could then give some portion of to an "investor" who, upon receiving it, would always triple its value. There was a catch, though. The potential investors could choose how much, if any, they wanted to give back. In this framework, giving any funds to the investor is a sign of trust; the more you give, the more you're willing to trust him, as the rules don't require him to return the investment, let alone the profits.

The researchers designed the set of possible investors to appear as if they differed in stores of willpower. Capitalizing on the established fact that fatigue reduces self-control, the scientists manipulated how exhausted and overworked the various investors appeared to be. What they found clearly supported the notion that, unconsciously at least, our minds sense that the ability for self-control matters for trustworthiness. Study participants not only indicated that they viewed exhausted investors as less trustworthy, they also agreed to give them less funds to invest.

Who Wants to Be a Statistic?

The third problem with current views of trust work is that, as we've seen, they usually all involve statements that end with the words *on average*. Now, I don't know about you, but I don't like to think of my outcomes as a statistic. If choosing to trust someone and cooperate is a better strategy on average, it necessarily means that it wasn't a better strategy for everyone. Someone, somewhere, got the short end of the stick. It's a fundamental rule of life: if someone wins big, someone else doesn't. So while using mathematical models and iterated PDs to determine what decision strategies characterize successful populations and which of them give individuals the best outcomes across spans of time can be informative at times, it's cold comfort when you're standing face-to-face with someone to whom you're about to sign away a chunk of your life's savings. At such moments you don't care much about what strategies work best on average, you care about what you should do right now.

As I described earlier, traditional models of trust solve this dilemma in one of two ways. First, if you know a potential partner through past interactions or reputation, use that information to calculate odds for how trustworthy she'll be. Second, if you don't know anything about the potential partner, then it's probably best just to trust her unless you can be absolutely sure you'll never interact with her again and no one will find out about your defection. Although the first option appears logical, I've just shown you (and will continue to do so throughout this book) that past actions and reputation aren't good predictors for how trustworthy a person will be in any future moment. If you follow that fact to its logical conclusion, you enter the realm of the second option—you know nothing about a potential partner, so you might as well trust him. Yet if this route were really the best way to go, we wouldn't often feel that pit in our stomachs when deciding whether we can trust the salesman or new business partner in front of us. Our minds would simply impel us to trust strangers. But that's not what we feel; it's not how the mind works. When we're put in a position where we have to trust someone, especially someone new, we get hunches— intuitions, if you will—regarding their trustworthiness. We do the same for those we know, too, but we often make the mistake of failing to attend to such hunches, preferring to make decisions by reputation. Many times, though, that can be a costly mistake. Using reputation may appear to work at times, but that's no guarantee it will always do so.

The reason we have these intuitions about others' trustworthiness is that our minds are striving to optimize our outcomes by leveraging whatever information is available in the moment. If you think about it, this quest for accuracy makes great sense. The ability to gauge another's trustworthiness, even at slightly better than chance levels, would offer huge potential for enhancing resources. It would replace the problems caused by the vagaries of reputation and increase the odds for success in any given situation. In essence, it would be like entering a casino with your own loaded dice— loaded such that snake eyes were less likely to occur than other possible combinations.

There are good theoretical reasons to expect that humans should possess a capacity to assess the trustworthiness of others. Yet there has been very little evidence to confirm it. For decades, scientists have searched for the clues without much success. I realize that there are many books that promise to teach you how to read everything from intelligence to deceptiveness from body language. With respect to trust, and for that matter with respect to a majority of motivations and feelings, these books are of questionable value at best. Scientific understanding of how nonverbal cues and physiological markers might be used to identify feelings and motives is being rapidly redefined. Traditional methods for using cues to assess emotions, trust, and deception have been shown to be virtually useless. Even current programs developed by the government to identify possible threats using nonverbal behavior possess no strong empirical validity.

The state of the art in trust detection is in fact so poor that, as I noted in the preface, IARPA—a major research unit for the Department of Homeland Security—announced a funding initiative in 2009 to jump-start novel approaches for assessment. What's most interesting about this initiative is that a primary goal is to fund research to look for markers of trust in observers' bodies and minds, not in those of actors. That is, the initiative is designed to examine and magnify any subtle markers in people that suggest they believe they can trust a person they're viewing. In essence, the program works on the assumption that the human mind can sense a signal of trustworthiness from others, but that this signal may be a relatively weak one that can often get lost in the noise. The trick, then, becomes finding a way to extract the signal from the noise.

The question, of course, is why we haven't yet identified the signal. To my mind, there are two principal reasons. First, like many signals, it's meant to be subtle. The signal for trust shouldn't be an

easy one to read. Walking around with a big *T* on your head to sym-
bolize you'd be trustworthy would open you up to all types of exploitation. As a consequence, we can expect people to play their
cards close to the vest, revealing the signal only through extended
and dynamic interactions. Second, we've been looking for the signal
in entirely the wrong way. There won't be one "golden" cue for trust
like an averted gaze or a fake smile. Signals will consist of many
discrete elements that can only be correctly determined within
context. Like the individual sounds that make up speech, different
cues will have different meanings as a function of the other cues
with which they're paired.

It's Not Just Integrity, and It's Not Just Rational

One of the best parts of my job is that I have opportunities to chat
with people from a variety of backgrounds who have one important
feature in common: they have their fingers on the pulse of their
respective fields. So it was that I found myself one summer after-
noon sitting across the table from Adam Russell, who is a program
director at IARPA and heads its initiative on trust. Now, Adam is
one of those people who is as charming as he is intimidating. He's a
cultural anthropologist by training, a Rhodes scholar, and a rugby
player. This means he could easily pummel most anyone (me included) mentally or physically. This day, though, we were discussing his views on the problems with how trust has been traditionally
studied.

"Dave," he said, "let's just say you had a brain tumor. Now, I really want to help you. You know I'm honest, and you know I like
you. I'm going to do everything I can to help you get rid of that
tumor. Would you hand me the scalpel?" Of course I wouldn't.
Adam's not a surgeon; he doesn't have the right skill set. Trust him

to give me honest feedback on a new project, sure. Trust him to have my back if we were about to be mugged on the street, yes. Trust him to open my skull, no way. But that was exactly his point. When most of us think about trust, we usually focus on integrity. Our main question is: Does this person intend to hold up her end of the bargain? Although it's true that integrity is important, when it comes to trust it's not the only question that we should be asking. Competence can matter just as much. Good intentions, without the ability to bring them to fruition, don't count for much in the end.

Adam's clever thought experiment was designed to highlight for me a fairly large lacuna in research on trust. Most scientists train their lenses on integrity, thereby giving less weight to related, but no less practically important, components. Yet a multifaceted view of trust makes good sense. Whether you're a CIA agent trying to assess if an informant can actually gain access to the relevant information he thinks he can, or you're a cancer patient trying to evaluate whether to trust a homeopathic doctor's belief that he knows how to heal you, the issue of competency is clear. Yet most of us often tend to ignore the issue of ability when we're thinking about others' trustworthiness. One reason this occurs among scientists likely has to do with the use of dilemmas like the PD, where competence is rendered irrelevant. The task at hand is to give or take money. Anyone can do that; no special skills are needed. As a result, the issue of competence doesn't enter the equation. This is not to say, however, that our minds don't consider it.

Work by the psychologist Jessica Tracy has clearly documented the human mind's penchant for assessing status, power, and leadership potential. Through painstaking work, both in the lab and in different cultures across the globe, Tracy has shown that our minds rapidly encode clues related to signals of competence. Utilizing sets óf co-occurring cues related to ancient markers of status (e.g., expanded vs. contracted torso posture, tilts of heads, placements of arms), our minds evaluate the social standing and expressed expertise of others within milliseconds. And as we'll see later in this book, such cues directly affect the trust accorded to their expressers.

The central point of these findings is twofold. First, we have to remember that competence and integrity both need to be considered when studying trust. Second, and perhaps more far-reaching, we have to realize that much of the computations our minds make concerning trust happen without conscious guidance and often outside of awareness. This shouldn't come as a surprise. If we had to evaluate each interaction with every person that in some way involved trust in a rigorous manner, we wouldn't have much time left in the day for anything else. *Can I trust the guy who just gave me directions to the subway stop? Can I trust my dentist that I really have a cavity, and can I trust him to fix it correctly? Can I trust my girlfriend not to cheat on me on her business trip? Can I trust what's written in this book?* Human social life regularly involves intricate cooperation over extended periods, so much so that the need to navigate social interactions successfully is posited to be one reason for the large size of our frontal cortices—brain areas integrally involved in social computations. With increasing complexity comes the need for increasing bandwidth with which to process it. And for humans, computations related to social interaction are among the most central to life.

Unfortunately, there's also usually a downside that accompanies increasing complexities in systems; "bugs" become more likely. The systems underlying the mind's judgments of trust are no different. There are glitches. Some are relatively harmless; others can easily be exploited. My goal throughout this book, then, is to provide you with something of a user's manual. Knowledge not only about how trust truly works, but also about how you can optimize your own trustworthiness and your ability to detect it accurately in others.

Key Insights

• **Aesop had it right: it's not good versus evil; it's the ant versus the grasshopper.** The minds of most of us aren't looking to cause others harm. Optimizing our outcomes—at least in a biological or evolutionary sense—is all about considering whether there are more benefits to be gained through short-term expediency or long-term perseverance and loyalty. Often, our rewards are greater if we can forestall immediate impulses and aggregate benefits over time. But then again, sometimes much is to be gained by taking the money and running, especially if we think we won't get caught. These are the calculations that underlie trust—the calculations your mind is always making even without your awareness. To make better predictions, you should think carefully about why a distant reward seems less attractive. Is it truly not worth it to wait? Stop and calculate the potential gains from investing—both in money and people. Don't simply go with your gut estimation of value by default; see if you can bring your reason and your intuition into consensus on what to do.

• **Everybody has their price, even if they don't know it.** We like to think that we can predict how people will behave based on reputation, but decades of findings show that this just isn't the case. Consistency in trustworthiness comes from stable situations—situations where the costs and benefits don't change very much. Once the nature of rewards is altered, all bets are off. And to make matters worse, we usually don't even see it coming. Factors as subtle as emotional states, stress, or even the power of suggestion can significantly alter the calculations going on below a person's consciousness and, thereby, tip the scales of trustworthiness. As you read this book, you'll discover the subtle factors that impinge on your mind's trust computations. That knowledge will prepare you to foresee sources of external influence and to adjust accordingly.

- **Don't be a statistic.** Sure, mathematical models can suggest that always trusting others leads to better outcomes on average, but having odds for an average outcome isn't what always drives success. Every individual mind is out to maximize its own resources, and that means always trying to discern two things: whether a potential partner can be trusted and whether he or she is likely to be encountered again. Answers to those two questions, far beyond anything else, will determine what any of us will be motivated to do in the moment. Recognizing this fact will help you realize why context matters—why you can't possibly succeed by following a one-size-fits-all rule.

- **Look for competence.** Nice guys don't always know best. There are two facets to trust: integrity *and* competence. Some of the best partners or teachers you may ever have had may not be the warmest people in the world, but they knew their stuff. Yes, integrity is important in that you want others to be honest, but honesty buys little if expertise is lacking. A friend could believe he's giving you good advice, but if he doesn't have the requisite skills or knowledge, you're going to end up failing if you trust him. As we'll see later in this book, your mind comes equipped with ways to assess competence as well as integrity. So don't be lulled into trusting others simply because they're good souls.

- **You are not special.** If you think you can always trust yourself, think again. The same forces and mechanisms that determine the trustworthiness of others determine your trustworthiness, too. So while trusting yourself not to overspend, overeat, or gamble in the present moment may seem easy, the picture can grow much murkier when trying to decide if you can trust yourself not to behave in such ways in the future. There's no guarantee that your future self will see things the same way as your current self does. In fact, there are some built-in mental biases that suggest it won't. How to overcome these challenges is an issue we'll consider down the line.

CHAPTER 2

BUILT TO TRUST?

How Our Biology Determines Whom We Trust and Why

It was a beautiful summer evening as I sat on a grassy mesa outside Telluride watching the golden sunlight reflect off the aspens as dusk approached. I was in Colorado for a conference on the science of compassion that was sponsored by Stanford University, and on this evening, all the presenters were being treated to an al fresco dinner at one of the most picturesque spots in town. The food was wonderful, the view even better, and the company the best of all. My fellow diners consisted of dozens of the world's top scientists studying the virtuous side of human behavior. It could have been the nature of the conference, or the fact that the air was a little thin at nine thousand feet, but the feeling of community, openness, and comfort was surprising. Scholars who typically are very hard-edged and competitive were sharing thoughts, unpublished research findings, and family stories in ways that were not typical for professional meetings. Opening up about new ideas or findings can be risky, as it often can lead to getting scooped—every scientist's worst fear. Yet it was as if we were all among old friends that we trusted, even though most of us had never met before. Perhaps the most interesting part of this phenomenon was that people didn't seem to be making a conscious decision to feel at ease and trust those around them. They just felt comfortable, felt safe, and with that, the trust flowed forth.

My dinner companions for the evening were Stephen Porges and Sue Carter. There are probably few individuals in the world who have done more to advance understanding of how biology shapes social behavior than this husband-and-wife team. Steve is one of the foremost experts on the links between human physiology and behaviors like bonding, emotional support, and communication. Sue, in addition to her many other accomplishments, is the person who initially identified the importance of the hormone oxytocin in mammalian bonding and loyalty. As we talked that evening, it reinforced two central points of my views on trust. The first is that trust, like most of social interaction, is driven as much by feelings—or more specifically by changes in physiological states—as by the rational calculations of the conscious mind. The second is that humans aren't built for trust any more than they are for betrayal. We're built for both. The goal—at least at the biological level—is to determine which option serves our interests best in any given situation.

What these points imply is that our feelings—the pits in our stomachs, the rapid heartbeats in our chests, the calming effects of another's touch—all play a role in whether we choose to trust someone or even act in a trustworthy manner ourselves. As we saw in the last chapter, simple alterations in feelings like gratitude can significantly determine whether we're likely to support or exploit a partner. One of the most central facts to realize, however, is that these emotional responses don't always derive from our own conscious analysis of what's going on around us; to the contrary, they often occur automatically without our intent. We don't always decide whether to trust someone and then feel comfortable or anxious as a result. Often, it's just the opposite; we feel first and decide whether to trust afterward. As we'll see in this chapter, the human mind and body have built-in systems that have guided decisions to trust and bond for much longer than we've had the brainpower to analyze situations rationally. And even though we now have the mental capacity to deliberatively consider dilemmas of trust—sometimes obsessively so—we're still influenced by those older systems.

A final point that was confirmed from my discussion with Stephen and Sue was that, to put it bluntly, there is no simple way to understand the biology of trust. Contrary to what you may have heard or read, there is no such thing as a "moral molecule," whose presence in the brain turns people to trusting saints. Human biology mirrors human social life; it's a complex balance between competing tensions. So, while some scientists, bloggers, and writers hail hormones like oxytocin as the gateways to trust, the emerging evidence confirms that so-called moral molecules have a dark side as well. Like trust in general, it all comes down to context.

From Reptile to Mammal and Back Again: What's a Person to Do?

Understanding how our biology influences our willingness to trust and be trustworthy requires taking a bit of long view on evolutionary history. The easiest way to do this is to consider from whence we came. As you probably know, one of the most basic principles of evolution is that mutations—random alterations in our genetic codes—happen all the time. Most of the resulting changes aren't particularly useful; in fact, they can be downright problematic.

Mutations can result in alterations of any part of the body: extra or differently shaped fingers, changes in eye structure and sight, extra or missing arteries or veins attached to organs, and the like. Once in a while, though, a "change" ends up being something helpful—an alteration that increases an organism's ability to survive and propagate. These are the changes that matter over time; these are the ones that end up being passed on to more and more progeny in each generation. Put simply, these are the mutations that drive evolutionary development.

It's important to remember, however, that evolutionary changes don't only occur in the body; they also occur in the mind. The abilities to think, to reason, to have automatic responses to or intuitions about threats and rewards in one's environs, are as important to survival and reproductive success as are changes in physical features like lung capacity and hand structure. Sure, an opposable thumb is an important adaptation, but so is a mind that can imagine new solutions to problems and remember past mistakes. As a consequence, we have to consider changes to both the body and the mind when we attempt to discover how trust works—changes, as we'll see, that have tracked each other.

When scientists talk about what makes human physiology unique, they often paint a picture with broad strokes that compares us with a common, simpler denizen of the planet—the reptile. In many ways, this tack makes some sense. After all, humans (and in fact all mammals) evolved from common reptilian ancestors known as synapsids. As a result, we've retained some ancient remnants of body and brain from our scaly forebears. So, while I concede that using the term *reptile brain* to refer to older circuits of our minds is a bit of a simplification, I also agree that it can make for a somewhat useful analogy. For now, then, let's go with it.

When you ponder the differences between reptiles and mammals, many obvious facts emerge. Reptiles are cold-blooded, mammals warm. Reptiles have scales, mammals hair or fur. But if we're interested in trust, it's not differences in metabolic structures that matter; it's differences in social interaction that hold the key. By and large, reptiles aren't a social bunch. Most reptile mothers do not devote themselves to taking care of their children. They don't form a social bond with offspring. They just drop an egg and keep on moving, leaving junior to fend for itself. Reptiles aren't big into building coalitions or friendships, either. When's the last time you saw two snakes grooming or seeking comfort from each other? Parental care, social bonding, cooperation with non-kin—these are hallmarks of mammals, especially as you follow the progression to primates. Human survival depends on the ability of infants to trust their moms, romantic partners to trust their mates, and coalition members to trust their teammates. As we saw in the last chapter, the ability of humans to flourish requires a fundamental dependence on others—a requirement that placed a firm pressure on our evolutionary development. Put simply, mutations that benefited social interaction were going to be retained.

A way to see how evolution has shaped our physiology with respect to trust, then, comes from comparing the results of mutations over time. One of the most influential models in this vein is Porges's polyvagal theory (PVT). As you might surmise by its name, PVT centers on the form and function of the vagus nerve—one of the most important cranial nerves in the human body. The term *vagus* comes from a Latin root meaning "to wander," and that's just what this nerve does. After exiting the brain stem, its branches innervate much of the body's viscera. The vagus both monitors and partially controls the working of the heart, the lungs, the stomach, and related structures. In a sense, it informs the brain what these organs are up to while also relaying orders from the brain back to them. As such, the vagus stands as a fundamental link between the mind and body, allowing each to inform and influence the other. That's the *vagal* part of polyvagal theory. It's the *poly* part, though, where things get interesting.

The prefix *poly* refers to "many," which, when we're taking about PVT, means quite simply that the vagus nerve is a bit more complex than used to be thought. As Porges has argued, the vagus nerve in mammals really consists of two sections: an ancient unmyelinated (i.e., nerve cells lacking electrical insulation by a covering known as myelin) part and an evolutionarily newer myelinated part. Combining these two aspects of the vagus nerve with the rest of the sympathetic nervous system, whose activation puts the body into a fight-or-flight state, results in a set of three definable stages in the development of the vertebrate nervous system. Considering the function of each system in turn provides a glimpse into the biological basis of sociality and trust.

The first system, represented by the ancient or unmyelinated vagus, is tied to an immobilization response. Its activation results in freezing and feigning death. Why would you want to feign death? Well, when an animal is under extreme threat (e.g., about to be caught by a predator), one of the simplest but most effective strategies it can follow is to play dead. Carrion eaters aside, most predators don't want to eat already dead things. As a result, freezing, fainting, or playing dead is an excellent way to remain silent and not be caught, or to avoid being eaten if found. Thus, activation of the unmyelinated vagal circuit produces the oldest and simplest response to threat—a behavioral pattern that is seen in reptiles and mammals alike.

The second system, like the first, also deals with environmental challenges, but does so in a different way. What Porges terms the sympathetic-adrenal system (SAS) constitutes the second level of response to threats. It's the system that guides what is commonly referred to as fight-or-flight; it prepares organisms for action. It increases heart and respiration rates, drives blood to the muscles of the limbs, and releases adrenaline and stress hormones. It's what you feel in your body when you're anxious, worried, or downright terrified: the churning of your stomach as you face issues at work that you can't overcome, the racing heart and sweaty palms you sense when you're caught in a lie or when you feel you have no one to turn to for help, the overriding impulse you feel to pound on someone who is harming you and from whom you can't escape. Like the unmyelinated vagus, the SAS is fairly well represented in most vertebrates. However, its sensitivity to social threats, as opposed to solely environmental ones like being eaten, is what makes it particularly relevant to social species like us.

The third system—that of the myelinated vagus—is uniquely associated with mammals, especially higher-order, social ones like primates and humans. The myelinated fibers of the vagus serve several functions. The two most relevant ones for our purposes are its links to the heart and the stress response. With respect to the heart, increased vagal tone (i.e., increased electrical activity in the vagus nerve) has a calming effect. It serves as a cardiac brake; it slows the heart and respiration. With respect to stress, increased vagal tone decreases activity in the hypothalamic-pituitary axis; that is, it decreases the release of stress hormones. Perhaps the most interesting part of the myelinated vagus, however, is that it is also reciprocally linked in the brain with nerves controlling parts of the body relevant for social engagement—muscles in the face that are central for emotional expression, muscles that alter the inner ear's ability to hear frequencies most associated with the human voice, and throat muscles that influence the larynx's ability to provide intonations to human speech. Taken together, what these facts suggest is that the myelinated vagus functions to tune social engagement. It places the body in a calm state where successful social interaction can occur—a state characterized by feelings of safety and serenity that subsequently fosters sharing, listening, comfort, and trust.

Why does the newer vagus work this way in mammals? Put quite simply, some biological mechanism has to play this role. Unlike many nonsocial animals, mammals in general, and humans in particular, face challenges that can't always be successfully dealt with by fighting, fleeing, or playing dead. We need to work together, to cooperate, to trust at times, if we're going to survive. We need to be able to rely on our parents, our spouses, and our friends to get what we need, and that's not going to happen if we run from them, punch them, or faint in front of them. Increased vagal tone puts our bodies in a state that is conducive to communication, sharing, and the building of social support. Without it, we'd never experience a state where we could even contemplate trusting another.

Although polyvagal theory is relatively new, findings supporting the link between vagal tone and superior social outcomes continues to grow. Work on children, for example, has shown that chronic increased vagal tone corresponds to less emotional negativity, fewer behavior problems, and heightened social skills. Among adults, the picture is the same. Greater vagal tone predicts increased social connectedness, greater well-being, and even greater compassion for the suffering of others. All these are, of course, qualities that increase the odds of being trustworthy. When we're calm, when we feel bonded to others, we are in a state in which we value the long-term gains that can come from supporting others—gains that build our reserves of social capital even though they might require some sacrifice in the moment. In fact, heightened vagal tone has also been shown to influence not only the virtue of our actions, but also the accuracy of our perceptions. Application of the vagal brake often results in greater acuity in our ability to correctly identify the feelings of others. Why does it do all this? Again, because it calms the threat response of the body, thereby allowing the mind to focus on the social challenges at hand, many of which require both the ability to ascertain what a partner is feeling and the motivation to act accordingly.

Before moving on, I don't want to leave you with the sense that the myelinated vagus is the answer to all of our problems. Trust, fairness, and bonding are certainly central to human success, but they're not the only elements. That's why the other two systems still reside within us. Sometimes trust and cooperation just won't cut it. It takes two people with the right motives for trust to be successful; if one of them isn't interested, it's every person for herself. As a result, these three systems are organized in a hierarchy. Our minds start with the highest-level system—the myelinated vagus—and move backward if it doesn't solve the problem. If, for example, we suddenly feel that trust isn't warranted as a potential partner intends to cheat or harm us, the vagal brake is removed and we turn to fight-or-flight. When you can't trust your partner, you have two options: get away from him or clobber him. We'd much rather look to a partner for social support when we're faced with a challenge, but if that doesn't seem likely—as is especially the case when the stress is due to a potential partner him- or herself—we go it alone.

But what about those times when the threat is overwhelming—when it's just more than we can stand? In such cases, our bodies move back to their most primitive response mechanism—the unmyelinated vagus. When it comes to trust, this fact implies that although moderate feelings of mistrust or moderate betrayals by a partner might lead us to leave or to vent our fury, larger betrayals engender something entirely different. If the breach of trust is of such a magnitude that we feel our world crashing down around us, the experience will likely be a feeling of numb paralysis enveloping us in our shocked disbelief, followed for some by a sense of all going black as they pass out.

Of course, we all possess different thresholds for each of these steps. Take public speaking as an example. Some of us see it as a chance to connect, and so our vagal tones rise. Others see it as a threat to be avoided, and so they sweat and feel their hearts race. Still others are so frightened by being put in the spotlight that they freeze or even faint. It's the same with trust. We all move up and down the physiological hierarchy from systems of the thriving social primate to those of the frightened reptilian turtle, depending on how we evaluate the levels of loyalty and deceit of our others.

From the preceding discussion, you might be tempted to see vagal tone as the biological panacea for trust—the more, the better. Doing so, however, would go against one of my basic rules: balance is what's important. We all know you can have too much of a good thing, and vagal tone is no different. In most of the findings I have just presented, the term *heightened vagal tone* referred to an increase of vagal activation over a fairly low level. It shouldn't be taken to mean that continual increases in vagal tone are always better. In fact, it turns out that ultra-high vagal tone isn't always a great thing. As you might suspect, a person can be *too* social or *too* positive, such that these characteristics approach pathological levels.

Work by the psychologist June Gruber clearly ties ultra-high levels of vagal activity to overly high self-confidence and motives for social connection. The problem here is that a sense of invulnerability combined with a constant desire to connect socially can lead one not only to be exploited by others, but to become unreliable and untrustworthy him- or herself. Simply put, if you're trying to connect with and please everyone, there's just not enough of you to go around. If you're promising different people opposing things, it's unlikely you can deliver. And if you're chronically feeling calm and safe, you don't experience those pangs of anticipated guilt or worry that remind you that promises to some people are more important than responsibilities to others. You feel like everyone will love you no matter what.

Interestingly, such high and nondiscriminating vagal tone appears linked to mania, a psychological disorder in which a sufferer's trustworthiness goes out the window for these very reasons. It's also a phenomenon that our minds intuitively recognize; people with ultra-high vagal tone are readily judged to be less reliable social partners than those possessing more moderate levels. Although we wouldn't recognize the basis for our judgments, they would prove to be quite functional in nature.

This last fact raises an important point. We don't usually control our physiological responses; they control us. Although the notion that any person's trustworthiness might not be completely under conscious control can be a bit disconcerting, if you think about it through the lens of evolution, it makes great sense. Analyzing, planning, and running simulations in our heads requires a lot of effort. Given the centrality and import of trust, it seems quite reasonable that our minds would have developed ways to complete the relevant calculations in a more efficient and automatic way. Plus, it's also the case that many of our primate cousins don't quite have the cognitive complexity to plan and analyze that we humans have, yet they still need to depend on each other to survive. This fact alone suggests that strategic planning and analysis can't be the only routes to detecting trustworthiness and acting accordingly. There must be something else.

The nature of that something else is what much of this book is about. Although many terms have been suggested to cover the intuitive mechanisms in question, one of the most frequently used was coined by Porges himself: *neuroception*. The idea behind neuro-ception is that the mind constantly scans the environment for signs related to safety or threat, adjusting physiology in response to what it sees. These changes in physiology subsequently alter the probabil-ities of what we'll do next. We've seen some examples of this phe-nomenon already in the research on gratitude and stress I discussed in the previous chapter. Subtle changes in feelings directly altered how fair, helpful, and trustworthy individuals were likely to be.

If we examine events in our own lives, we're likely to find simi-lar instances—instances when we spontaneously acted in a way that may have surprised us. The feelings of comfort at that dinner in Telluride I described undoubtedly heightened the sense of trust and community that the usually cautious scientists involved were feel-ing. As a result, they were willing to share information about their work while trusting that others wouldn't scoop them. Yet all the anecdotes, experiments, and examples I've offered possess a funda-mental shortcoming. They all involve humans. If I really want to show you how deeply rooted trust and cooperation are in biology, we need to take a few steps down the evolutionary ladder.

The Monkey Economy

The first ability any organism needs to have if it's going to trust is a way to tell when it gets cheated. Put simply, if you can't recognize when someone is exploiting or betraying you, you're going to keep being exploited or betrayed. That's not an adaptive situation for any animal, human or otherwise. In fact, humans are so averse to feeling that they're being cheated that they often respond in ways that seemingly make little sense. Behavioral economists—the econo-mists who actually study what people do as opposed to the kind who simply assume the human mind works like a calculator—have shown again and again that people reject unfair offers even if it costs them money to do so. The typical experiment uses a task called the ultimatum game. It's pretty straightforward. One person in a pair is given some money—say $10. She then has the opportunity to offer some amount of it to her partner. The partner only has two options. He can take what's offered or refuse to take anything. There's no room for negotiation; that's why it's called the ultimatum game.

What typically happens? Many people offer an equal split to the partner, leaving both individuals happy and willing to trust each other in the future. Of course, such decisions drive economists crazy; their basic assumption is that people are rational money maximizers. If you don't have to share any money and won't be subject to subsequent punishment for not sharing, why in the world would you share? It only makes you poorer. But if one adopts a more psychological view, splitting the resources begins to make sense; it builds bonds for the long term. As a result, the human mind possesses mechanisms that habitually push a sense of fairness.

Not everyone acts fairly, however. Remember, I said *many*, not *all*, people offer equal splits in the ultimatum game. Perhaps the more interesting case, then, is what happens if one individual does make an unfair offer in the game. What happens, say, if she offers her partner $1 and keeps $9 for herself? Time and again, most partners contemptuously refuse the offer. It just seems so selfish and unfair that they can't bring themselves to accept it. But here again, the economists shake their heads. If the partner took the $1, he'd be leaving the game ahead; he'd be $1 richer than he was at the start. You can't argue with the logic. Yet people across cultures tend to refuse offers when the split is greater than 80 percent/20 percent. In their gut, they know the other person isn't treating them fairly, and they're willing to sacrifice their own profit to make the point.

In humans, it's certainly true that one could make an argument that these responses are consciously driven—a reasoned protest, if you will. I wouldn't agree with that argument, but it is a tenable one. To see why it's likely not true, however, and why the idea of neuroception makes good theoretical sense, we need to turn our lens toward our closest relatives. And in this endeavor, there are few better scientists to whom to turn than Sarah Brosnan. Brosnan has spent years working with different species of primates in an effort to understand the evolutionary origins of fairness, trust, and cooperation, and her resulting research has begun to illuminate the origins of these phenomena in ways previously unimaginable.

One of Brosnan's most robust findings is that many species of monkeys and apes show a decided aversion to inequity, just as do their human cousins. You may be wondering how she knows this, as it would be pretty difficult for a monkey to play the classic ultimatum game. But primatologists are a clever bunch. They've developed a procedure that easily adapts to fit the monkey economy. Although versions vary slightly at times, the basic framework is as follows. Two monkeys are placed in nearby enclosures so that they can easily see what the other is doing. An experimenter then trains both monkeys to complete a simple task to get food. For example, monkeys may learn to hand the experimenter a token in exchange for a morsel to eat. After the monkeys get accustomed to the procedure (which happens fairly quickly), the main part of the experiment begins. One monkey continues to get the usual boring food item in exchange for a token. The other, though, suddenly gets a much more desirable item (e.g., a grape or other fruit) for doing the same thing. Monkeys don't much care about dollar bills, but they do care about tasty treats. And in this procedure it rapidly becomes clear that the human is treating the two monkeys inequitably. One is getting "paid" much more than the other for doing the same work.

Watching these experiments always makes me smile. Not because I like seeing some monkeys treated unfairly, but rather because this research shows just how much we have in common with other primates. The work of Brosnan and others has confirmed time and again that chimpanzees and capuchins don't only recognize when they're being treated unfairly, they also appear to get quite angry and indignant about it. After only a few trials in which inequity is clearly manifested, these monkeys act out. They either refuse to participate, throw the less desirable food back at the experimenter, or otherwise let it be clearly known that they're not happy with the situation in the least. As you'd expect, the researchers run several control conditions to make sure this behavior truly stems from a sense of inequity. For example, they've shown that the monkeys don't become upset simply by seeing a desired food that they can't have, or by the experimenter unintentionally dropping the treat before she can give it to them. They only become agitated when another monkey is getting better food for the same price.

What these and related findings clearly show is that these monkeys are readily capable of sensing when someone's not treating them fairly. With chimps, one might question whether there's some explicit analysis going on. Though certainly not at the level of humans, the minds of chimps do evidence some ability to engage in reasoning. For capuchins, though, this is certainly not the case; their analytic capacity is much more limited. Yet capuchins demonstrate the same aversion to being cheated as do chimps—a finding that makes conscious analysis unlikely to be the source.

If inequity aversion did stem from a capacity to reason as opposed to from a more intuitive calculus, we'd not only expect capuchins not to show it, we'd expect all primates that possess brainpower similar to chimps to provide evidence of it. Interestingly, though, orangutans, one of the smartest and most cognitively capable of nonhuman primates, show no such aversion. They don't become upset at all in the face of inequity. The reason has to do not so much with their mental acuity as with the evolutionary pressures that shaped their automatic responses. Unlike chimps and capuchins, orangutans live very solitary lives in their native habitats. As a result, they don't engage in cooperation or need to be sensitive to issues of trust at nearly the levels other primates do. Their physiology, in essence, isn't tuned to these challenges, meaning that they don't reflexively become upset in the face of unequal treatment.

If responses to inequity and cheating don't stem from conscious analysis, what is likely happening in the minds of capuchins and chimps to cause these behaviors? Much as I suspect is the case in humans, the minds of these primates are automatically identifying unfair behavior. Decades of research on humans have consistently confirmed that our minds often size up a situation before we even know what's going on. When we hear a loud sound, or see a snake in our path, our body is already reacting before we can consciously make sense of our environs. We feel our stomachs tighten before we're sure the loud sound we just heard truly represents a danger. We sense our hearts race before we know for certain whether the squiggly black thing on the ground is a snake or just an old rubber hose. Neuroception is fast and it doesn't require conscious thought. And while it's true that it can sometimes lead to an incorrect result, it works more often than not, which is why it has been evolutionarily retained.

For social species like humans, chimps, and capuchins, it's fair to say that many of our responses to being treated unfairly can happen even if we don't take time to analyze the situation. Anger at being treated unfairly or in response to broken trusts is in our DNA; it's who we are. But as I noted at the outset, issues of trust don't only involve our responses to betrayal or loyalty, they also subsume

the abilities to demonstrate our own trustworthiness and to correctly predict it in others. Here again, a perusal of the primate lit-
erature shows just how deeply ingrained in the mind and body such
phenomena are.

Until now, we've been considering events from the perspective
of the monkey who gets cheated. But what about the one who benefits? Being the one who reaps unfair rewards isn't always helpful in
the long run. Sure, in the moment the extra money, grapes, or similar reward might be great, but in the long term, a willingness to
profit at another's expense marks one as less than trustworthy. Here
again we can see why, contrary to economists' predictions, people
often make fair offers in the ultimatum game; they want to make
sure others view them as fair and reliable. Interestingly, this concern is evident in many social primates as well. Chimps, for instance, easily recognize when they have been "paid" more for a task
than their neighbor and will sometimes refuse the preferred food
reward when this happens. Likewise, capuchins will often offer a
superior reward to their less fortunate partners. The only reasonable explanation for such behaviors is that the monkeys are attempting to demonstrate their moral bona fides; they're attempting
to show that they would be fair and trustworthy partners in future
endeavors.

This explanation could only be valid, of course, if monkeys
in fact take notice of such actions by others and utilize them in
their decisions. Recent evidence confirms that they do. Alicia Melis
and colleagues at the Max Planck Institute have shown that chimpanzees are quite capable of discriminating among potential partners. When they're presented with a task to solve that requires two
individuals to cooperate in a trustworthy manner, chimps choose
partners who have previously proved themselves. For example, in
one experiment, chimps selected as work partners others that had

equitably shared food rewards with them in the past over others who didn't. In another, they chose partners who had demonstrated competence at solving the problem at hand over less able others. Remember, trusting someone isn't only about determining if they will treat you fairly; it's also about determining if they can accomplish what they say they can.

As was the case with inequity aversion, neither the behavior of rejecting unfair rewards nor the decision to select more trustworthy partners necessitates conscious awareness and rational analyses on the part of the primates involved. A physiological response or emotional impulse on its own is sufficient and would have been retained through evolutionary development. Just as we automatically respond with physiological changes and warm feelings toward a cute baby or puppy without having to be taught to do so, we, like our primate cousins, similarly respond without conscious intent to markers of inequity and fairness when trust is on the line.

The Misnomer of the Moral Molecule

Anyone interested in the biology of trust has probably heard of the supposed magic of the neuropeptide oxytocin. It's often referred to as the moral molecule, given that early findings suggested it promoted trust, love, and basically any related feelings you might have while singing fireside rounds of "Kumbaya." Newer research, however, is recasting the view of oxytocin's role in human interaction. In line with my mantra that trust and betrayal always exist in a delicate balance between short- and long-term gains, it now appears that the functions of oxytocin do so as well. Yes, oxytocin can breed harmony, but it also has a darker side. To understand why this makes sense, we need to start at the beginning—birth.

Many mothers—whether they know it or not—are quite familiar with the effects of oxytocin. At a very basic level, oxytocin is
what birth is all about. No oxytocin, no labor. For any of you who
had to have your delivery kick-started with something called Pitocin, you know this to be true. Although you might not recognize it
from its name, Pitocin is a synthetic form of oxytocin. Of course,
labor pains on their own are a bit removed from trust. But we're not
done. Oxytocin also stimulates lactation and nursing behaviors. It's
what allows women not only to produce milk for their newborns
but also to be willing to spend many sleepless nights awakening
repeatedly to feed and cuddle them. That's where the trust and
social connection come in. The hormonal rush of oxytocin holds
one other secret: it strengthens emotional bonds with babies. And
it was this fact that gave rise to the belief that oxytocin might be a
panacea for distrust.

If you stop to think about it, though, there are two sides to a
mother's bond with her child. She usually loves that child dearly,
and as a result believes it to be perfect and worth her undying efforts aimed at nurturing it. But on the flip side, this also means she's
willing to see her child as more perfect than any other baby and to
protect it, to borrow a term from Sarah Palin, like a mama grizzly.
If we apply this fact to issues of trust, it generates some interesting
predictions about oxytocin that many people missed at the outset.
Yes, oxytocin might increase attachment and willingness to trust
those close to us, but it also might result in greater discriminatory
behavior toward those we see as different. Much like new parents—
moms *and* dads—oxytocin may make us see the world in a slightly
polarized way. Some people—specifically those affiliated with us—
may be more worthy of our trust and support than others.

At the start of this chapter, I introduced you to Sue Carter,
whose initial work on oxytocin was central to showing that its

effects reached far beyond the confines of birth and lactation. Working with species of voles (small social mammals), Carter repeatedly demonstrated that oxytocin played a role in social bonding for both females and males. Evidence explicitly linking oxytocin to trust in humans, however, comes primarily from a groundbreaking paper by the behavioral economist Ernst Fehr and colleagues that appeared in 2005. The researchers began with the idea that, due to its role in strengthening social bonds in mammals, oxytocin might also lead to increased trust in humans. The design of their seminal experiment was simple but elegant. They had participants play a version of a trust game I described in the previous chapter. Participants (i.e., investors) were endowed with a sum of money that they could give to another individual (i.e., the trustee) to invest. The trustee would always triple the money that was given to him by the investor. The catch was that he didn't have to give any back; he could keep as much of the tripled money as he liked.

As a consequence of the rules, the investor is confronted with a dilemma. He can keep his initial small amount of money or give some to the trustee to triple. If he trusts the trustee, giving increasing amounts of money to him makes great sense; it will be tripled and both partners end up with more. But if the trustee is untrustworthy, the investor might end up with nothing—a situation worse than that with which he began the game.

To examine the effects of oxytocin, the researchers administered it to half the participants through a nasal spray. The results were striking. A simple snort of oxytocin significantly increased the amount of money investors were willing to put under the control of trustees; they forked over almost 20 percent more cash on average. Of import, this behavior didn't stem from stupidity; it wasn't that oxytocin made people feel silly or reduced their ability to think rationally. When the researchers changed the game so that it involved gambling risks from things like rolling dice or drawing cards, oxytocin didn't increase the amount of money people were willing to wager. It only seemed to have an effect when the risk involved trusting another person to do the right thing.

Following up on this initial work, Fehr and colleagues demonstrated that increased oxytocin perpetuates trust even in the face of a betrayal. This time, they used the same trust game but manipulated how the trustee behaved. Sometimes she acted fairly by splitting the profits with the investor; other times she acted selfishly and kept the profits for herself. Investors who had not received oxytocin quickly learned not to trust a trustee who betrayed them. Those who sniffed oxytocin, however, showed no such decrease in trust; they continued to give greater amounts to the crooked trustee for a few more tries. Taken together, these findings clearly indicate that oxytocin doesn't impair reasoning in general; its impact appears to target feelings of trust specifically.

To this point, you can easily see why oxytocin came to be viewed as trust in a bottle. It didn't matter who you were or where you came from. Take a shot of oxytocin and it appeared you were ready to trust anyone. But as work on the so-called moral molecule continues, its true dual nature is becoming clear. Yes, oxytocin can increase trust and bonding, but it can likewise fuel distrust, envy, and discrimination. It all depends on context, which, when we're talking about trust, means the nature of one's potential partner. As noted earlier, the fundamental truth that one of oxytocin's principal purposes involves caring for offspring makes the notion that it would increase trust for anyone a bit odd. Trust for family and friends? Sure. Trust for the guy from the neighboring tribe, ethnic group, or religion? Not so much. In the end, biology all comes down to protecting and providing resources for people on your own team.

Supporting this view, emerging research demonstrates that

oxytocin, much like the rest of human morality, is a bit biased. In most of the experiments I've noted, partners came from the same social or cultural groups as participants and, thus, benefited from oxytocin's effects. Yet many of the most compelling findings showing oxytocin's dark side, which come from the work of Carsten De Dreu, employ a slightly altered paradigm. Using tasks in which participants made financial decisions that involved themselves, their social ingroup, and their social outgroups, De Dreu and colleagues found that oxytocin could both increase *and* decrease trust and cooperation. The main determinant, as you probably have guessed, was simply the identity of the partners involved. When decisions impacted people close to participants (i.e., members of their ingroup), oxytocin functioned as first theorized; it increased trustworthiness and decisions that benefited the group as a whole, even at immediate cost to oneself. But when decisions involved members of outgroups, oxytocin wasn't a source of the warm fuzzies. Quite the opposite; it produced decisions that were discriminatory in nature—decisions that evidenced a clear bias toward favoring you and yours over the interests of others.

When De Dreu and colleagues examined issues of morality, it was much the same. Oxytocin regularly increased people's willingness to make decisions that benefited ingroup members over outgroup members. For example, in scenarios involving hypothetical life-or-death trade-offs, participants were more willing to make decisions that asymmetrically saved their fellow citizens over foreigners. At base, increases in oxytocin lead to greater ethnocentrism and bigotry.

The dark side of oxytocin isn't limited to intergroup interactions, either. Although it usually increases trust, oxytocin's effect has a limit depending on the likability of the other person involved. For example, when individuals play economic games with a partner who always beats them and treats them unfairly, increased oxytocin leads to greater feelings of envy. As a result, when the time arrives that this partner does lose, increased oxytocin produces greater gloating in the face of the partner's misfortune.

While it's true, then, that oxytocin may lead you to trust another person even in the face of some initial defections and betrayals, it certainly won't turn you into a love zombie for all eternity. After a while you'll start to despise untrustworthy people and, perhaps most interestingly, the more oxytocin you have coursing through your veins, the more you'll despise them and take pleasure in—or even willingly cause—their pain.

Built to Optimize

Are humans built to trust and be trustworthy? *Yes.* Are they built to distrust and betray? *Yes.* Although these answers appear to defy logic, they don't. It's the nature of the questions themselves that misses the mark. When you realize that successfully navigating social life isn't always about being a saint or a sinner, questions that focus on following one route or the other fall away. Optimization, not virtue or vice, characterizes the evolutionary chisel. And when it comes to social interaction, we often need both sides of morality to succeed.

So, yes, we humans possess physiological mechanisms that make us more likely to trust others and act loyally ourselves, but we also possess mechanisms that do the opposite. As we've just seen, we have systems that calm us in the presence of safe others—systems that motivate us to communicate, to support, and to trust. We also have systems, like our primate cousins, that work to calibrate these responses by automatically attempting to determine whom we can trust based on their actions and skills. And when we sense that the people in front of us cannot be trusted, these same systems motivate us to act against them, whether by avoiding them or behaving in ways that benefit us at their expense.

To return to the motif of the ant and grasshopper, each instance in which issues of trust emerge necessitates a calculation about whether trust is really warranted. Trust and trustworthiness always involve risk—a cost in the short term that might to lead to a greater benefit in the long term. Solving this problem—determining which outcome it will be—is what our minds and bodies continually attempt to do, often without our even being aware of it. Our brains form intuitions and modify our physiological systems accordingly. Those systems in turn influence each other, thereby shaping the next assessment our minds make.

The end result, then, isn't a simple one. The biological systems, taken as a whole, aren't there to increase trust or dispel it. To the contrary, the systems are there to build bonds when it's appropriate and to be selfish when it's not. To trust when we're likely to be repaid, and to exploit or discriminate when we're likely to be cheated. We're not completely controlled by these automatic responses, of course. Our conscious minds can overrule our biological intuitions. But it's when there are disagreements between the conscious and nonconscious minds that we're often most confused. When we think we should trust a friend but our gut says no. Or when our conscious mind tells us our chronically lying sibling is never to be trusted, but we have a hunch that he's really sincere this time. These are the occasions when knowing where our intuitions come from become so important. After all, it's only with such knowledge that you can begin to make an informed assessment of whether you should listen to your intuitions or not. Unlike most animals, we humans possess the wonderfully adaptive ability to reflect on the workings of our minds and bodies and to use that information, rather than be completely controlled by it. We just need a clear understanding of how everything works. As we move forward in this book, it's my goal to help you gain that knowledge and put it to good use.

Key Insights

- **There's a reason you have two sides.** Maximizing outcomes in this world often requires flexibility. Issues of morality aside, much is to be gained by trust and trustworthiness, but certainly not all. Although it's true that we profit by refusing to trust dishonest others, it's also true that we sometimes profit by being untrustworthy ourselves. And while I'm certainly not advocating such behavior, overall success—not virtue—is what drives biological adaptation. As a result, we're built to trust and deceive as a function of the risks and payoffs involved. Accepting this fact will not only allow you to come to terms with the biologically derived impulses you feel, but also prepare you to manage them as you see fit.

- **Trust is a force of nature.** Dilemmas of trust aren't particular to humans, and as a consequence, neither are the psychological mechanisms meant to address them. Our ancestors weren't self-indulgent savages who only learned cooperation and loyalty through the development of civilization. As the behavior of many of our primate cousins shows, mechanisms to manage one's trustworthiness and to read it in others derive from the conflicting pressures posed by social living.

- **Calm and assertive is where it's at.** On this point, I agree with Cesar Millan of *Dog Whisperer* fame. Social mammals—humans included—find it difficult to trust or bond unless their

physiology is in the right state (unless the stress comes from social anxiety and a related desire to bond and be accepted). This
means having a high (but not too high) vagal tone, resulting in
a sense of calm and certainty that allows communication and
sharing with others. Nonetheless, the importance of a calm, assertive state for breeding trust should also raise red flags for
you, as we've seen that feelings from one situation can sometimes bleed over to others, influencing how they are perceived.
If you enter a new situation angry or nervous, you've already
unwittingly constrained your ability to trust. Even if you normally might have trusted the person in front of you—and rightly
so—those residual feelings decrease the odds that you will do so
now. Similarly, if you enter a situation feeling exceedingly calm,
you might just trust someone you shouldn't. Both these facts
point to the importance of understanding context. If you want
to be able to trust as you should, take a moment before negotiating with someone new to allow any feelings from a previous
event to dissipate.

• **There is no moral molecule.** Oxytocin won't make you a
saint; it'll make you a team player, for better or worse. Its dual
nature means that while it will increase your trust and support
for those similar to you, so, too, will it increase your distrust
and exploitation of those different from you. At base, it's a
chemical tied to parenting, not to piety. And as such, it biases
evaluations of others along lines of affiliation. Remember, biology is about optimization, not virtue.

CHAPTER 3

IN THE BEGINNING

Learning to Trust and Trusting to Learn

Learning never exhausts the mind. That may well be true if you're Leonardo da Vinci—from whom I drew this quote—but I'm not sure it's a sentiment with which all my students would agree, especially on those nights when they're studying at two in the morning before an exam. Still, there are few other types of work we do that regularly keep us up that late. Whether it's cramming for an exam, writing a paper, or finishing a project for a new client, learning occupies much of our mental efforts. In fact, learning is pretty much what human life is all about; if we weren't continually learning, our respective lives would end up being a lot shorter and less rewarding. In this respect, Leonardo was right; our brains are made for it. From the moment we awaken to the moment we drift off to sleep, our minds are scanning and analyzing information in an effort to soak up knowledge that we may need.

The intensity of this thirst for knowledge isn't always constant, however. Although the mind continually learns, the rate at which it does so is another matter. And nowhere in our lives is the need to learn—and learn quickly—more central to success than in child-hood. The minds of kids, more so than those of adults, are seem-ingly insatiable. They have to be, as, for the most part, sparkling new brains don't come preloaded with the information necessary to survive and flourish. Kids' minds have the *capacity* to learn and the specific tools to do so. They're just lacking the relevant content and, as a consequence, are unwavering in their attempts to acquire it.

This quest for knowledge, as any parent knows (or will remem-ber), can at times be trying. The questions often seem relentless. *Why aren't people at the South Pole walking around upside down? Why do I have to share with my little brother? Are you sure Martians don't exist?* Yet, in spite of this seeming onslaught, there is an upside—most adults gain a sense of satisfaction in being sought out by their young protégés for advice and answers. Yes, at times repeated queries can make even the most patient of us begin to search in desperation for the television remote to divert a child's attention, but for the most part it feels good to be asked—a fact I know all too well.

When my kids were younger, I loved that they'd ask their mom and me tons of questions. When they first thought about what it means for the sun to set, they'd ask either of us where it went at night. When they didn't understand why a bat was a mammal and not a bird, they'd look to either of us for an answer. And when they wanted to know how to spell a word, they'd ask whomever they saw first. In their minds, we were both fonts of knowledge. But as they grew, I began to notice something subtly different in their questioning. At times the fonts didn't seem to be equally val-ued. When my kids wanted to know what they should buy their cousin for her birthday, how they should deal with nerves before a music recital, or what they should take with them on a trip, they'd walk right by me to seek out their mom. Trying to be helpful, I'd at times offer an answer to the question before they could find my wife, but that didn't seem to satisfy them. They'd still go ask their mother.

At first this puzzled me a little. Why didn't they want to hear what I had to say? They certainly knew that both parents loved them equally and neither would ever give them poor information on purpose. But they also came to realize something else. In certain domains, information from one of us tended to be a bit more reliable. I have to admit it; answers I'd given in the past about what the kids should pack have not always turned out for the best (think shivering kids without coats). Ditto for dealing with recitals and with what a five-year-old girl might like for her birthday. Unlike their mom, whose expertise is as great in science as it is in managing social interactions and logistical planning, my skill set tends to be a bit more limited. As a consequence, my kids learned early on that they couldn't trust my answers to certain questions. It wasn't because I meant to be untrustworthy. I didn't; they knew that. It was simply because my competence was suspect, and they knew that, too.

Trusting to Learn

Both integrity and competence hold consequences for all of us when issues of trust are involved. There are numerous people out there who will attempt to deceive or take advantage of us on purpose, leading us to experience failure and loss. But failure and loss can also come from those who, while earnestly trying to uphold their end of the deal, fall short simply because they don't have the requisite abilities or resources. Although our feelings toward the deceptive and the incompetent may differ, the outcome of trusting them will always be the same: failure and loss. For children, the issue of competence takes on an even greater significance. Think for a moment about the ways kids learn and how these ways differ from those of adults. When we adults want to know something, we have multiple avenues at our disposal. We can research questions using libraries or data repositories. We can conduct our own experiments to determine if an idea is correct. Or, in cases where neither of these options is available or practical, we can simply take someone's word for it; we can choose to trust the information people give us.

Unlike adults, young children don't have the same variety of options readily available. Before the age of seven or so, there's not much in the way of research that they can easily access. They don't have the vocabulary, let alone the reasoning ability, to consume and analyze statistics, to acquire and read technical information, or even to navigate Google and Wikipedia successfully. As for conducting experiments on their own, they're also constrained. Kids can and do learn basic scientific principles through observation and play, but the level of knowledge they can acquire this way is limited both by a lack of available materials (most kids don't have easy ways to purchase everything they want to learn about) and a mind that hasn't yet learned the logic needed for advanced reasoning.

A wonderful example of kids' limitations as naïve scientists—which will become important for understanding where trust enters the picture—comes from work by the psychologist Bruce Hood. Hood was interested in how children learn and reason about basic gravity-related concepts. He couldn't ask them how they go about learning, as most kids don't have the insight to analyze the process of their own learning through introspection. So Hood tried a different tack. He constructed a simple bi-level structure comprised of six cups. The cups were placed in two rows of three, with one row positioned six inches above the other. Since this was going to be a gravity experiment, each of the top cups had a hole in its bottom, allowing anything placed into it to fall through to the corresponding cup below.

Hood was clever, though. He realized that if he wanted to study how kids learned about gravity, he'd have to present them with cases that would require different predictions. If kids only saw balls dropped into top cups fall into lower ones, it was very unlikely that their minds would ever be taxed. So Hood sometimes added a twist to his contraption. He would connect upper and lower cups with either opaque or transparent tubes that ran at angles. These diagonal connections meant that a ball dropped into a cup in the top row would be diverted to land in a cup in the bottom row that was off to the side.

The point of the different versions was to see whether kids could learn through simple experimentation. When Hood asked two- and three-year-old children to find the balls he dropped into the cups, he found very different levels of success depending on what version of the apparatus the kids saw. If no tubes were present, the children had no difficulties. The balls always fell into the cup below where they were dropped, and that's exactly where the kids looked to find them. If the tubes were transparent, results were much the same; the kids made few errors in looking for the ball in the correct place. They could easily follow the progression of a ball as it rolled through the tube to a lower cup off to the side. But when the tubes were opaque, the story changed; most of the kids kept looking for the ball in the lower cup directly under the upper cup into which it was dropped. They just weren't able to grasp that the opaque tubes were diverting the balls in the same way as the clear ones did. Based on their prior experience, kids believed gravity pulls stuff straight down. Unless they could actually see a ball being diverted, they stuck with their intuitive theory: a ball should land below where it was dropped.

What was perhaps most interesting about this experiment was the kids' clear inability to learn from their mistakes. Even after making repeated errors, the children didn't change their minds. The hallmark of learning through experimentation is to follow the data—to update your knowledge based on whether your predictions are confirmed. Yet these young children continued using their basic assumption about how gravity works, ignoring the data at hand. If you needed any evidence that kids cannot learn entirely through their own experimentation and observation, this was it. While some learning can occur through playing the role of a naïve scientist, kids' minds are not always mature enough to overcome previously ingrained ideas, thereby stifling intellectual advancement.

This constraint begs an obvious question: If kids can't access facts from repositories and face limitations even when viewing data with their own eyes, how do they learn some concepts successfully? The answer comes down to the third way of learning: the testimony of others. As I noted earlier, adults use this strategy as well. For answers to highly specialized questions—questions for which we can't quite find or interpret the evidence ourselves (What is a quark? Is there a heaven?)—we often have to accept the statements of experts at face value. For kids, though, almost all new knowledge is highly specialized. As a result, they're stuck relying on testimony to a greater degree than the rest of us.

When you're young, the world can be a confusing place. Remember how fascinating and counterintuitive it was when you first learned that the earth was round. Neither you nor I would probably have come up with that realization on our own, but we accepted it when our parents or teachers told us. That's how we came to learn it. Same thing with the kids in Hood's experiment. Although they couldn't learn on their own where the balls would end up in the opaque-tube version, they quickly stopped making errors when an adult told them how it worked. Suddenly the kids stopped looking again and again for a dropped ball in the cup under the one where the experimenter placed it. Quickly internalizing the advice of an adult, they followed the opaque tubes with their eyes and easily found the balls where they actually landed. For these children, seeing wasn't believing; hearing it from an adult was what made the difference.

For all its seeming efficiency, learning from what other people tell you isn't a perfect strategy. There's an inherent problem: the credibility of the source is always a risk. How do you know if the person explaining something knows what he's talking about? How do you know if you can trust him? When you're a kid, every day is filled with people telling you things that are difficult to accept. *Numbers can be negative. Dolphins aren't fish. The Loch Ness Monster does exist.* You see the problem. If you simply believed everything you were told, you'd probably end up pretty misinformed, which in evolutionary logic translates to pretty dead. Extreme gullibility is not an adaptive feature, and precisely because of this fact, the minds of children are a lot less gullible than most people think—a fact that holds important consequences not only for how kids learn, but also from whom they're willing to learn.

Today, when most of us consider the process of education, we think of it as a simple transmission of knowledge. But in so doing, we're missing a meaningful distinction. *How* knowledge is transmitted is as consequential to learning as is the substance of the knowledge itself. The human mind didn't evolve to learn information in isolation; it evolved to learn information from *someone*. And exactly who that *someone* is can make a profound difference. In life, especially in the early years, we all face a fundamental problem: we not only have to figure out who wants to help us, we need to determine who actually *can*! That means kids need to be sensitive not only to issues of whom they can trust to have their best interests at heart, but also whom they can trust to teach them correctly. In fact, when it comes to learning, it may really be the latter that matters most.

Picking the Right Teacher: Whom to Ask? Whom to Believe?

Amanda Ripley—an author and journalist whom I had the pleasure to meet when we both spoke at a PopTech conference—had written an article for the *Atlantic* on evaluating schools that was drawing a lot of attention in 2012. It centered on a simple yet provocative question: If one really wants to evaluate teachers, why not ask their customers—the kids? For decades, most procedures to evaluate teachers and schools were based on standardized test scores or the views of outside experts. Yet, for all the effort put into test construction and systematic observation, it was clear that the resulting evaluations weren't very good metrics for how much kids actually learned in a given classroom. As you might imagine, average test scores for schools are tremendously influenced by factors like family income and the education levels of students' parents—factors that have nothing to do with the actual performance of the teachers who work there. And while the use of outside observers to evaluate teachers might get around this difficulty, such tactics suffer from another equally problematic issue. External observers only tend to be around for a few days. This limited time not only means that the evaluators don't have a wealth of information on which to base their opinions, it also suggests that the information they do have might not be entirely reliable or representative. Teachers know when they're being watched, and if there's anything we know from decades of psychological research, people behave differently when they know they're being evaluated. Anyone in their right mind would be performing at the top of his or her game during those few days—a level at which most also would not perform during the rest of the year.

How to solve the problem? Ripley's take, based on discussions with innovators at Harvard's Graduate School of Education, suggested a novel two-part answer. The first involved the source of information: school administrators needed to ask the people who knew the teachers best—their students—as opposed to outside experts. The second involved the nature of what was being asked in the first place: true precision in assessing an instructor's abilities required changing the questions posed to the student evaluators. Through detailing work by Harvard's Thomas Kane and colleagues, Ripley showed that the questions administrators thought would matter to kids weren't really the right ones. How much kids liked a given teacher had little bearing on how much they actually learned from him or her. On the other hand, whether kids believed they could *trust* a teacher's competence did.

Asking students to report whether a teacher could show them how to fix mistakes, whether the teacher provided correct information, and whether the teacher was efficient in directing and controlling the class strongly predicted how much the kids ultimately learned. It wasn't that the children necessarily liked these competent teachers more that mattered for learning; it was whether they believed they could rely on them. Time and again, the data supported this view. The classrooms that had teachers the students felt they could trust in terms of competence were the classrooms where students learned the most.

Although these findings hold great import for altering how educators should be evaluated, they might not be entirely surprising from a psychological perspective. After all, the kids involved in these studies were all far along in age. You might well expect that students studying math and science in a magnet school would be able to determine which teachers were more competent based on repeated interactions with them. Still, the findings resonated with my view that trust was central to learning. And since learning begins way before high school, I began to wonder just how deeply embedded the relation between trust and education was. How early does it emerge? Based on my own kids' behaviors in differentially directing questions to my wife and me, I suspected the answer was going to be earlier than most of us thought.

As I pondered this question, I turned to my colleague and collaborator Paul Harris, who, like Thomas Kane, is a professor of education at Harvard. Rather than studying education on the fairly macro level of classroom and school district dynamics, Harris focuses his efforts on the mechanisms by which individual children acquire, process, and internalize information. Probably more so than anyone else, Paul Harris is responsible for revealing how early and how deeply issues of trust impact learning. His work demonstrates that trust isn't just important for kids in junior or senior high. It's not just central for those in elementary school. It reaches back even further. By three years of age, trust is already influencing how we learn.

Harris's research is driven by two basic insights: children are vulnerable, and those who are vulnerable should never seek advice indiscriminately. Throughout human history, there have always been people who attempt to prey on the weak or gullible. As a consequence, kids who were selective about from whom they would learn were also the kids who had better odds of survival and success; they knew whose input they could trust. Over time, these propensities, like any adaptive trait, became predominant in the species. As such, decisions about to whom to turn for information aren't ones kids need to be taught; at some level, the process is automatic.

As a first step in proving the point, Harris and his colleagues conducted an experiment with preschool children in two different day-care centers. The design of the experiment was as simple as it was elegant. In each center, two caregivers (one from each of the respective day-cares) would show kids unfamiliar objects. The kids could choose to ask either caregiver—the familiar or unfamiliar one—to tell them the name of the novel object and what its purpose was. Irrespective of whom the children asked—or even if they asked at all—both caregivers volunteered information after a minute or two. The central feature of the experiment, however, was that the two caregivers provided different names and purposes for each of the unfamiliar objects. For example, a caregiver from a child's center might tell him that Object A was a "linz" and was used to look at stars, while a caregiver from the other center would tell the same child that Object A was a "slod" and was used to breathe underwater.

Although both caregivers appeared similar—meaning that they looked and acted in ways kids would expect of a day-care teacher— the children showed a clear preference for whose information they valued. They were twice as likely to ask the familiar teacher for information about the objects and to accept her responses over those provided by the unfamiliar teacher. Now, you might protest that this preference simply stems from habit. If a child is accustomed to asking Ms. Smith his questions, then why not just keep doing it? Fair enough. That's why Harris and colleagues conducted the experiment a second time, but with two interesting twists.

The first twist was that the role of the familiar instructor was filled by kids' mothers—the person who typically is not only the most familiar to children, but also the one of whom they ask questions most habitually. The second twist was that each of the kids in the experiment, all of whom were four years old, had had their attachment styles assessed when they were only fifteen months of age. Attachment style, as made famous by the work of John Bowlby and Mary Ainsworth, refers to the mental models that underlie children's assumptions about relationship dynamics with important others. Broadly speaking, children can be characterized as possessing one of three styles of attachment based on early interactions with their primary caregiver. Securely attached children are confident in their mother's (or other primary caregiver's) support. They know she's always there for them, values them, and will do whatever she can to nurture them. In short, they know they can trust her. Avoidant children are just the opposite. They've learned through neglect that their mother isn't to be trusted; she's been indifferent to their needs in the past. Ambivalent children, as you might guess, fall somewhere in the middle. Their mothers can and do attend to their needs, but they often require a bit more nudging to do so.

These differences in attachment style lend themselves to making pointed predictions about how trust guides learning. Since securely attached kids hold beliefs that they can trust their moms, they should preferentially seek them out for information. Yes, secure kids are willing to venture further from their moms to explore their environs—a typical finding from the scientific literature—but when they need to know something, Mom's where it's at. For ambivalent kids, it should be much the same. Their mothers have shown themselves to be competent; it's just that they need a bit more coaxing to engage with their children and meet their needs. Avoidant kids, however, are another story completely. Their mothers have proven to be untrustworthy; they can't be counted on to meet the needs of their children. For avoidant kids, Mom is no more reliable than a stranger, even though she's certainly more familiar.

When Harris and his colleagues conducted the experiment on

these children, even though two and a half years had passed from the time their attachment style had been assessed, they found exactly what you'd expect if it were trust and not familiarity alone that was driving learning preferences. Kids who were securely attached asked for and accepted information from their moms about novel objects more than twice as often as they did from the strange day-care teacher. For ambivalent kids, the pattern was similar if not slightly more mom-focused. For avoidant kids, though, the effects of a lack of trust couldn't have been clearer. They showed no reliable preference for their mothers; they were as willing to seek out and learn from a stranger as from their own parent. Trust, not familiarity or habit by themselves, was what mattered.

Of course, kids of even three to five interact with new individuals from whom they must learn fairly frequently. Whether it's a substitute teacher, an instructor in a new class, or a new friend's parent, children often have to acquire information from new individuals with whom, by definition, they don't possess a long-standing affiliation. This necessity raises the question of how trust might influence learning when familiarity with the past behavior of potential instructors doesn't exist. In such instances, a viable alternative might come through quick assessments of competence. Simply put, if you aren't sure who to believe based on their previous ability to meet your needs, it might make sense to go with who was correct a moment ago.

To examine this possibility, Harris and colleagues again used the method of having two people present opposing names and functions for novel objects. This time, though, both of the people providing the information were unfamiliar to the kids, having been introduced to the children only ten minutes before. Something important happened during those ten minutes, however. The children watched videos of the two individuals providing names for familiar objects. One individual always named the objects correctly (e.g., calling a hammer a hammer), while the other referred to them using incorrect names (e.g., calling a hammer a fork). When the second part of the experiment began and it came time for the three- to five-year-olds to learn about the unfamiliar objects in front of them, they did not ask their questions randomly. They directed their questions three times more often to the "smart" individual than to the seemingly incompetent one.

This preference in selecting a teacher demonstrates that the kids had stored information in their minds about which of the strangers they could trust—information that they readily applied to a new learning situation. Even the three-year-olds adapted quickly. More surprising, though, was that this effect was durable. When the children were brought back a week later and again were exposed to new unfamiliar objects, they continued to prefer to learn from the individual they had earlier deemed competent. Yet perhaps the most profound effect of competence on learning came not from kids' decisions about whom to ask for information, but from their actual ability to retain the knowledge itself. Recent research has confirmed that children actually remember information better—the *same* information—if they hear it from a trustworthy source as opposed to an untrustworthy one. The implications of this fact are immense. When it comes time for exams, for instance, how well any of us can remember information not only depends on how hard we study, but also on how much we trust the teacher who taught it to us.

Familiarity and competence, then, are both central to deciding whose information you can trust. But what about when these two variables are at odds? What about when the person you know and with whom you feel a warm, supportive bond—like a favorite teacher—just doesn't seem to have as much expertise as a new instructor? In those cases, when push comes to shove, knowing the score might be more important than trusting a friend. After all, if the friend is wrong, you'll both be in dire straits.

Once again, Paul Harris's research provides support. This time, he and colleagues tweaked their usual procedure by adding a competence difference to the familiar-unfamiliar teacher experiment. Kids could again choose which of two day-care teachers to ask about the names and uses of novel objects—their usual teacher or an unfamiliar one. As we saw in the past, children overwhelmingly prefer their familiar teacher. The difference this time, however, was that, prior to having the opportunity to learn about novel objects from the familiar and unfamiliar teachers, the kids saw their usual teacher, at the behest of the experimenters, provide incorrect names and uses for some well-known objects. In short, they saw her repeatedly make errors. What happened? Well, for three-year-olds, not much. They continued to favor their familiar teacher irrespective of whether she displayed expertise. But for four- and five-year-olds, the situation changed dramatically. They rapidly abandoned seeking information from their usual teacher and turned to the stranger, whose competence they could trust. Although they might have loved their usual instructor, they dropped her like a stone when it came to learning. Much as Amanda Ripley reported happens with teens, the minds of four-year-olds direct their attention to teachers who are effective and not just nice.

Competence, then, trumps basic familiarity when it comes to trust. But what happens in those cases when children don't even have the chance to assess competence? What happens when they have to decide whom to trust when they have nothing to go on? It's in these cases that we can see how deeply social the mind is in its efforts to shape learning. Consider the following. You are confronted by two people who, though both speaking intelligible

English, speak it with slightly different pronunciations—one with a "standard" English pronunciation and one with a Spanish accent. Each is volunteering different information about how to use an unknown object. Whom do you trust? If you're four years old, the answer is easy: trust the person most like you—the person without the accent (or who matches your accent if you have one). In the absence of any other information about two seemingly well-meaning individuals, differences as subtle as accents can impact a willingness to learn. If kids have to pick someone from whom to accept information, their minds, even though they don't realize it, push them to learn from the "safer" person—the one who is most like them and thus likely to share some level of affiliation.

Although these findings are interesting in terms of sheer science, it's their implications for education that, when we take a step back, shake some long-held assumptions to the core. It's becoming clear that whether and how our children learn is influenced to a great degree not only by the skill levels of the teachers providing information—something teachers can themselves control—but also by subtle factors that are outside most teachers' usual domains of concern. When preschoolers in certain classrooms show more academic success than do those in others, it might not be because the teacher uses a superior curriculum or set of classroom demonstrations; rather, it might be because he or she looks or sounds more like the kids do. When certain kids in a specific class perform better than others, it might not be because they are innately smarter, but rather because their expectations about whether they can rely on their teacher differ. At heart, learning often comes down to believing you can trust what you're told, and by as early as three years of age our minds are already categorizing informants—parents included—as trustworthy or not.

If we're to improve learning in the classroom, findings such as these suggest that educators will have to take the social aspects of instruction into account. Improving curricula is well and good, but additional success is likely to come from helping teachers shape the social persona they display to students. This means educators have to pay attention not only to ways to maximize their competence and intellectual authority, but also to ways to identify links to young students. A teacher may not speak with an accent similar to that of a new pupil, but if he or she lives in the same neighborhood, has the same kind of pet, or experienced a similar past challenge as the student, highlighting this fact will allow a link of association to be made. There's nothing magic about accents in determining similarity. Any marker of association will do. Learning to find and highlight such links can thus be one of many items in a teacher's toolbox. Using it can make all the difference in a young student's taking the first step toward trust and, thereby, toward increased academic success.

Learning to Trust

To now, we've been examining how trust impacts learning. But to truly understand how trust interacts with the developing mind, we have to flip the question around and ask how the mind learns to trust in the first place. I've shown you some evidence that the minds of children are sensitive to competence early on, but what about the other facets of the trust equation: fairness and integrity? Earlier than most would imagine, the minds of children are already engaged in calculations that determine not only whom they feel they can trust, but also whether they themselves will act in a trustworthy manner.

Let's begin with the latter. If you have ever spent time perusing parenting books, especially those from a few decades back, you learned that they often subtly, or sometimes not so subtly, promote a view that infants and toddlers are selfish. They cry not just because they need something, but because they're trying to manipulate you. They smile not only because they're happy, but because they're trying to get something from you. Now, it is certainly true that being a baby is difficult—you can't do much of anything on your own. You have to depend on others. It should come as no surprise, then, that babies enter the world with a magic bag of tricks. As we saw in the last chapter, they stoke oxytocin in their parents' brains to increase bonding. They also arrive with those beautiful round heads with big eyes—features meant to evoke a caretaking response in almost everyone. But it is also true that babies and toddlers do not enter this world hell-bent on manipulating and deceiving their tired parents. Just like the rest of us, they need to strike a balance, and so their minds come pre-equipped to promote their own trustworthy and helpful behavior.

Attempting to understand the psychology of babies does pose one big problem, however. It's not easy to ask infants questions; they can't really tell you what they're thinking. They can't readily say whether they trust someone, let alone tell you if they'd cooperate with him. They can't even read information in order to learn about potential partners. What these limitations mean is that those who study infant cognition have to be quite creative. They need to use tools that present and collect all the information a baby requires without relying on any introspection or verbal responses by the subject in question. As a consequence, these scientists need to adopt strategies where everything occurs by observation. This way, the babies and the researchers can get all the info they need simply from what they see.

One of the modern classics using this strategy to investigate children's motivations to be helpful comes from Harvard psychologist Felix Warneken and colleagues. Warneken began with a basic question: Are very young children innately prosocial? Could they be trusted to lend a hand without being told that they should do so? To find out, he sat eighteen-month-olds down, one at a time, to watch a series of actors confront a series of unfortunate events—events with which the little ones could help if they so desired. The main questions centered on whether the toddlers would be able to distinguish when help was needed and, if they felt it was, whether they would do anything about it. For example, an actor in the experiment might drop a pen and say, "Oh, no, my pen!" or conversely intentionally drop the pen. Other times, she might accidentally drop a spoon through a small hole in a box and look upset versus intentionally placing a spoon inside the box in a calm manner. In each case, the basic action was the same, but the emotional expressions, or absence thereof, differed.

The results couldn't have been more striking. Clear majorities of toddlers quickly came to the actors' aid in all situations where she appeared to need it. They retrieved her pen for her when she seemed distressed that she'd dropped it; they showed her a hidden flap on the box (which they had previously been shown) that would allow her to retrieve her spoon when she was unable to retrieve it on her own. At the first sign of an unintentional mishap, these kids were on the job. They were there to help the adult and thus prove themselves reliable. By a year and a half of age—before most can do any more than string two words together—the instinct to support and cooperate with others is already active.

Of course, kids aren't saints any more than we adults are. Like us, they have a dual nature, simultaneously possessing impulses that make them worthy and unworthy of trust. Yes, they will certainly come to a person's aid when there is no real cost to them for doing so, but when faced with the opportunity for selfish gain at the same time, their actions can be a bit more nuanced.

By three, kids are already struggling with issues of this type—issues of me vs. you. To see the struggle in action, Warneken and colleagues conducted a different experiment where they had children work on a coin-retrieving task with a puppet. The puppet, which was operated by an adult, and the child were asked to combine their efforts to use fishing-pole-like devices to remove coins from buckets for a reward—a fun, but difficult, task. Unbeknownst to the child, the task was rigged so that the child would be able to remove either two or four coins. If she removed two, the puppet would remove four; if she removed four, the puppet would remove two. In some conditions, then, the child outperformed the puppet on the joint task; in others, the puppet outperformed the child. At the end of the coin-fishing endeavor, researchers gave the children six stickers—a *very* valuable reward for three-year-olds—to divide between themselves and the puppet for completing the work.

Now, a trustworthy partner would, and should, divvy up the stickers based on the amount of work each individual completed. It's a simple rule of the workplace: more work equals more reward. At some level, the three-year-olds already understood this fact even in the absence of anyone ever making it explicit. When the puppet performed in a superior manner (i.e., retrieved four as opposed to two coins), the children gave it more stickers—three of the six on average—than when the puppet performed poorly. In those poor performance cases, kids gave the puppet two stickers. At first glance, this seems right; the puppet can trust (as much as puppets can) that their work partner will give them more of the financial reward when they perform better. But you may have noticed a slight glitch in the system. Puppet laborers are being treated differently than their human counterparts. When the puppet outperforms the child, rewards are divided equally; kids give the puppet three of the six tokens. When the child outperforms the puppet, there is a difference; the child keeps four stickers for him- or herself and gives the puppet only two.

What we're witnessing is a fundamental conflict between psychological mechanisms pushing three-year-olds to be trustworthy and others pushing them to be selfish. Yes, they'll reward their partner with more when he performs better—three as compared to two stickers—but never with more stickers than they'll give themselves! Tricky accounting, to say the least. At five years of age, the same pattern emerges. As kids grow, however, they learn that dividing rewards in this way will probably get them into trouble in the long run. In fact, by eight years of age kids are quite aware of this fact; like adults, they show a strong aversion to inequity, at least in public. They realize that the short-term benefit of unfairly taking a greater reward will result in larger losses in the long term, and consequently, children of this age regularly reject rewards that unfairly favor themselves over potential partners who are present (and thus aware of the distribution of rewards).

Of course, this fact doesn't mean that older kids won't be untrustworthy at other times. The mechanisms favoring short-term self-interest still reside in their minds, and will, given the right situation, lead them to seek immediate, selfish advantage. For example, five- and six-year-olds who readily share resources equally with others when the resources are public knowledge will hoard said prizes for themselves if they believe others won't know about it.

Taken together, these findings support the notion that the seeds of trustworthiness emerge on their own. Children don't need to be taught to act fairly and honorably to be virtuous; these motivations are part of their nature. Sure, they'll sometimes break trusts to serve their needs, but, like adults, they'll also at times stand firm in their loyalties and obligations, even in the face of temptation. Mechanisms for trust, cooperation, and their antipodes reside in the minds of babes and, like much of the rest of the young mind, blossom on their own schedule. Children don't enter the world as selfish imps or tabula rasae. They arrive with a fledgling morality that, as in their adult counterparts, is a bit more complex than most of us realize.

It would be a mistake, however, to assume that, just because the minds of children possess moral mechanisms, moral education isn't necessary or can't serve a purpose. As I mentioned in the first chapter, trustworthiness, like all moral behaviors, is jointly determined by both the conscious and the nonconscious minds. Teaching your little ones—whether they're your own children or kids in your classes—the value of keeping one's word can certainly increase the odds that they'll do so more frequently (especially if they *trust* you). Internalizing these values will shape the reactions of the conscious mind a great deal, but these reactions aren't the only ones that matter—a fact that's important to remember when trying to fathom why in the world little Johnny just ate more of his sister's candy than he promised he would. As we'll see throughout this book, there's an entirely different level of moral calculations going on below awareness.

Deciding to be fair and reliable makes up only half the picture when it comes to learning about trust. For every kid considering whether to cheat a partner, there's another kid contemplating whether or not to trust the first kid. And if we're talking about children deciding whether to trust adults, the potential consequences become even greater. Due specifically to their heightened vulnerability, kids need to figure out early and quickly upon whom they can rely. Even if all a child can do is cry if a "bad" person approaches—a person who can't or won't take care of him either by design or ability—it may be enough to ensure his survival. Mom and dad are less likely to leave a child with someone if the kid is pitching a fit about it. This precarious aspect of childhood alone argues strongly for the need to gauge the dependability of others— a need that should direct even the minds of babies to engage in a trust-relevant analysis of those around them. The question, of course, centers on how early such an ability arises.

To find the answer, I turned to the work of my friend Paul Bloom. Paul and his wife, Karen Wynn, run one of the most famous labs on child development in the world. Few research duos are more proficient at probing the minds of babies than these two, and their research suites at Yale have produced some of the most intriguing findings to date on the social thoughts and evaluations of the pre-verbal set. I have had the good fortune of speaking with Paul several times over the years, and am often in awe of the creative methods that he, Karen, and their students have devised to observe the moral thoughts of children. Their work has turned back the clock for the emergence of the earliest hints of moral judgment. Together, Bloom and Wynn continue to demonstrate that the minds of infants don't busy themselves just with learning facts about how the world works; they're also focused on figuring out how the people living in this world are likely to behave.

As I noted earlier, working with infants means confronting the problem of not being able to ask your research participants what they think. One way Bloom and Wynn get around this difficulty is by using a *violation of expectancy* task. As its name suggests, the task works by showing infants different events to see what, if anything, surprises them. How do you measure if babies are surprised? Easy— time how long they look at something. It's a well-established fact that babies will look longer at objects or scenes that diverge from what they expect to see. If, for example, you placed a red ball under a box and then subsequently raised the box to reveal a yellow ball, infants would stare for a significantly longer time at the yellow ball than if it had been red. Even though they are unable to say they expected to see a red ball when the box was lifted—as they didn't see anyone replace the red ball with a yellow one—their surprise can be assessed by attending to their gaze.

Bloom and Wynn's genius was to use this looking-time strategy to gauge babies' judgments about social beings instead of objects. How to present trust-relevant events in an easy way for the infants? Again, we turn to puppets. Small, wooden, geometrically shaped, puppets. Picture the following: a small stage with a rolling-hill landscape below a blue-sky backdrop. Enter from stage right a little red wooden circle with googly eyes. Animated by the invisible puppeteer, the red circle—known as the climber—winds its way across the landscape until it comes to a big hill. It then tries valiantly to scale the hill, much like the Little Engine That Could, but to no avail. After it fails to reach the summit twice, a second puppet suddenly appears as the climber begins its third try. The new puppet, also taking the form of a googly-eyed geometric shape, does one of two things. In the *helper* condition, it approaches the climber, and as the climber looks at it in anticipation while stalled at the halfway point, the new puppet helps the climber by pushing it all the way up the hill toward its elusive goal. In the *hinderer* condition, as its name suggests, the opposite occurs; the new puppet pushes the climber back down the hill, thwarting its goal. The ten-month-old babies watched several similar scenes of this "play," seeing the helper and hinderer an equal number of times.

You would probably agree that the resulting interpretation, for adults at least, is quite straightforward: the climber can trust the helper but not the hinderer. But how about the babies? Are their minds already making inferences about morality and dependability before they even know what these words mean? To see, Bloom and Wynn took the infants who had watched these interactions and sat them in front of a new stage. Here, all three puppets suddenly appeared, with the climber at center stage and the helper and hinderer flanking the opposing ends. The big question became, which puppet would the climber approach when given the chance? If you think like a baby, the answer should be easy: you approach people you can trust. When that's what the climber did—when it bounced over to the helper—the babies didn't spend much time looking. Everything happened as they expected; their world made sense. However, when the climber bounced over to its nemesis, the hinderer, the babies looked much longer. Their gaze was fixed on the new pair, almost as if staring in disbelief.

Pushing the developmental clock back even more, Bloom and Wynn repeated the same experiment with six-month-olds. Even these infants—barely able to sit up on their own—could interpret which of the puppets was trustworthy and thereby deserving of interaction. When offered a chance to pick which of the two puppets—the helper or the hinderer—to hold and cuddle, *all* of the infants reached for the helper. It didn't matter what color or shape it was—the researchers made sure to alternate the physical characteristics of the two puppets—no one wanted to interact with the puppet who proved unsupportive of a friend in need.

Wednesday's Child Who's Full of Woe or Thursday's Child with Far to Go?

When children enter this world, they confront a social landscape of sorts—a landscape riddled with forked paths leading to treasures and traps that daily unfold before them. It's no surprise that the goal of a life well lived is to follow the paths that take one far, as opposed to those that dead-end in woe. That's what every parent wants for her or his child—a desire mirrored implicitly in the minds of children themselves. As kids approach each juncture on the road of life, a choice must be made of which route to follow, and when such choices involve human interaction, issues of trust will frequently be central. Who can you trust to teach you? To take care of you? To share equitably with you? Should you yourself be trustworthy? Treat others fairly? Help them or ignore them? The answers to questions like these are fundamental determinants of where a journey finally ends. There's just one slight problem kids face along the way—there's no map.

The absence of an unfailing guide or similar metaphorical map for ensuring which route or option to take isn't as debilitating as it might initially seem. As we've seen in the preceding pages, kids aren't left to decide whom to trust or whether to cheat by flipping a proverbial coin. It's not a random process, nor should it be, by any stretch of evolutionary logic. This would be leaving survival to chance, and there's little more anathema to the process of evolution than that. Consequently, the minds of children come preloaded, so to speak, with trust-relevant software. To borrow the cognitive scientist Steven Pinker's phrase—the mind is no blank slate. Before we can even sit up reliably, we're trying to figure out whom we can trust. Before we can talk, we already recognize the importance of fairness and cooperation. And before we get our first grade in school, we already are selective about whom we will rely on to teach us.

These innate and precocious abilities aren't static, of course; they grow as we grow. Children's intuitions about what to expect from others get regularly updated through early interactions with caregivers and teachers. In essence, the initial hunches about how likely it is that someone new will be trustworthy— the expectations we're all born with—become more finely tuned each day. Early experiences alter children's expectations, and the resulting attachment styles partially explain why certain older kids aren't so surprised that others will cheat or neglect them. These learned expectancies function much as does the setting of different base rates for cooperation in simulations using the prisoner's dilemma. They influence the odds that any given individual will choose to trust someone else and act in a trustworthy manner herself, which then sets the stage for subsequent interactions.

In the case of learning, though, we can see that the effects move beyond issues of integrity and extend into those of competence. If a child correctly identifies a competent teacher, she is likely to learn more and thereby serve as a competent instructor for others in the future. She'll be someone these others can trust to provide information; she'll be someone with whom they want to work. If she selects a teacher incorrectly, it's as if she is destined to be a defector; by virtue of a poor choice, she'll have less expertise and thus be shunned more frequently as a potential partner or source of knowledge. Low competence is, after all, functionally equivalent to defection. Irrespective of whether the "problem" comes from immoral intention or low ability, it leads to failure of a partnership.

As you undoubtedly now recognize, trust is about integrity and competence—about wanting to do the right thing and being able to do it. If our children are to reach their full intellectual potential, we have to provide their young minds with the type of instructors they perceive as optimal—the type of instructor from whom the brain evolved to learn. This strategy also means paying attention to changes in the trust-relevant qualities that are paramount at any given time. The brains of the very young are focused on learning from those who are similar and comfortable, much as a mother or father might be. As children progress through the early years of primary education, however, their concerns with comfort and similarity ebb in favor of competence and expertise. Parents and educators must follow suit if they're to maximize any child's learning potential. They must demonstrate their expertise, lest they be ignored as nice but irrelevant. They must earn the kids' trust, but learn to do it in different ways. The data exist to show what kids want and need in order to excel in school. We, as a society, just need to listen.

Key Insights

- **Telling kids to trust you doesn't work.** From nearly the moment they're born, the minds of children begin to keep score with respect to whether an adult is trustworthy or not. Before they can speak, they know if you treat others fairly. And before they begin kindergarten, they know if you're competent in certain areas. So, while you can try to convince their conscious minds to trust you, their nonconscious ones already know the deal. Past behavior, of course, never guarantees future behavior—reputation isn't perfect—but it sets an expectation that you'll have to work harder to overcome if you've let kids down in the past.

- **Instructors should be mentors, not friends.** A good mentor is someone who holds the expertise to guide you in an endeavor and shepherds you through the challenges you face along the way. A good mentor, then, is someone you can trust both to support you and to give you expert advice, even if it's not the advice you want to hear in the moment. For children, this means finding teachers whom they respect and like. But if they can't find a teacher with both qualities, they tend to err on the side of respect. As we've seen, by the age of five, kids intuitively favor receiving information from people they view as experts over people they view as just nice. They also remember that information more, which can make all the difference when it comes exam time.

• **When it comes to being trustworthy, children are no less complex than adults.** People often assume that kids' decisions about how to behave are simplistic. If they want a cookie they're not supposed to have, they take it and worry about consequences later. But in reality, their minds, at least at the intuitive level, are subject to the same competing mechanisms as ours. They recognize inequity at the same time they want to maximize their own rewards. They want others to view them as trustworthy, but also understand the benefits of anonymity. So, although they may split cookies evenly with a friend if she's present, it's also likely they'll take more cookies for themselves if she's not and unlikely to find out. Their minds, like ours, are trying to find the right balance between immediate and long-term reward. Unlike ours, however, it's often more difficult for kids to override their intuitive impulses, meaning next time little Johnny says he doesn't know why he broke a promise, he may really be telling the truth.

CHAPTER 4

THE HEART OF THE MATTER

Trust in Romantic Relationships

Although it's true that all types of adult relationships—friendships, business partnerships, team memberships—involve some level of joint dependence for success, their spheres of influence are usually fairly narrow, meaning that individual breaches of trust, though unwelcome, don't necessarily make one feel universally vulnerable. But this statement comes with one big caveat: love. When it comes to romantic relationships, most adults can have their seeming self-sufficiency momentarily obliterated. It's not that we become paralyzed or cognitively helpless. We can still reason, research, and analyze. We can still work, cook, and plan for retirement. What we can't do, though, is turn off that burning desire to connect with a partner—to share, to merge, to depend on, to bare our souls to him or her.

As a result of these desires, it can often be exceedingly difficult to just "move on" when a valued romantic relationship fails. Try as we might, consigning the memory of a romantic partner to the junk heap can be tough. Few events cause the level of emotional turmoil and searing pain as the betrayal of a trusted spouse or significant other. The losses, real and emotional, that accompany knowing the person you love has decided to leave you—or at least wants to leave you—can make almost any other loss seem trivial by comparison.

The reason for this emotional tumult stems precisely from the magnitude of the costs and benefits attached to romantic relationships. Love builds ties between two people, and for adults, one main goal of these ties, whether you want to admit it or not, is the production and support of the next generation. Historically speaking, it took two individuals to make a baby and at least two to care for it optimally. In an evolutionary sense, then, the trustworthiness of a coparent often holds more implications for one's success than the loyalty of most anyone else. Disloyal spouses directly equate to lower odds for passing on one's genes. And since that's the engine behind natural selection, it counts for a lot in terms of shaping the mind.

Yet, as important as reproductive concerns are, the benefits of love and fidelity don't end with child rearing. Study upon study continue to document that the physical and psychological health of people in satisfying long-term relationships outstrips that of those who are single. On every metric there is—economic, social, physiological, or otherwise—being in a long-term relationship serves as a plus. It provides you with a constant cooperator—a person who, hopefully, will provide loyal support across many domains of life. As such, a good relationship will serve as a buffer for challenges due to stress, finances, social dilemmas, and anything else that has potential to darken your future.

The upshot is that while betrayal by a business partner is certainly a negative experience, the likelihood that it would adversely affect one's life to the same degree as betrayal by a spouse is close to zero. This simple fact explains why the complexity of the mechanisms the mind uses to manage trust in nonromantic relationships doesn't come close to that reserved for relationships with those we love. Still, even this view of how trust works seems to leave one piece of the puzzle unexplained: Why does it hurt to get rejected by someone new? Why do people spend hours obsessing over whether the person they met at last week's speed-dating party might have liked someone else more? The answer, as we'll see later in this chapter, is found through recognizing that even though the context of romantic relationships adds some additional twists to how trust functions, it still maintains the common element of being sensitive to the future. Trust within couples isn't only sensitive to the costs and benefits of the present; it's also responsive to the costs and benefits yet to come. After all, the guy you met at the speed-dating event might just turn out to be the father of the three children in your future.

Love: What's Trust Got to Do with It?

At heart, all romantic relationships are about give and take. What differentiates good ones from bad ones is the relative balance between the two. Decades of research and centuries of common sense tell us that relationships characterized by roughly equivalent costs and benefits to the partners are the ones that are most satisfying and likely to endure. The exact lines along which the costs and benefits break down don't really matter much. One partner might provide more income while the other tends to family needs. One might provide more emotional support while the other provides expertise in managing finances. The key to making the relationship work is simply that each provides benefits in areas the other values. And as long as the benefits being received are subjectively equal to the costs incurred, the relationship keeps chugging along.

I realize this description of romantic bliss might sound a bit cold and businesslike, but at the most fundamental level that's how romantic relationships operate. This dynamic doesn't preclude the fact that relationships can feel magical at times; our hearts can still flutter from the benefits we receive. Still, whether we enjoy and therefore decide to remain in a relationship depends on just how much we're willing to do to continue to experience that warm glow. No one can afford to give continuously without receiving, and as a consequence, managing relationships comes down to a balancing act between protecting oneself from exploitation and gaining benefits that can only come from fostering long-term, intimate social bonds.

A fairly basic way to manage this balance simply requires keeping track of who did or will do what for whom. Peter agrees to come home early and cook dinner for Olivia, who is working late. *Check.* Olivia, in turn, stays up later that night to finish reconciling the pair's banking statements. *Check.* Peter then agrees to get up early to run the next day's errands. And on it goes, with individuals adding items to their respective mental tally sheets and checking the boxes when their partners come through. On the surface, this system appears straightforward; it seems to provide a way to ensure that costs and benefits don't become too asymmetric. In reality, though, this system is not only hugely effortful, but also ridden with potential for bias.

Think for a moment about how many promises, favors, and related cooperative acts most people in relationships make or do for one another in a given day. We rely on our partners to run errands, take care of kids and pets, balance our checkbooks, invest our retirement funds, plan vacations, pick up the groceries, etc. In reality, there is no way the human mind can keep an accurate running tally of the success or failure of each instance in which one partner depended on the other. This limitation is especially true when you consider that many instances of cooperation occur over time delays. Unless you're running a spreadsheet to track your partner's reliability in real time, there are bound to be errors in remembering who was suppose to pick up the dry cleaning or whether it's the fourth or fifth time one of you forgot to mail the rent check. You might try to remedy the situation by only keeping track of the "big stuff"—the events that really matter. The problem here, of course, is that what's big to one person might not be as big to the other. Olivia might be really upset that Peter didn't spend enough time providing emotional support to her when she was describing an argument with her boss; yet to Peter this might not have seemed to be a big deal at all. He was more upset that Olivia made plans for the two of them to have a friend over on the night he intended to watch the game.

Here's where trust comes in. It eases the mind's computational load in long-term relationships by functioning as a cognitive shortcut that removes the need to track costs and benefits in a detailed way. If we trust our partners, that trust, assuming it is well placed, allows us to read their minds when it comes to reliability. It's a bet that our partners will hold up their end of the relationship. On average, they'll do their share of errands, pay their share of bills, compromise with us on issues we care about, and offer the support we need and expect. Of course, the exact balance of effort need not be fifty-fifty; it depends on the two people involved. Some couples may be happy with a sixty-forty split or other alternative. What ultimately matters for trust to emerge is that individuals are meeting the expectations their partners set, thereby freeing their partners from having to consistently check.

The moment when trust emerges in a relationship often marks a sea change in comfort, as it signifies that the relationship is entering a new and more durable phase. A colleague of mine at Yale,

Margaret Clark, refers to this transition as moving from an *exchange-based* to a *communal* relationship style. As the names suggest, exchange-based relationships are characterized by explicit attempts to keep track of the costs and benefits incurred. For most people, it's that early phase where they're feeling the other person out. *If I buy dinner today, will he buy it tomorrow or be a mooch? I've been there this week when she needed a shoulder to cry on, but will she take the time to listen and support me now that I just lost my job?* As individuals pass through those early periods, most keep tallies, if for no other reason than trying to determine if they can trust the other person.

After some time—how much depends on the people involved—many relationships graduate to the communal phase. Once there, people stop keeping track and engaging in "if I do this, she'll do that" type thinking. They uphold their responsibilities and assume their partners will do the same, thereby freeing up a lot of mental capacity that had been directed toward monitoring exchanges. Although there are numerous experiments that attest to this fact, one of my favorites comes from Clark's early work. It demonstrates the phenomenon in question in about as straightforward a way as possible. In the experiment, she simply asked people who were either communal- or exchange-focused in a relationship to work on a joint task together. They were told that money would be given to one of the pair to divide between the two based on the amount of work they each completed. There was one catch, though: each person had to work on solving problems in a separate room. After a few minutes had passed, the problems would be swapped between members of the pair so that the individuals could provide answers to the questions their partners didn't. It seems simple enough, but there was one final, minute detail to be considered: ink color.

On the desk in front of each participant lay two pens with which to record their answers—one with red ink and one with black. As innocuous as it may at first appear, the presence of the two pens sets up an interesting choice. If you circle answers using the pen with the same color ink as the one used by your partner, evidence of individual contributions vanishes. If you use a different color ink, an objective record exists for who did what. As you might now expect, pen selection didn't turn out to be random. People who were oriented toward a communal framework tended to use the pen that matched the one used by their partner about 75 percent of the time. Those who were oriented toward exchange did the converse; they chose to use the pen with the opposite color ink more than 90 percent of the time. They wanted to ensure the existence of an explicit, objective record of each person's efforts. Trust but verify—plain and simple. Well, mostly just verify, as the objective record removes the vulnerability of getting cheated.

If these differences in relationship orientation can influence variables as minor as pen choice, imagine what they can do to tallying efforts when large costs and benefits are on the line. Trust is the key to solving the problem. It not only removes the motivation and need to verify, it also allows you to cooperate when the ability to verify might not be readily available. It allows a relationship to grow in the face of obstacles that might otherwise prevent it. Those who were communally oriented possessed faith that their partners would give them the money they deserved. They didn't worry about having an objective record or keeping a tally; they used the same pen. They just trusted their partner to do the right thing.

The Benefits of Trusting the One You Love

Although reducing mental fatigue is certainly a desirable thing, if it were the only benefit of trusting a partner, trust would long ago have been replaced by accounting devices. Think of the multiple ways humans have developed to keep track of financial transactions. We could have done the same for exchanges with romantic partners. It might have been difficult to devise the mechanism, but if all the benefits of trust came down to bookkeeping, we would have found a way. That we didn't do so suggests that trust must possess an additional benefit. But what?

Jeffry Simpson, a psychologist at the University of Minnesota, has put his finger on the answer. Simpson has studied the role of trust in close relationships for decades. In so doing, he has developed influential theories for how trust shapes and perpetuates strong interpersonal bonds. One reason his views hold such weight is that his methods are about as precise and valid as one can get in studying romantic relationships. Simpson is a big proponent of what is commonly referred to as strain-test paradigms. Yes, it's what you're probably thinking. He brings couples into the lab and puts their relationship under a strain and then looks to see what happens.

Imagine the following. You and your significant other arrive at a lab and are escorted into a relatively comfortable room, having previously completed online measures related to trust. The room you enter has inviting chairs, pleasant lighting, and, possibly to your discomfort, video cameras. After a few minutes of chatting with the experimenters, though, the salience of the cameras fades. At this point, the researchers make a fairly straightforward request. One of you will bring up a desired goal for yourself that would require major sacrifices from your partner to obtain. You'll discuss it for seven minutes with him or her, and then switch roles. When each of you has had your turn, you'll fill out some questionnaires inquiring about your views of the discussions and your partner. The process may not sound fun, but it usually provides valid insights into the dynamics of a given relationship. Attesting to the procedure's

ability to capture real-world interactions, the most commonly dis
cussed goals in these experiments involved areas of conflict familiar
to those of most established couples: relocation to pursue a career,
leaving a job to go back to school or to change professions, making
an expensive purchase, or taking a vacation to a place that one's
partner dislikes.

Jeffry Simpson's view for how trust works centers on its ability
to grease the wheels of romantic relationships—to keep them going
strong by biasing not only one's own behaviors but also one's inter-
pretations of a partner's actions. Trust, in essence, functions as a
kind of relationship buffer—it smooths rough spots. You can think
of it as a kind of love drug. Like many pharmaceutical substances
you might take to cope with a stressful event, trust can alter your
behavior both by lowering hostility in the moment and by positively
biasing your recollections of the past such that potentially problematic events don't seem to be so troubling after all.

In Simpson's experiments, like the one just described, such
benefits of trust emerge time and again. The video recordings made
during couples' discussions reveal a consistent pattern: individuals
who entered discussions with higher levels of trust for their partners demonstrated much greater accommodation and collaboration.
Not only were they more willing to listen to their partner's desires
and take them seriously, they also were more motivated to try to
find a solution that would be acceptable to both parties. It's not that
trusting individuals were discussing goals that were any less stressful in scope than the ones discussed by their less trusting counterparts; both groups face off over similarly consequential possibilities.
The decreased tension and resulting greater success in negotiation
derived solely from the subtle effects of trust itself.

At each juncture in the conversation—at each point when a
snap decision has to be made about whether to escalate conflict to

protect one's interests—trust intuitively tips the scale back toward de-escalation and compromise. Simply put, trust alters the mental calculus running in the background of our minds. It makes us consider what we have to lose in the long run if we harm this relationship in pursuit of a short-term victory. Is it really worth damaging or potentially ending a relationship that can bring you years of joy and support simply because you don't want to go to Disney World next month with your spouse? Hopefully, the answer is *no*, and that's why trust works to combat the mind's usual focus on favoring short-term gains over long-term ones. It works in the background to make you value the long-term more, and thereby be willing to engage in greater sacrifice or cooperation in the present.

Conflict, even in the face of successful resolutions, can leave scars, however; the strain of somewhat tense discussions can negatively color individuals' views of one other. While a partner may have ultimately collaborated, it's possible that the simple act of negotiating itself may have altered your views of him or her. *Wow, that was more difficult than I thought it would be. She's more selfish than I thought. Gee, I didn't realize he doesn't value X.* Put differently, the tendency of negotiation to unmask competing motives and goals holds the potential to raise questions about a relationship's health and trajectory. Here again, though, Simpson envisions trust as a panacea of sorts.

One way to combat any potential damage negotiations may produce is to change the impressions left by said negotiations after the fact. Simpson's research demonstrates exactly this phenomenon. Individuals who entered discussions already possessing a high degree of trust in their partners regularly overestimated the amount of accommodation they received. As an example, if a husband agreed to his wife's request that he work ten more hours a week to allow her to go back to school, the subjective value she attached to his concession was much greater if she had higher levels of trust in him prior to the negotiation. Put simply, the more trust you have for a partner, the more you view his or her actions as noble sacrifices. Now, you might also guess that it works the other way as well— seeing a partner's sacrifices as more substantive leads to even greater trust in her or him. And you'd be right. The ultimate effect of the biasing influence of trust is just that—it self-propagates, assuming your partner wasn't completely selfish and refused to cooperate at all. As Simpson's findings confirmed, individuals who trusted their partners more at the start of the discussions in his lab trusted them to an even greater degree at the end, even when holding constant the objective amount of accommodations made.

At this point, it's possible that you might be feeling a bit troubled. Isn't a bias of any type problematic? After all, this research shows that trust in a partner appears to be fostering a bit of a positive illusion; it tends to make you believe a partner is more trustworthy than he or she may actually be. Yet if you think back to the arguments proffered at the beginning of this book for how trust works, your focus will likely change from wondering why this bias exists to considering the trade-offs it offers. Although it is certainly true that these inflated views of a partner's trustworthiness could lead to negative consequences, it is also true that they can hold benefits as well. The key to understanding why is *noise*—noise in the cooperative system that is our social networks.

The reinforcing rounds of trust begetting trust that Jeffry Simpson identified combat opportunities for damage to relationships— damage that itself might stem from bias. Remember that in Nowak's simulations, tit-for-tat strategies weren't the big winner. While performing well, they nonetheless possessed a fundamental flaw. They were unable to recover from a mistaken defection—an instance when someone meant to act in a trustworthy manner but didn't. In

TFT, once a partner shows an inkling of disloyalty, he's written off. The partnership enters a downward spiral of distrust from which there is no return. Generous tit-for-tat, however, possesses a feature that overcomes this threat. It accepts that an isolated act of untrustworthy behavior could be aberrant; it is forgiving and still allows one to assume that a partner is worthy of more trust than an instance of his or her objective behavior might indicate. As such, it allows a relationship, whether it's preexisting or new, to advance rather than end. And with that advancement comes the continued benefits of cooperation and support. Herein lies the payoff for the bias; there's often more to gain in the long term by keeping a valued romantic relationship going than there is by ending it over a possible transgression.

Think about it. There are many instances in which, whether due to stress, a bad mood, or even mishearing something, we can respond in a manner that is less than accommodating—a manner that doesn't truly represent our usual willingness to support a partner. Although these instances may appear aberrant and nondiagnostic to us, a less than supportive response often seems just that to a partner. Unless he or she devotes the time and energy to dig more deeply into its causes, it will be interpreted as an indication of selfishness. Another intrinsic bias of the human mind—the fundamental attribution error—often pushes us to ascribe specific actions to a person's disposition as opposed to situational forces. As a consequence, such "noise" in relationships has the potential to set an otherwise healthy relationship into a death spiral by mistake.

The biasing power of trust—its ability to cause the mind to see negotiating behavior as more trustworthy than it actually was—functions as an analogue to GTFT. By producing asymmetric errors in reflection—errors that make it more likely we'll overestimate a partner's support and trustworthiness—it leads us to be more forgiving of selfishness even though we don't know it. While it's true that on a conscious level we may at times intentionally excuse people we trust for sporadic selfishness, we have to be motivated to do so. The bias discovered by Jeffry Simpson is more efficient; it continually and effortlessly operates at the nonconscious level. It colors our hunches and feelings toward our partners, pushing us at an intuitive level to keep trust high—not because we forgive our partners for acting less supportively, but rather because we misre-member exactly how supportive they were. The results, however, are functionally the same: smoother-running relationships. In fact, Simpson has shown chronic levels of high trust among relationship partners not only increase levels of relationship satisfaction, but also lower variability in those levels. In line with trust's buffering abil-ity, partners who have high trust perceive their relationships to be less bumpy, even when to an objective eye this isn't the case. Trust grinds mountains into molehills, both in the present and in memory.

Not to worry, though; trust doesn't completely blind us. If a partner acts extremely unaccommodating, no amount of white-washing will matter. This is as it should be, too. Intentional mali-ciousness or complete disregard for a partner should be taken as a sign that trust may be misplaced and will likely lead to continual loss. It's in those borderline cases, though, where the adaptive role of bias can most readily come into play.

The Head and the Heart: Two Routes to Trusting Your Partner (or Not)

Sometimes it's difficult to shake a nagging feeling that something is amiss in a relationship. Your significant other just isn't acting right. Do you confront him and risk showing insecurity or provoking his retreat? Or do you ignore the feeling, thinking you may be overreacting? It's a question that plagues almost everyone at one time or another. It's also one that often requires making a choice between trusting your head or your heart. How to make that choice correctly, though, is no easy matter. It's not as simple as blindly going with your intuitions or with your reasoned analysis. As I said at the outset of this book, neither deliberate nor intuitive mental calculations always provide the best answers when it comes to trust. Both aim to solve the problem, but neither is perfect. To make the best choice, you need to understand how both systems work together.

Intuitive trust, or impulsive trust, as it's sometimes termed, refers to evaluations of a partner's trustworthiness that occur outside of conscious awareness. You can think of it as a result of Porges's neuroception—a sense of another's trustworthiness derived from an automatic, continuously updated calculation. Exactly how those calculations take place will be a topic for later chapters; for now, it's sufficient to know that the mind uses the resulting information. Reasoned, or reflective, trust is just the opposite. It's an assessment based on deliberate analysis. It's the kind of trust we often call into question when we're engaging in what-ifs. *What if my partner's refusal to go to the party with me means he's losing interest in our relationship? What if the many late nights my spouse has been working means she's having an affair?*

As you might imagine, how the mind deals with these questions and concerns—whether they even arise in the first place—holds important consequences for the success of relationships. While it's certainly true that actual breaches of trust can spell the end of a relationship, so, too, can misplaced suspicion stemming from an incorrect analysis. So, for a second, let's put aside issues of how people respond to actual infidelity or related events where trust is clearly decimated in favor of examining how intuitive and reflective systems jointly determine responses to those we love when cases are a bit more ambiguous.

Challenges to trust in the romantic realm usually begin with a *hmmm*—a pause where we reflect on just what a certain questionable behavior means. Does a partner's working late or reticence to discuss future plans suggest he might not be as enamored of the relationship as once thought? Trying to find answers can often call reflective trust into question. It motivates us to reconsider our current relationship in an attempt to determine if a partner continues to be trustworthy. Trust, after all, entails vulnerability, and if a partner isn't going to provide support, one way to guard against being exploited is to reduce your own level of trust in him or her. To determine the best course of action, most people will analyze a partner's behaviors—sometimes obsessively so—to discern the truth. As rational as it may at first seem, this strategy is nonetheless rife with limitations. As one example, the attributions we make for the causes of past behaviors are often erroneous. Yet even if this analytic process were entirely objective, its results alone would not provide a perfect prediction for what we would ultimately decide to do. Remember, assessments of trustworthiness operate at two levels. Whether a troubling *hmmm* leads to a true recalibration of trust hinges as much on the analysis going on outside of awareness as on the one the conscious mind is directing.

One way to get a sense of how these two systems interact comes from work by psychologist Sandra Murray. Murray has spent years examining how couples navigate challenges to trust on both the conscious and nonconscious levels by focusing on exactly the type of *hmmm* issues we've been discussing. Say, for example, Olivia asks Peter to come home early for dinner and a movie, but Peter refuses, telling Olivia he already made plans to watch the game with the guys from the office. *Hmmm.* Some alarm bells may begin to go off in Olivia's head, especially if this isn't the first time something like this has happened. "Can I trust him? Can I trust that he's really going to watch the game and not be out at a bar or club?" she may wonder. That instance of wondering, according to Murray, sets off two parallel processes in the brain.

At the conscious level, Olivia begins analyzing Peter's behaviors—how often he goes out, who his companions are likely to be, the existence of any other signs suggesting a lack of interest in her. In short, she begins to recalculate the level of reflective trust she holds for him. Unbeknownst to her, however, a similar process is occurring on the nonconscious level. Her mind is retrieving the most recently updated evaluation of trust attached to Peter—a datum that may, to Olivia, seem like an unsubstantiated hunch. The results of these two processes, and how they are integrated, will determine what Olivia does next. If both evaluations conclude that Peter is trustworthy (i.e., she trusts him in her gut and she believes he is where he says he is), Olivia will continue to trust him and likely endeavor to build even closer bonds. If both evaluations conclude that he is untrustworthy (i.e., she had a hunch that he was not to be trusted and this instance is the last straw, as there isn't any game on television tonight), the relationship is toast.

The more interesting cases, however, occur when the conscious and intuitive evaluations of trustworthiness disagree. For many individuals, the results of the conscious evaluation will carry the day. If Olivia's rational analysis gives her reason to trust Peter, she will likely do so. This doesn't mean that she might not harbor a nagging sense that something's wrong, but, like many people, she can probably talk herself into ignoring that gut feeling if she so desires. Individuals do, of course, differ in the weight they give to their intuitions. For some—those who value their hunches—the gut feeling that a partner isn't to be trusted may be enough to override a conscious analysis and lead them to distance themselves. However, mistakes come from assuming that the favoring of one type of evaluation over the other is always under your control. In some instances you may have a choice, but don't get used to it; there are times when this luxury won't be the case.

One general principle to emerge from the past two decades of psychological science has been that intuitive responses guide behavior when the conscious mind isn't inclined or able to override them. This fact isn't a failure of design; it's a feature with a purpose. Thinking is costly in terms of time and resources. If you had to daily evaluate the costs and benefits of every decision you made in a deliberate fashion, you'd be mentally exhausted way before lunch. By contrast, intuitive decisions are quick and effortless; that's their plus. Sometimes you don't have the option to consider every detail. You may want to do a comprehensive analysis, but you may not have the time or the expertise needed. Better to have an intuitive decision in such cases than no decision at all.

To see how the interplay of these systems influences trust, Murray conducted an elaborate long-term study of over one hundred cohabitating couples (most of whom were married). To gauge their intuitive levels of trust toward one another, she administered a cognitive task known as the implicit association test, or IAT, separately to each. Although the computations involved in scoring the test are a bit complex, the task itself is fairly simple. Different words and images rapidly flash on a computer screen, requiring participants to categorize them. The words reflect positive and negative themes associated with trustworthiness (e.g., good, honest, awful) while the images reflect text associated with a partner (e.g., first name, last name) or pictures of him or her. The speed with which participants categorized different sequences of items provided insight into how their minds associated trustworthiness with their partners at a nonconscious level. In addition to the IAT, Murray asked participants to complete another series of cognitive tasks designed to assess their level of executive control—a fancy word that basically refers to how facile one is at conscious analysis and the inhibition of intuitive responses. The more executive control you have, the less your analytic capability is constrained by distractions or time pressures in your environs, meaning you're more able to override intuitive responses.

After taking these measures, Murray released her participants back into the "wild" of their daily lives with the requirement that they complete trust and relationship activity questionnaires daily for two weeks. If trust worked as she suspected, the influence of intuitive trust on relationship bonds would diverge as a function of differences in executive control. That is, the less executive control a person had, the more his or her subsequent opinions and actions toward a partner would be dictated by gut responses.

As you might expect, instances that set off alarm bells occurred somewhat regularly across the two weeks for many couples. Some partners had disagreements over desires or goals; some didn't do things they promised they would, etc. In the face of such events, Murray's predictions held up. Individuals who possessed high executive control—those who were able to devote mental capacity to a deliberate analysis of their partner's behaviors—were principally guided by reflective trust in how they dealt with their significant others. After considering all the data at hand, if they believed there wasn't sufficient reason to doubt their partners, they continued to trust and drew closer to them. If, on the other hand, their analysis raised a red flag and supported their initial concern, they began to distrust their partners and withdrew from them.

For those low in executive control—those who habitually didn't like to analyze things or were too tired or busy to do so—it was another story completely. Their intuitions tended to shape their responses. For example, if a husband stopped to wonder why his wife was scheduling extra appointments with her attractive athletic trainer, whether this pause led to continued trust or to its withdrawal depended on what the husband's underlying intuitions were. If on a gut level he possessed a deep and abiding sense of trust in her, he simply disregarded the incident and continued to feel confident in her loyalty. But if his gut harbored suspicions that he couldn't trust her, even if he wasn't quite sure why, he readily assumed she was up to no good even though a reasoned analysis wouldn't have led most individuals to make that assumption. The subsequent impact on relationships was just as you'd expect. Those who intuitively trusted reinforced bonds; those who intuitively distrusted distanced themselves from partners.

The implications of these findings couldn't be clearer. Whether you like it or not, there will be times when your intuitions about a partner's trustworthiness will completely color your views of him or her. Even those of us with high executive control will face times when our mental capacity is taxed—times of emotional upheaval, cognitive burnout, or slight inebriation. If something calls your trust for your partner into question during one of these times, what your nonconscious mind thinks of him or her will have unfettered rein to determine whether you remove the concern from your mind or remove the trust you placed in your partner.

Earlier, I suggested that the existence of intuitive responses is an adaptive aspect of the mind. Better to have a quick-and-dirty evaluation than none at all, is how the story usually goes. You might wonder, though, if this view continues to make sense in light of the aforementioned findings. Unlike deciding whether you like a certain product, vacation spot, or dinner entrée, decisions involving trust are always accompanied by some degree of vulnerability. Is it adaptive, then, to allow the intuitive system to rein supreme at times? Why not have the intuitive system always adopt a generous tit-for-tat or similar forgiving strategy? Why let intuitive distrust possibly ruin a good relationship—one where a reasoned analysis would suggest trust is warranted?

To answer this question, it's important to recognize a common misconception about intuitive processes. Although they're often generally referred to as quick and dirty, when it comes to discerning trustworthiness, the "dirty" part is a bit of a misnomer. As we'll see in the coming chapter on detecting trustworthiness, intuitive processes likely provide more accurate information than reflective ones. Although neither type of mechanism is perfect, a combination of the two often provides the best results; two heads—or minds, in this case—are always better than one. Yet in absence of having access to both, reliance on intuition for assessing trustworthiness is often a better choice.

Unleashing the Green-Eyed Monster

Until now we've been considering the costs and benefits of trusting a partner and how the mind goes about making those calculations. But there's another, equally important facet to consider when it comes to romantic relationships. What happens when you strongly suspect—or, worse, are confronted with evidence—that the person you love actually has or will betray you to be with someone else? What happens when cheating occurs? The answer boils down to one word: jealousy.

Some of you may disagree with me at first, believing you'd just throw your partner out. If he or she shows interest in someone else, fine—it's over, case closed. But if you think about it honestly, relationships don't usually work this way. If you can dispatch a partner without any emotional tumult, you probably weren't that invested in the first place. Even if you know ending the relationship is the right thing to do, it is almost always intensely painful if you value your partner at all. In fact, the searing feeling of betrayal is so difficult to avoid in such situations that Freud himself—not one known for finding normalcy in many things—argued that jealousy's absence, not its presence, is indicative of pathology. In other words, if you're not feeling jealous in these situations, you're suppressing it.

As familiar as it is, jealousy can be a difficult emotion to describe easily. It's often best captured as a combination of fear, anger, and sadness that gnaws at the soul. This constellation of more basic feelings makes great sense when you view jealousy through the lens of trust. Fear stems from anxieties about the costs—social and economic—that losing a partner entails. Anger derives from a belief that one was cheated, that a partner violated the rules. And sadness comes from the realization that a significant other—someone whose judgment you value—views another as more desirable. Take comfort in knowing, however, that even though the composite of feelings we call jealousy is painful, it doesn't solely exist to torture you. The distress you feel has a purpose; it's there to motivate action.

To fathom exactly what this purpose is and why it's useful, two steps are required. The first is to recognize that jealousy isn't all about sex. It can seem that way at times, as the media has an almost insatiable appetite for stories about jealousy and sexual infidelity. The periodicals at checkout lines and the celebrity gossip shows on television are fixated on who is sleeping with whom. Most people, too, will tell you, assuming they're willing to admit to being jealous, that it's the idea of their partner sleeping with someone else that is the ultimate cause of their distress. In reality, though, this is somewhat of an illusion. It's not how jealousy works. Jealousy is about trust, not sex. Contrary to their statements otherwise, most everyone would be jealous if a partner decided to leave them to spend time with another even after taking a new vow of celibacy. At the most fundamental level, jealousy's purpose is to increase the odds of trustworthy behavior, whether that means preventing the loss of an existing relationship and its associated benefits, or working to ensure that future relationships will be characterized by greater loyalty. Sex is only one benefit; jealousy is sensitive to all benefits. If you don't believe me, hold on for a few minutes. Empirical proof is coming shortly.

Before we get to that proof, though, I need to mention the second step required to appreciate jealousy's unique functions. As is likely clear, trust can be breached within the context of romantic relationships in many ways. A spouse can siphon money from joint retirement savings to feed a gambling habit. A fiancé can refuse to be emotionally supportive. A boyfriend or girlfriend can blab to others about something that was supposed to be kept confidential. Yet none of these events will spark even a flicker of jealousy. Anger, to be sure, but not jealousy. The reason is that jealousy only occurs when there's a triad. While most instances of trust involve two people, jealousy requires three. You'd certainly be angry if a physician you trust provides an incorrect diagnosis or a business partner you value cheats you out of profits, but you won't lie in bed at night with unrelenting pangs of jealousy keeping you awake. However, if you're worried that a partner is beginning to desire someone else— someone who might entice him or her to violate a trust with you— the green-eyed monster becomes unleashed.

It's the triadic nature of the situation—what is sometimes referred to as a lover's triangle—that stokes jealousy. Unlike situations where trust is broken because one person favors his own interest over another's (e.g. skimming profits, engaging in fraud), breaches of trust that give rise to jealousy occur when there is a relative asymmetry in value between two options. A partner isn't choosing simply to cheat you out of something like money; he's choosing to cheat on you with someone else. Put another way, a man might still like his fiancée, but he might like another woman just a little more. And it's precisely because of the relative difference in value that the existing yet threatened relationship could be saved. If one could tip a partner's affections back the other way, trust might be restored, and with it, the benefits of the existing relationship. This possibility is why anxiety forms part of the jealousy composite. Unlike anger, which motivates punishment of a cheating significant other (we'll get to that shortly), the anxiety one feels when contemplating the loss of a partner to a rival is specifically meant to spur action to prevent or reverse that loss.

To drive the point home, one need only look to swinger culture. Yes, swingers—the folks who regularly swap partners for sexual liaisons. If jealousy were about sex and not trust, swingers would be the most insanely jealous people on the planet. But that's not the case; jealousy is extremely low in this group. The reason why may surprise you. It's not because swingers are incapable of maintaining strong, meaningful, and loyal relationships. To the contrary, their track record doesn't differ from nonswingers in this regard. The reason they aren't usually jealous is because they continually work to build trust and confidence with their long-term partner by reinforcing the idea that sex outside their primary relationship is just a different form of recreation. For them, swinging is like playing soccer. Sex outside of marriage isn't an indication of a lack of trustworthiness among swingers any more than is joining an intramural sports team. It's just a hobby. And since it doesn't suggest a breach of trust, there is no jealousy.

When jealousy does strike in the rest of us, though, the anxiety we feel is often mixed with anger. Which feeling is salient depends on how far along the betrayal is. As just indicated, the anxiety component of jealousy is meant to push people to save the relationship before it's too late. The anger part becomes more prominent when betrayal is no longer a possibility but rather a fait accompli. At that point, one may try to wrench the relationship back, but, absent success, anger may best be used to punish the perpetrators and thereby reduce the odds of subsequent disloyal behavior by them or by witnesses to the wronged's fury.

If this view of jealousy is correct, it leads to two somewhat counterintuitive predictions. First, if jealousy is about trust, it should, at early stages of threat, push one to be more accommodating to a partner, not less. If you're worried that a partner may leave you for someone else, being angry at or punishing him will only end the relationship faster. Second, jealousy should be sensitive not only to the real costs and benefits of a relationship, but also to potential ones. In other words, jealousy, like all trust-relevant phenomena, should be sensitive to the shadow of the future.

To find support for the first of these predictions, we need only turn again to work by Sandra Murray, this time charting the daily experience of over two hundred newlywed couples for several weeks. Each day, individuals reported any worries that arose concerning their partner's possible romantic interest in others, as well as their own emotional states and behaviors. What Murray found is exactly what I predicted. On days when concerns were high that a partner might have a better option, jealousy led spouses to alter their behaviors to foster their partner's degrees of dependence. They would do any number of things—look for something their partner lost, cook a favorite dinner, fix something their spouse broke—that might lead their respective spouses to feel more dependent on them. In short, rather than push the "superior" spouse away into the arms of another by being angry, the inferior-feeling spouse strove to make her- or himself indispensable—a partner on whom the other could rely. And it worked. On days following such dependence-enhancing behaviors, jealousy-inducing partners reported diminished doubts about their commitment to the relationship.

One aspect of jealousy, then, does appear to center on enhancing, or at least maintaining, a partner's desire to bond and trust. But how about the second prediction—that jealousy is sensitive not only to what is occurring, but also to what the future holds? We'll approach this one in two different ways, both stemming from my own work.

The first way to observe jealousy's link to preventing possible violations of trust involves its application to warding off failures of willpower by partners. In chapter 1, I described how sensing the willpower of others is used to estimate their trustworthiness. We're less willing to rely on or cooperate with individuals who we know are fatigued, impulsive, or otherwise possessing characteristics that make us doubt they can control themselves in the face of temptation. Many times when we make such judgments, we haven't yet entered into an exchange relationship; we're deciding whether we can trust someone new. As such, it's quite easy to avoid people we view as unreliable. But when we're already in a relationship, we don't always have that option. The best we can do is attempt to manage the temptations that an existing partner is likely to face.

Here is where anticipatory jealousy can serve an important function. If jealousy were simply a negative response to infidelity, we wouldn't feel it until cheating had occurred. If it's related to trust, it makes great sense that we'd feel it earlier—those moments when we're attempting to make predictions about a partner's loyalty. If I'm right about this, it also means that the intensity of jealousy we're likely to feel will vary as a function of how much a potential rival has to offer. Think of it this way. If you believe that your intelligence is your defining feature—the one that attracted your partner to you in the first place—then it's a good bet that he or she will be more tempted by a rival who is also intelligent than by one who is a party animal. So, if you had to keep tabs on a partner's potential wandering eye at a cocktail party, it would make sense to be vigilant concerning his or her chatting with other guests who were clearly brilliant as opposed to those who kept visiting the punch bowl.

Testing this idea was quite easy. I simply recruited Yale undergrads (I was completing my doctoral work at Yale at the time) for a purported experiment on dating. I had them answer some basic questions about themselves—age, likes, hobbies, views of their attractive qualities and defining characteristics—and similar ones about their dating partners. Their responses allowed me to assess the qualities they and their partners most admired about themselves. Then I presented them with scenarios that went something like this:

> Imagine you and your partner are at a cocktail party. You lose track of him (her) for a few moments but then notice him (her) across the room striking up what seems to be an engaging conversation with someone of your gender. They really look to be enjoying each other's company. How jealous would you feel if this person were [fill in the blank].

The blanks were filled with different descriptions of rivals: smart ones, athletic ones, popular ones, etc.

What I found confirmed my suspicions that jealousy motivated people to prevent breakdowns of trust. The jealousy individuals felt

peaked when the rival with whom they imagined their partner so-
cializing possessed a quality that they and their partner valued.
Given the participants were Yalies, a large majority believed intelligence to be the most important quality; as a result, they were
much more jealous of potential rivals who possessed great brainpower. The athletes among them, however, also showed the predicted response; they were more jealous when their partner was
conversing with a fellow athlete than with a member of Phi Beta
Kappa. While chatting and flirting by partners didn't overly distress
most people, jealousy kicked into high gear when they believed
their partner was likely to be tempted—when he or she was spending time with a rival who was superior on a valued characteristic.
At a very basic level, jealousy was tracking the odds of a future
betrayal.

Although suggesting a close link between jealousy and trust, all
the examples I've discussed so far have a common feature: the loss
of benefits attached to a strong, current relationship. Yet, if jealousy
is really about trust, then it shouldn't only occur when there is pres-
ently a lot to lose; it should occur even when the gains have yet to
be realized. If you follow this logic to its conclusion, it ends at a
surprising prediction: people should be jealous over someone they
barely know. What I mean by this is that people should be jealous
of the poaching of any relationship, even if that relationship is only
a few minutes old. The key to understanding why is simple. When
looking at a relationship through the lens of trust, what matters are
not the benefits already gained—they're in the bank—but the benefits yet to come. If a partner fails to be trustworthy, those future
gains are lost.

Putting this prediction to the test required the most difficult
experiment we've ever conducted in my lab. By *difficult* I don't mean
complex, I mean interpersonally difficult. Imagine the following.

You arrive at the lab thinking you're about to take part in an experiment examining whether people work better in teams or on their own. Sitting beside you is another participant of the opposite sex—Carlo or Gillian. The experimenter informs you both that there are a bunch of tasks to complete, and since this is an experiment on team vs. individual performance, you can either work on the tasks individually or together. At this point, Carlo or Gillian (who ·in reality worked for me at the time) always suggested the two of you work together. As the minutes passed, they had an overriding goal: make the experience of working together a positive one while also subtly flirting. As fate would have it (well, really by design), the experimenter then ushers in a third person who is ostensibly late. This new person, again either Carlo or Gillian, depending on which one is already acting as your partner, is the same gender as you. He or she sits next to the two of you, but directs attention primarily to the partner with whom you have been enjoying working. At this point, the experimenter enters a final time, saying that since there are now three people, one of you will have to work alone.

Here's where the difficult part comes in. The rival—the new third wheel—always invites your partner to work with him or her. And in some conditions, your partner agrees, leaving you to fend for yourself.

The results were more intense than we ever predicted. The "dumped" participants not only reported feeling jealous, they often shook their heads in disbelief, sneered, or hurled an insult under their breath at Carlo and Gillian, and almost universally chose to punish their erstwhile partner and rival when given the opportunity.

Assessing this desire to punish was also accomplished through a little subterfuge. After everyone completed their tasks, we had them take part in a supposed second study—one purportedly about taste perception. Here, participants had to prepare taste samples for each other, and true participants (as opposed to confederates) found out they were randomly assigned to prepare samples of hot sauce for the other two, spicy flavors being one of the taste categories to be examined. Participants were also told that whatever amount of hot sauce they put into the sample cup would be placed into Carlo and Gillian's respective mouths. In cases where Gillian or Carlo left for a rival, participants poured it on. They intentionally wanted to cause as much pain as they could to their unfaithful partner and new rival. It was vengeance, plain and simple. Perhaps even more compelling, though, was that the intensity of jealousy they felt directly predicted how much hot sauce they poured; more jealousy equaled more hot sauce.

With respect to trust, two features of these findings come to the fore. The first is that people became jealous over someone they had known only a few minutes. No solid relationship had been built; no benefits had been exchanged. All that existed was the promise of a future—the potential that a longer-term partnership might be coming. As I suspected, that was enough; jealousy arose because a potential long-term partner wasn't trustworthy. During the moments of the brief three-way interaction—when the rival was flirting with a participant's partner—many individuals tried to woo the partner back. But when the budding relationship was finally severed, anxiety about loss was useless, and jealousy became characterized by anger.

This anger and ensuing retribution brings us to the second important feature: punishment. By the time the opportunity to punish the guilty parties arose, the nascent relationship was over; the partner had betrayed and left. Why, then, engage in punishment when trust no longer appears to be an issue? What's to gain? And perhaps most puzzling of all: Why punish rivals? They didn't engage in betrayal. The answers to all these questions become clear when you consider the adaptive benefits that arise from working to enhance future trustworthy behavior.

There's a well-known phenomenon in behavioral economics called third-party punishment. In a nutshell, it refers to the human propensity to punish others who transgress against a third party. Experiments have revealed time and again that people will pay money to punish others who cheat even when they themselves were not victimized by the cheating. The basic idea is that if everyone exerts effort to punish rule breakers, the number of people who engage in such behaviors will quickly be reduced. And this fact in and of itself means that the next person you or I are likely to meet will be less likely to cheat us. In punishing the untrustworthy partner and the rival who sought to encourage disloyalty, people are, in essence, paying it forward. They're working to discourage the untrustworthy among us from behaving this way again. If the system is working well, the next romantic partner you encounter may just end up being more faithful to you than he or she might otherwise have been, specifically because of a jealousy-induced punishment experienced from a previous partner.

In saying this, I'm not in any way advocating punishment and vengeance. Rather, I'm pointing out why jealousy's role as a primary cause of domestic violence has been so difficult to stamp out. In an evolutionary, game-theoretic sense, punishment can serve a function when it comes to relationships. Whether we choose to tolerate that function, and I hope that we would not, is up to us as a society. Just as we've come to outlaw and condemn violence as a response to violations of trust in business, we should do the same for violence stemming from breaches of trust in romantic relationships. Yet, as I write this, there are still several cultures in which physical punishment for infidelity is regrettably widely accepted. As we've seen, trust certainly can have great benefits when it comes to fostering relationships, but it can also have considerable costs when it is broken. The increased magnitude of these outcomes should not come as a surprise, however; they follow directly from the formidable nature of the rewards at stake.

Key Insights

- **Positive illusions can be good.** Trust begets trust more often than not. Although common sense may seem to suggest that illusions are always to be avoided in favor of hard objectivity, sometimes a softer-focus lens, one capable of smoothing the rough edges, is to be preferred. If you've developed a strong sense of trust in a partner, it will function in just that way. When there's ambiguity about how trustworthy he or she is, that sense of preexisting trust will burnish your view; it'll blur the lines in an effort to push you toward continuing to trust. And, in reality, that's not a bad thing. As I noted in the first chapter, many instances of perceived untrustworthiness are errors or aberrations. Consequently, forgiveness is a great strategy, even if you don't realize you're doing it. Of course, taken to extremes, positive illusions can be blinding. But your intuitive systems don't go to extremes. If you're pushed too far, that pit in your stomach will soon let you know something questionable is afoot.

- **Trust your hunches.** As I just noted, intuitions, or hunches, are usually less variable than conscious evaluations. As a result, they often (though not always, as we'll see later) provide more accurate assessments of another's trustworthiness. There are two reasons for this superiority. The first, as we'll see in chapter 6, is that the nonconscious mind is more attuned to reading the true indicators of trustworthiness than is the conscious one. The second is that the nonconscious mind is also less amenable to our own influence. We've all had the experience of trying to talk ourselves into or out of something, meaning that we've all had the experiencing of trying to override our intuitions. When it comes to trust and romantic partners, this often translates into talking ourselves into continuing to trust someone even when we shouldn't. Why? For some, maybe it's convenient to stay in the relationship. For others, maybe it's a fear of being alone. In all such cases, though, the long-term outcomes will be poor. So I urge you to listen to your hunches; hear them out. While intuitions may not always be right, they are more often than not—a fact alone that warrants their consideration.

• **Jealousy is about the future, not the past.** Contrary to conventional wisdom, jealousy isn't an emotion to be avoided. It's a crucial part of the mind's arsenal for trust. The primary reason, as we've seen, is that jealousy isn't about the past as much as it is about the future. The reason we feel jealous is to motivate us to protect or repair a valued relationship—one where we can rely on a partner for mutual support. The pain of jealousy isn't meant to torture us, but to spur us to figure out how to save a relationship—new or old—that has the potential to offer many benefits down the road. It's also why, if a relationship does end, the urge for retribution can be so strong. Although it won't help us directly, a person who's felt the rage of a spurned lover is unlikely to want to be in the same situation again. And the biological benefit of this behavior—the use of aggression to punish violations of trust and thereby inhibit future transgressions—is also what makes the link between jealousy and domestic violence so difficult to break. As I said, the goal of evolution is not to produce saints; it's to propagate one's genes by whatever strategies work. That doesn't mean we have to accept such behavior, of course; rather, it provides insight into how, when, and why such behaviors occur, which hopefully will aid in limiting their frequencies and repercussions.

CHAPTER 5

POWER AND MONEY

Trust Among the One Percent and Their Wannabes

Critics often say that great films—the ones we watch time and again—share an important feature: they crystallize shared sentiments in iconic ways. It's as if each time we sit back and watch them, we remind ourselves of facts we need to know, or at least reaffirm their supposed truths. Now, I'm no film critic, but when it comes to issues of how trust divides along the socioeconomic spectrum, there's probably no greater classic than Frank Capra's *It's a Wonderful Life*. Sure, there are lots of other films about characters differing in social class and greed—*Wall Street* with Gordon Gecko is difficult to forget—but none that have become classics quite in the way that George Bailey and *It's a Wonderful Life* have. Every December, in good times and bad, we're treated to George's trials and travails in Bedford Falls.

For those few of you who haven't seen this film or have forgotten it, it's the quintessential little guy vs. big guy showdown, where *little* and *big* don't refer to physical stature but rather to social class. On the lower end we have George Bailey—frustrated owner of a small building-and-loan who gives his own honeymoon savings to keep his institution afloat and keep his commitment to customers sound. On the upper end we have Henry Potter—banker, slumlord, and genuinely heartless bad guy. These two—the man who puts his own interests behind those of the Depression-era townspeople who count on him to hold their money, and the man who would exploit these same people at every opportunity—exemplify our notions of what "commoners" and the "rich" are like.

Objectively speaking, those lower in socioeconomic status, or social class, are by definition characterized by possessing fewer economic resources and educational opportunities, less access to elite schools and clubs, more subordinate positions in the workplace, and increased levels of stress. For their upper-class counterparts, it's just the opposite—more resources, more leisure, less stress. From the realities facing each group, you might assume that members of the lower class would be more focused on meeting their own survival needs and, thereby, prioritize their needs over those of others. As a result, you might also expect them to be less trustworthy as compared to members of the upper class, who, given their greater resources, have the luxury to trust. But if you do, you're missing a central point about how trust really works. Trust isn't a luxury. It's a tool we need to get by when we can't make it on our own; it's a means of survival for those who must depend on others. Viewed this way, predictions about trust and class get turned on their heads.

If you don't have a lot of expendable income, if you can't hire nannies and personal assistants, if you can't always afford to keep your car in top working order, you're going to need to depend on the cooperation of others. Put simply, success by those lower in SES requires mutual support; complete self-reliance isn't an option. They *need* to trust each other. As George Bailey reminds his customers at a moment of great shared financial peril, "We can get through this thing all right. We've got to stick together, though. We've got to have faith in each other." Those on the upper end of SES, like Mr. Potter, already possess all the resources they need. As a consequence, they have the luxury of being selfish in order to acquire even more; they have the freedom to rely on money as opposed to people to provide what they need.

From this perspective, you wouldn't predict that members of the lower class would be selfish takers; to the contrary, you'd expect they'd place a greater emphasis on cooperation and fairness, meaning they should both trust others more and behave in a more trustworthy manner themselves as compared to members of the upper class. If that's right, it suggests there may be some truth to the cultural stereotypes on display in classics like *It's a Wonderful Life*. Our route to finding out begins at a nondescript intersection in San Francisco.

Get Out of My Way

Most of us don't usually stop to think about it, but the simple act of crossing the street necessitates some level of trust. Unless you're crossing the road in a ghost town somewhere in the Midwest—a place where there are no cars for miles—stepping into an intersection makes you vulnerable to being hit. Remaining safe, then, usually involves trusting that approaching cars will slow down or stop and allow you to proceed. Now, you might say that you never actually think about trusting a driver, but I'll bet you do. Most people have had that experience of trying to decide whether cross in front of an oncoming car. Does it have a lot of collision damage? Is the driver blaring his music and revving his engine? My guess is that if the answer to either of these questions or ones like them is yes, you'd probably choose not to cross the street when you might have done so if the car were a cute VW Bug being driven by a nun. You see, the choice to cross isn't just influenced by the physics of velocity; trust plays a role.

To understand how this fact relates to social class, consider the following. You're standing on a corner in downtown San Francisco. It's a four-way stop, meaning cars are supposed to pause before entering the intersection. As you're sipping your latte, you look to your left before stepping off the curb. The car approaching is a shiny BMW. Do you cross? How about if it's a Ford Fusion? The model of trust I've been describing suggests you might want to pause if it's the BMW. There's really only one way to tell, though. You've got to put yourself out there. And that's just what Paul Piff and colleagues from the University of California at Berkeley did.

As cars approached this busy intersection in San Francisco, a researcher would enter the crosswalk. Unbeknownst to drivers, he also noted the make of their auto and their perceived age and gender. The main datum for each car was whether the driver paused to let the researcher cross at the stop sign (as is required by the California Vehicle Code) or sped up to cut him off and thereby proceed more quickly toward the driver's goals. Piff and colleagues divided drivers into five SES categories based on their cars—think Hyundais on one end and Ferraris on the other. The results were quite remarkable. At the lowest end of the class gradient, every single driver stopped to let the pedestrian entering the crosswalk continue on his way. Midway up the class ladder, about 30 percent of drivers broke the law and cut off the pedestrian so that they could keep going. At the upper end of SES, almost 50 percent of drivers broke the law to put their own needs first. At the most basic level, these findings offer a provocative warning. When you're vulnerable, upper-class individuals are more likely to disregard the trust you place in them if doing so furthers their own ends.

You may think my statement is a bit of hyperbole. After all, we're simply talking impersonal interactions at traffic intersections. Fair enough. If the data ended there, I'd agree there might not be much to it. But it doesn't end there. Suspecting their view of the upper class's trustworthiness—or lack thereof—was correct, Piff's team began a multipronged investigation that examined class-based effects both on a willingness to trust others and on trustworthy behavior itself. In all the experiments, they first divided individuals into distinct class levels based on typical measures of SES and then exposed them to different situations. What follows is a sampling.

One experiment was presented as an investigation of negotiation tactics. The participants—here members of the upper or lower class—were told that they would play the role of an employer negotiating a salary with a job candidate. These "employers" were given a lot of information about the job (e.g., salary ranges, details about responsibilities), but one piece was central to the researchers' concerns: the job was scheduled to be eliminated in six months. As the participants reviewed the file of the job candidate they were to interview, it became clear that he was looking for a long-term job and wouldn't consider a position unless it was likely to provide at least two years of employment. The employers then produced a written script of how they would describe the position to the job-seeker. What instantly became clear is that as social class increased, so did the likelihood of concealing the fact that the job would soon end. The experimenters even asked these faux employers point-blank if they would tell the job applicant the truth about when the position would end if he asked directly. Again, significantly more upper-class individuals indicated that they would lie—that they would intentionally betray the trust the job-seeker placed in them as an honest supervisor. Strike two for trustworthiness.

Next, the team had participants of different classes play a

gambling game on computers. It was a dice-rolling game where higher numbers corresponded to more money won. The task was quite simple: roll the dice five times and report the results to the experimenters. What happened is just what you'd expect based on the previous findings. More upper-class individuals inflated their rolls, thereby ensuring they'd receive larger sums of money from the experimenters than they deserved—a fact that was easy to determine, as the computers surreptitiously recorded the totals of the actual roles. Strike three.

These and many similar findings make the link between higher social class and unethical behavior clear. What they don't do, however, is provide any indication of whether this untrustworthy behavior is intentional. Do those in the upper echelons knowingly decide to be untrustworthy, or are they unsuspectingly nudged into dishonesty by their nonconscious minds? It's a question Piff and his colleagues have wondered about, and somewhat surprisingly, their work suggests that it's likely the former. Many of the upper class appear not only keenly aware of their lack of trustworthiness, but also embrace it. When the researchers presented individuals with scenarios depicting other people engaging in unethical and untrustworthy behaviors, social class was a strong predictor of whether these individuals were troubled by the events described. Members of the upper class not only judged actions where one person increased her benefit at another's expense to be more acceptable, they also indicated that they would be more likely to engage in these behaviors themselves.

As a whole, then, these findings certainly suggest that increasing untrustworthiness and acceptance thereof comes with increasing class. But trust is a two-sided phenomenon. It's clear that one's own fairness and honesty go down with rising class, but what about a willingness to trust others? If it were simple selfishness that drove the untrustworthy actions of the upper class, we might not expect to find any influence of SES on a willingness to trust others. After all, why not trust people of a different class? All the mathematical models we covered earlier suggest that, on average, trusting others can lead to greater resources when you need them. But that's just the point. With increasing class comes less of a need for the resources supplied by others, and correspondingly little motive to accept any vulnerability. If this view is correct, increasing class should not only be associated with less trustworthy behavior, but also with a reduced willingness to trust others in general.

To put this prediction to the test, Piff and his colleagues employed one of the most classic measures of trust available—the trust game. As you'll remember from my earlier description of it, the game works by endowing people with a bit of money. They can choose to give it to a "trustee" who will triple the money but isn't required to give any of it back. The choice, then, is a straightforward one. If you trust the trustee to act fairly and at least split the profits, you'll end up with a lot more money if you give him yours to invest than if you choose to keep it all yourself. As is usually the case, you have to make yourself vulnerable if you're going to reap greater rewards. How did class affect trust in this game? Just as you'd expect if self-reliance were the factor driving the behavior, increasing social class was directly associated with a decreased willingness to trust others. And, as in all of the experiments described, the link between class and trust held even after controlling for lots of other factors (e.g., gender, ethnicity, etc.).

These findings offer what seems to be a straightforward message. Members of the upper class—the better off among us—are self-serving. They don't need to rely on others and would rather members of the lower classes—just like the pedestrians in the San Francisco intersection—just get out of their way. But is this a fair assessment? The data are certainly clear: higher social class often equals lower trustworthiness. But this fact alone doesn't say anything about why this relation holds. Is it because members of the upper class have lived a life of privilege, being taught from a young age that they are the elite? Is it because the social circles to which they belong foster a subculture of dishonesty or a drive to win at all costs? If so, there's really not much to be done. Trustworthiness, or lack thereof, has been ingrained in the minds of the one percent and it's not going to change easily.

To me, though, this view doesn't make much sense. I've spent much of the time up till now arguing that trustworthiness is dynamic—it comes from calculations that are constantly being updated. Like the rest of human morality, it's not fixed. Past behavior only predicts future behavior when the situation hasn't much changed. In the case of social class, this view suggests a very different way to understand why trust varies. Yes, members of the upper class have been raised in privileged environs, but that's not why they're on average less trustworthy. It's because they're still living in those environs—because they still, at this moment, have resources to burn. What drives trustworthiness is a sense that you need others, a sense that you're not invulnerable or able to achieve your desired ends all on your own.

Taken to its logical end, this view suggests that the lower class is more trustworthy because it has to be, but if I were to pluck someone out of a position of deprivation and suddenly place him or her on a higher rung of the status ladder, a decrease in trustworthiness should quickly follow. If you stop to think about it, it doesn't seem such an odd idea. The story of the little guy who makes it big is a fairly common one. Boy or girl from humble roots gains some power—gets a big promotion at work, lands an acting or music contract, wins the lottery, or otherwise begins to move in more affluent circles—and his or her personality changes. He's not the same any-more; he's somehow more self-absorbed and less reliable. Of course, it works the other way, too, if Hollywood is to be believed. Rich, snobby girl suddenly loses it all and learns to become a caring and honorable member of the lower or middle class. If I'm right about this, it means that it's not so much the class you're raised in that determines your trustworthiness, it's where you are right now rela-tive to those around you. Put another way, it means that, at least when it comes to trust, being in the one percent is a state of mind as opposed to a result of breeding.

Power Corrupts

The notion that power corrupts is not a new one. History and lit-erature are replete with numerous examples of how the powerful go astray. What's not clear, though, is how quickly it can happen. Yet if my view of trust is right, we should find that increases in class or power give rise to unethical behavior not through a slow learning or enculturation process, but by quick changes in the intuitive cal-culations for how much one needs to rely on others. Change the level of need; change the level of trustworthiness. It's as simple as that.

In line with this view, acceptance that class and power are mal-leable has been growing among social scientists. What truly appear to matter are immediate, relative differences—where one stands in comparison to those around her. A person earning $400,000 per year would likely feel needy in the presence of Bill Gates or Warren Buffett, while someone earning $50,000 per year might feel like the king of the world standing in a homeless shelter. It's the fact that the nature of our daily lives—the people with whom we regularly interact—doesn't usually change much from day to day that provides the illusion of a fixed sense of class or power. In reality, though, the process of determining where on the ladder we stand is dynamic; it's dependent on the situation. And that means trustworthiness should be as well.

One of my favorite demonstrations of this phenomenon involves a study Paul Piff and colleagues conducted involving stealing candy from babies. Well, okay, not really stealing candy from babies, but pretty close. As part of the experiment, participants were asked to complete some surveys, among which were measures of wealth, education, and job prestige. The catch was that these measures also provided information about the wealth, education, and job prestige of others. Sometimes these others were people near the top rung of the SES ladder; other times they were individuals near the bottom rung. The reason for varying comparison groups was to manipulate relative status. When the middle-class participants saw information about members of the one percent, they reported feeling diminished and more powerless than usual. When they viewed information about those on the lower end of the class spectrum, they felt empowered and respected.

Now comes the candy part. Before leaving the room with the collected surveys, the experimenter paused and asked the participants (who were always alone) to hold a bowl of individually wrapped candies that were meant for children in the next room who were taking part in another study. The experimenter told participants that they could have one if they liked, but that he'd be back in a minute to pick up the bowl and take it to the waiting kids. He was, in essence, trusting participants to watch over the candy; at least this was what it seemed like to them. What followed is exactly what you'd predict if it were a relative sense of power and resources that drove differences in trustworthiness. Participants who reported feeling increased power and prestige—those who had just compared themselves with others lower in SES—took significantly more candy from the bowl than did participants who reported the opposite. Remember, these two sets of participants didn't actually differ in SES; the experimenters just made them feel as if they did based on altering their targets of comparison.

The effects of power reach much deeper, though. Relative increases in power of any type—even those not explicitly focusing on differences in incomes, education, and the like—can lead an individual to see the world through a self-serving lens. No one knows this more than Adam Galinsky of Columbia Business School, who is known for conducting some of the most creative work on the effects of power. Galinsky realized that it is quite easy to manipulate people's sense of power in an experiment. All one need do is invite them to take part in a simulation in which they are given a position of influence over others.

As one example, he had participants take part in a role-play requiring them to solve different problems, but before they began, he selected one person to be the boss and dole out the assignments to the others. Following the simulation, Galinsky asked participants to judge the acceptability of certain ethical lapses that either they or others might commit. For example, participants were asked whether it is okay to keep a stolen bike they took if they really needed it, or whether it's acceptable for someone else to break the speed limit and related rules of the road if he was late. Here again, simply being put into a momentary position of power—a position where your outcomes don't depend on others—led individuals to increasingly say that breaking the rules was more acceptable if they did it than if someone else did. At a very basic level, power increased hypocrisy—a behavior anathema to trustworthiness.

Perhaps most troubling, though, is the fact that power appears not only to make people less reliable, but also to enable them to get away with deceit. Dana Carney of Berkeley's Haas School of Business has demonstrated that temporary increases in power make people better liars. Using a procedure similar to Galinsky's, she had individuals play roles in a simulated business. The bosses got bigger offices than the workers, got to assign the workers salaries, and so forth. Following a brief period of this role-play, half of the participants were instructed to "steal" a $100 bill from the next room before meeting an interviewer to end the experiment. The interviewer interrogated all participants without knowing whether they were instructed to take the money, but those who were told to grab the bill were also informed that if they could convince the interviewer that they didn't take it, the money would be theirs to keep.

This procedure meant that at the end of the experiment there were four types of participants: high-power thieves, low-power thieves, high-power controls, and low-power controls (controls were the ones not instructed to take the money). When interviewers asked the controls if they took the money, there were no signs of discomfort. As a result, these individuals weren't flagged as liars. It's when Carney looked at the thieves that the effects of power came into focus. Low-power thieves were often identified by the interviewers as being deceitful. No matter how hard they tried to put on an honest façade, their guilt leaked through its cracks. But for high-power thieves—the ones who spent a short time playing the role of boss—this wasn't the case. They lied with apparent ease. In fact, they weren't flagged as thieves any more frequently than were the controls—the people who actually were telling the truth! Unbeknownst to any of the participants, a slight change in status empowered them to be self-serving liars. Imagine, then, what larger and more long-lasting changes in power might have the ability to do to any of us. Whether we expect it or not, power degrades our trustworthiness while simultaneously sharpening our skills for deceit.

Money Changes Everything

If the effects of class and power on trust really come down to states of mind, it begs the question of how easily swayed this phenomenon truly is. If what's really driving power differences in trust is an increased sense of self-reliance—an increased sense that all the resources you need are at your disposal—then at a very basic level, simple signals of abundance might be all that's necessary to increase dishonesty. Remember, my basic argument is that decisions to be trustworthy derive from conscious and nonconscious calculations weighing the trade-offs of short-term and long-term gains. At the conscious level, most of us readily understand what this means. We compare the immediate benefits to be gained by acting in an expedient or insensitive manner to the long-term repercussions of so doing. With increasing power comes the belief that one's future outcomes don't depend as much on the support of others, and as a consequence the costs of treating them unfairly decreases.

At the nonconscious or intuitive level, however, the system works a bit differently. These mental mechanisms constantly scan the environment for clues about what people are likely to do or what resources are likely to be present. We've already talked a bit about neuroception in assessing individuals' trustworthiness; here, though, we need to focus on the intuitive system's responses to cues of abundant resources. Put simply, the presence of ample resources in close proximity might function as a cue that everything you need is within reach. If there's abundant food in one's environs, trust and cooperation in order to produce it and store it aren't necessary. If there are many people who want to date you, the losses that come from breaking a trust with one partner don't pose as much of a long-term problem. As a consequence, a plentitude of a relevant resource might lead the intuitive system to favor short-term, selfish behaviors. And when it comes to trust, no resource is likely more salient than cold, hard cash.

At an anecdotal level, this prediction seems like it might have some basis in fact. I don't know about you, but I have some friends who fit the bill. Usually they're pretty levelheaded rational types. But take them to a casino and a whole different side comes out. Suddenly one friend who regularly checks his retirement account is letting big bets ride on the roulette wheel, and another friend who promised he'd be ready to go home by ten p.m. is holding some big bills and denying he ever said he wanted to leave early. It's almost as if a fever takes over, turning normally ethical and prudent individuals into self-indulgent doppelgängers. The relevant question for our purposes, though, centers on whether it can really be just the presence of money that produces the change. Can it really be that subtle?

To find the answer, we turn again to the work of Francesca Gino, a behavioral economist at Harvard Business School. Gino believed that proximity to money would be enough to increase deceit and untrustworthiness. To prove her point, she recruited participants to take part in what they believed was a word fluency experiment. When they entered the room she had set aside, they found an experimenter standing next to a table with cash on it. After greeting them, the experimenter handed participants sheets of papers with anagram tasks and $24 in cash taken from the table. They were simply told that they would receive $3 for each correct solution, where a correct solution meant being able to generate twelve words from the set of letters on a given page; the task was much like Scrabble. The experimenter then left participants alone for twenty minutes, after which she returned, told them to grade their own work, take the appropriate amount of money from their pile, and leave.

It sounds straightforward enough, but there was one big difference between the groups of participants that I've yet to mention. For some groups, the pile of cash they saw when entering the room consisted of enough money to pay each of them $24 plus a few hundred dollars more. For others, the abundance of cash was much greater; more than $7,000 was on the table after accounting for the money that would go to pay participants. As Gino predicted, the simple presence of the extra cash significantly increased the amount of cheating on the anagram tasks. Unbeknownst to participants, the experimenter had a way to match up worksheets and score sheets to verify reported scores versus true scores. Across three different experiments, individuals who were in the presence of more cash inflated their performance so that they could keep more of the money than they deserved.

To now, I've been arguing that the presence of abundant resources—as in lots of cash—leads people to be more untrustworthy. That is, power, social class, and the like function to increase dishonesty not because of some stable subcultural ethos or slow acculturation process but rather because, in many ways, they're proxy measures for not needing to rely on other people. The more power or money you have, the less you have to depend on the cooperation and goodwill of partners to get what you need. Gino's findings clearly show that the presence of money can serve as a subtle cue to intuitive systems that resources abound, meaning that a short-term focus on expedience is fine. And when resources are plentiful, dependence on others necessarily decreases.

While certainly intriguing, it is true, though, that her findings don't provide a window into the underlying mechanisms of this phenomenon. Yes, more cash equals more abundance, but how do we really know that this abundance is truly associated in the mind with greater self-interest? How do we know that money really makes people care less about their interactions with others?

This is a question that has been pondered and answered by Kathleen Vohs of the University of Minnesota's Carlson School of Management. In a series of influential experiments, Vohs demonstrated that the simple presence or reminders of money caused people to become self-focused and to favor self-sufficiency over social interactions with peers. For example, after highlighting the idea of money to some participants (e.g., showing them money; having them write about money), Vohs observed fairly dramatic differences in interpersonal behavior. Making money salient not only leads individuals to be less willing to offer any type of aid or assistance to a partner who requests it, but also leads them to resist requesting help for themselves when faced with difficult tasks. Put another way, the cue of money increases motivations to be self-reliant and to reject others who display a need for help or cooperation.

To drive the point home and show that money can readily turn people into lone wolves, Vohs and her team conducted two additional experiments, both focused on preferences for communal versus isolated social interaction. In one, Vohs simply examined social proximity preferences—how close individuals were willing to get to one another. Proximity has a long history serving as one of the best markers for a person's willingness to engage another; distances separating two individuals correlate negatively with their intentions to interact. What Vohs found is that any reminders of money caused people to sit farther apart from each other. That's right, just thinking about cash led people to prefer a greater radius of isolation around themselves. In a second, related experiment, Vohs looked at the effects money had on social preferences in a different way. Here, individuals were asked to indicate whether they would like to work on a difficult upcoming task with another person or by themselves. People usually prefer to cooperate on unpleasant tasks, but Vohs found that those who were reminded about money (through the presentation of pictures of it) chose to work on their own significantly more often. They did not want to share credit with or rely on others for their successes.

Power Corrupts, Unless It Doesn't

Few have captured the seductive dynamics of power and trust better than Benito Mussolini when he mused, "It's good to trust others, but not to do so is much better." As I noted at the outset, most of us trust because we have to. It's the only way to get the resources and benefits we couldn't likely obtain on our own. Yet humans are a hierarchical bunch; we regularly sort ourselves into ordered categories of status, power, and class. But the categories aren't equal in size; they narrow by necessity as we approach the top. Whether we're talking about the one percent of American society or the individual who in his or her present surroundings is temporarily top banana, positions of privilege exert an influence on the calculus of trust. So while most of us need the help of others to get by, the "powerful" do not. By simple virtue of their status, they have access to social, physical, and economic rewards that most others don't. Put simply, they *can* stand alone. And as Mussolini says, what's not to like about that?

The answer to what's not to like comes from consideration of a different question: Where did Mussolini end up? If you'll remember, it was hanging upside down from a pole outside a gas station in Milan. For all its benefits, power can be corrosive if it's not managed well. In the trade-offs between short- and long-term benefits, power is usually focused on short-term gains. Despots, upper-class scions, and presidents of the PTA often feel unconstrained in their social responsibilities by virtue of their hierarchical positions. Other people have to listen to them, and so they usually can satisfy their short-term goals without fears of repercussion. They don't have to trust others; they can order them. The problem with this strategy for leadership, though, is that it is one that must regularly be maintained through force, fear, or similar coercion. And when a powerful figure loses the ability to coerce, those who suffered exploitation at his or her hand often seek retribution.

Given this fact, you might well wonder why power affects the mind this way in the first place. Why does the mind alter its trust-relevant calculations when a person becomes powerful if it can end badly? The solution comes from recognizing that *if* is the key word here. It doesn't *always* end badly. If a person can maintain his or her position of influence, acting in a self-serving way is extremely adaptive. It just means always being on guard to maintain those benefits. It's also the case that evolutionarily speaking, positions of power are only relevant if they allow greater success of offspring. Step one in such success is being able to reproduce, and higher status in most every mammal we know of is associated with greater access to more and better mates. Step two is raising offspring to the age where they, too, can mate. So, logically speaking, even if a despot is overthrown by his own son or daughter, he's an evolutionary success. Remember, it doesn't matter how long one lives; it just matters that one's genes keep being passed down more successfully than the genes of others. Combine this fact with the benefit that even momentary experiences of power can allow one to achieve a goal expediently, and the gains of power-induced short-term thinking make some sense, even when fraught with managing risks of retribution.

There's another path to power and leadership, however, one that can allow individuals to prosper without accepting such high risk. As work by my friend Dacher Keltner, a professor of psychology at Berkeley, shows, individuals who are highly socially engaged and responsive to the concerns of others are often initially elevated to positions of power. Keltner is quick to note, though, that these socially skilled folks—those possessing what is often termed high emotional intelligence—are as likely to fall prey to the pernicious effects of power as anyone else. Those few, however, who are smart enough to resist the short-term and self-indulgent impulses accompanying increased power are the ones who in the long term maintain their positions with less stress and acrimony. They are the benevolent leaders who strive to maintain honor, fairness, and trustworthiness.

Still, filling the role of the benevolent leader can be difficult, as it often requires one to forgo maximizing immediate rewards. If a one-percenter or other powerful person is truly behaving in a fair and equitable manner, he's likely not accruing as much asymmetric profit as he could. Nonetheless, the smaller short-term gains in such profit will likely be outweighed by the long-term stability and benefits provided by his position of privilege. In fact, whether we look at mathematical simulations by Martin Nowak or real-world studies of hierarchy dynamics in social groups, individuals who are fair, trustworthy, and forgiving tend to come out ahead in the long run.

Assuming this is so, why then doesn't power push people toward virtue? Evolutionarily speaking, not everyone makes it to the long run, and if you die or are otherwise sidelined before you realize your gains, they're essentially wasted. Here again, it's important to remember that individual outcomes can deviate from averages, and the final outcome of any given set of calculations is dependent on context. In truth, all these calculations, at both the conscious and intuitive levels, are really bets. Your mind is playing with probabilities—ones that you yourself calculate and ones that are automatically calculated outside your awareness. The trick to maximizing your outcomes from power, then, necessarily depends on understanding the ways in which it can influence you. If you don't understand how power and money affect your trustworthiness and that of others, your ability to prepare for and manage situations is compromised.

The basic fact that your mind may sense short-term benefits and thereby facilitate untrustworthy behavior doesn't mean that you necessarily have to accept it. Recognizing this fact can prepare you to deal with the problem effectively—to combat the corrosive effects of power and thereby to lead with a more empathic touch. Likewise, understanding how power can corrupt can also prepare you to deal with friends or partners who have recently experienced an uptick in status, either by helping them avoid its pitfalls or readying you for possible changes in loyalty. Most of us have had friends who were changed by power—people who suddenly didn't seem like their old selves. As we've seen, though, such changes don't necessarily stem from a personality flaw, but rather from forces in the mind to which we're all subject.

Key Insights

- **Being in the one percent is a state of mind, not a birthright.** Well, at least that's true when we're talking about trust. While not everyone can be a millionaire, anyone can feel higher or lower in status simply by changing comparison standards. And that means that, while those in the one percent might be more untrustworthy on average, they're not necessarily more untrustworthy by nature. Both trustworthiness and the willingness to trust others will ebb and flow as a function of how we feel we compare to those around us. The upshot is that a raise or other windfall can suddenly make any of us feel like we need others less, which in turn increases the probability that our usual trustworthiness might take at least a momentary hit. It's an easy enough trap to avoid, though. Simply pausing to think about your social ties—your links with people on whom you have depended and will likely need to depend again—will reset your intuitive calculus and get you back on track.

• **Power is a drug to beware of.** Like many drugs, power can change your feelings about and abilities to further a goal. It makes you see yourself as special and often above the rules. Indeed, as the psychologists Dana Carney and Amy Cuddy have shown, even temporarily inducing yourself to feel powerful can help you "fake it till you make it" by giving you the confidence and ability to portray yourself to others in ways that might be a bit different from reality. And as Carney's additional work makes clear, power can even make you a better liar. Yet the caution with power—whether it comes from a momentary increase or a chronic role—is like that of many drugs: it's incredibly seductive. Power can easily get you what you want in the short term, but in the long term it often is debilitating unless handled carefully. Unless you constantly remind yourself to be sensitive to and take under consideration the perspectives of others, those others will likely drop from your social circle the moment they have the chance.

• **Avoid the Midas touch.** According to legend, King Midas was a man who liked money, so much so that when he was offered a wish, he asked that whatever he touched would be turned to gold. But as Midas soon found, the lust for money caused several problems, not the least of which was that he could no longer touch or hug his family. The desire for money isolated him, and similar reminders and desires for it do the same to us, albeit by a different mechanism. Cues of abundance and even symbols of money focus our minds on immediate, selfish goals and rewards. In so doing, they turn our attention from the social rewards—family and friends—that usually surround us. As such, thoughts of financial gain can reduce willingness to keep a promise to a child to come home early from work. Money on the card table can make one a bit more willing to cheat old friends. It's not that all of us are somehow morally bereft; these impulses arise from an ancient calculus focused on maximizing resources. As we've seen, abundance means you'll need others less, and that means you can afford to lose their trust and cooperation more. Knowing this basic fact will allow you, as I noted earlier, to pause and recalibrate or override your instinctual responses as needed when the smell of money is in the air.

CHAPTER 6

CAN I TRUST YOU?

Unlocking the Signals of Trustworthiness

Until now I've been making a case for how and why trust plays a central role in much of life. In so doing, I've implied that the ability to infer another person's trustworthiness would offer powerful advantages. In fact, just the possibility of obtaining these advantages has led researchers—in academics, business, and the government alike—on a never-ending quest to find valid ways to detect trustworthiness and deception. Now, I know there are lots of corporations and products out there—books, computer programs, even brain-scanning services—that claim they can tell whether a person can be trusted. For the most part, they're all worthless. I don't say this with joy or malice, but rather with a sense of scientific objectivity. When it comes to detecting deception, meta-analyses—a term for statistical techniques that aggregate findings across large swaths of research—tend to show that people are only slightly better than chance at identifying liars. We can pick out a deceiver 54 percent of the time, but in reality that's not much better than flipping a coin. And when it comes to reading trustworthiness in the absence of deception—trying to tell whether you can trust another when he's not actively attempting to trick you—the data are even murkier.

This state of affairs might seem quite counterintuitive. If the trustworthiness of partners is so integral to success, why does it appear that the human mind can't read it? To me, the lack of success from decades of looking for the signals of trustworthiness suggests one of two possibilities. One, trust-relevant signals don't exist, leaving humanity flying blind when it comes to determining if we can trust others. Two, trust-relevant signals do exist, but we've been flying blind because we're not looking for them in the right way. For a number of reasons I'll explain shortly, I put my money on the second possibility.

The reason for my bet stems from everything you've read in this book so far. Trust offers great benefits but also poses great risks. We rely on it to find a path to success—a path that, for humans, often necessitates the cooperation of others. If we place trust correctly, it engenders success in learning, in intimate relationships, in building social networks, and, in reality, in most every interpersonal endeavor that requires joint action. If we place it incorrectly, though, failure awaits, sometimes of a debilitating nature.

Given what we know about evolutionary adaptation, it makes little sense that judging whether you can trust a partner would be a process left entirely to chance; the stakes are just too high. Yet, agreeing an ability would offer massive benefits is a far cry from finding it. Just because an ability would be adaptive doesn't mean it must exist, only that there's a rationale for why it might. So, while you now understand the basis for my prediction that humans should possess an ability to gauge trustworthiness correctly, I still haven't given you a good answer as to why, if this is indeed true, no one has found the signals yet. To my mind, there are two primary reasons. The first, identified by Cornell economist Robert Frank, is well-known in principle if not always appreciated in practice. The second is not. And in many ways, it's this second reason that has stymied the search the most. To put it bluntly, we've been looking for trust-relevant signals in exactly the wrong way.

Close to the Vest

Communication, whether verbal or nonverbal, has one principal purpose: to pass information to someone else. While it's no surprise that this happens through speaking, it's also an established fact that animals of many types, humans included, exchange information through nonverbal channels (e.g., gestures, facial expression, eye gazes, postures). These more ancient mechanisms—the ones that don't require abstracting meaning from what can at times be complex utterances—are both rapid and effortless. A dog snarls as you approach it and you know it's not very happy with you. A friend looks frightened while walking down a dark street and you sense potential danger. In most cases, nonverbal communication is meant to function exactly this way—to facilitate information exchange in as quick and easy a manner as possible. But trust isn't like most cases.

To understand why trust is different, consider the following. Imagine you possessed an easily detectable and unambiguous signal that indicated you were trustworthy—say a giant letter *T* on your forehead. What would happen? Everyone, and I mean everyone, would want you as a partner. But with this popularity would come one big problem: many of those desiring to partner with you might not be trustworthy themselves. They'd know you'd be easy to exploit; unlike them, you'd always hold up your end of the deal. In the end, you'd lose everything you had; you'd be popular but poor.

Now imagine that it wasn't just you who possessed this telltale mark. What would happen if everyone's trustworthiness could be readily identified? As Frank realized, it wouldn't produce a utopia where the virtuous thrive; the true result would be a bit more complicated. Initially, people who were trustworthy would seek each other out preferentially. Whenever you needed to find a partner, you'd just go find someone with a T on her forehead. Fairly quickly, the untrustworthy would be ostracized and driven almost to extinction, as their economic and social outcomes would be much worse than their cooperative counterparts. Over time, though, the situation would begin to change. Individuals would stop paying as much attention to the T's, as the informational value the signal offered wouldn't be as meaningful. By this time, most people left in society would be trustworthy; the need to check foreheads carefully would be pretty low. But, evolutionary pressures being what they are, some nefarious individuals lurking in the shadows would, by mutation or design, begin to mimic the signal for trust.

Over time, the ability to successfully mimic this signal would grow. Given that people in a mostly trustworthy society wouldn't be paying close attention to signals anymore, skilled cheaters would begin to run rampant. They'd fool everyone and rack up resources quite quickly. Suddenly you couldn't depend on a quick glance at a T on someone's forehead to provide a reliable indicator of potential fidelity. As a consequence, a new pressure would emerge to push people to look more closely for subtle distinctions in the signal in an effort to gauge its authenticity. In essence, as Frank recognized, there'd be an ongoing cold war of sorts—cooperators trying to find secret codes to identify themselves to each other and cheaters attempting to game the system by obtaining the passwords.

The end result would be a dynamic equilibrium of the honest folk and cheaters where any signals indicative of trustworthiness would need to be subtler—and thus a bit more difficult to detect—than other types of nonverbal messages. Simply put, cues for trust would need to be played close to the vest. Many times, especially when interacting with someone new, it's easy to see why revealing all your cards at once could lead to ruin. Signaling trustworthy intent has to be stealthy and slow, at least compared with other types of nonverbal signaling, as individuals "dance around" each other while attempting to infer their partners' motives. As a consequence, accuracy in identifying trust-relevant signals will be a somewhat tenuous endeavor, at least until we can train people to find and interpret the correct signals more easily.

The Blind Men and the Elephant

If subtlety were the only issue limiting the search for trust-relevant signals, it wouldn't necessitate a paradigm shift to find them; all we'd need would be stronger glasses. But it's not the only limitation. Decades of flawed theory about how to decode nonverbal cues have set some ideas in stone. Everyone's looking for the golden cue. Is it shifty eyes? A specific twitch or tilt of the head? Maybe a fidget or curl of the lip? I'm here to tell you it's none of those things—at least not in isolation.

There's a long history in psychology of believing that specific expressions or gestures provide unambiguous cues capable of revealing a person's motivations or feelings. A smile means a person likes you and will be accommodating. A furrowed brow means a person is angry. A sideways gaze means a person is being deceitful. It sounds like a good story; it feels right. It's a view that has been promulgated extensively both by famous behavioral scientists like Paul Ekman and popular television shows like *Lie to Me*. But the past five years of groundbreaking work have caused this view to begin to crumble. Contrary to long-held doctrine, isolated gestures and expressions aren't reliable indicators of what a person feels or intends to do. Two types of context—what I call configural and situational—are essential for correct interpretation. And they've been missing in most attempts to discover what trustworthiness and its opposite look like.

Let's start with configural context. If it were true that the link between nonverbal cues and feelings never changed, then a smile would always mean someone's happy and downward eyebrows would always mean someone's angry. But that's not how it works. To see why for yourself, take a look at the photo below.

Christopher Johnson

If most people saw this face coming at them, they'd be a bit nervous. The man depicted here looks quite upset, if not a bit aggressive. He clearly shows the downward-pointing eyebrows and open mouth with bared teeth associated with an anger expression. There's only one problem. Milos Raonic isn't upset or angry. As you will see when you turn the page, he's ecstatic after winning a match at the Australian Open—something we easily recognize when we see the picture in its entirety.

Some of the best evidence demonstrating the problems with linking specific expressions to specific feelings comes from the respective work of the psychologists Lisa Feldman Barrett and Hillel Aviezer. Each has separately shown that basic facial expressions often prove useless in isolation for figuring out what someone else is feeling. It does seem an odd assertion at first, but on further consideration it begins to make sense. Using images of athletes experiencing intense emotional states from winning or losing, both Barrett and Aviezer have shown just how poor humans are at correctly inferring what others are feeling from their faces alone. Think about the last time you saw someone win a race or a match. What did his or her face look like? It probably wasn't a gentle smile. Just like Raonic, it likely was some combination of an open-mouth, furrowed-brow expression accompanied by one or both fists pumping. It's the nonverbal equivalent of "Yes, I nailed it!" But as Aviezer and Barrett show, if images of athletes are cropped so that all you can see are their faces, most people guess that the given face belongs to someone who is angry or upset, not to someone who is pleased. Without seeing the complete configuration of body movements—without the pumping fist(s) or puffed-up chests—accuracy in reading nonverbal cues nosedives.

It's much the same with cues linked to motivation. Whether we're talking about postural poses or facial expressions, the entire bodily configuration, not its individual elements, is required for accurate interpretation. As an example, let's take the cue of leaning away from someone. It's long been thought that leaning away indicates a hidden desire to avoid or otherwise distance oneself from an interaction partner. That may well be true *at times*. But if you're looking to identify untrustworthy individuals based solely on body orientations, lots of people with bad backs are going to be labeled as threats. In any given instance, it's just as likely that I'll lean away

Christopher Johnson

from you because I don't like you as it is because my lower back hurts. The only way to figure out which interpretation is right is to do it in a semistatistical way. Rather than rely on single cues that might be ambiguous on their own, looking for a configuration, or set, of cues can allow a better extraction of meaning. So while leaning away might indicate simple discomfort in a chair, if it co-occurs with two or three other cues that are also sometimes related to social avoidance, it's more likely that the leaning does in fact stem from a desire to be antisocial and, correspondingly, that the person displaying it might not be positively disposed to his partner.

The second type of context we need to consider is situational. What a cue means and how it's expressed often depends upon the goals and environment at hand. In practice, this means that there probably isn't any golden signal when it comes to trustworthiness. What our minds will choose to emit and to encode depends on what facet of trust is most important at the moment. If you're trying to determine whether you can trust what your physician is telling you, the signal your mind will likely look for is one that denotes competence, not fairness.

Situational context also means that the same cue can signal different intentions depending on who shows it. Fascinating work by the psychologists Max Weisbuch and Nalini Ambady reveals that whether our minds interpret someone's smile as a signal of support or malice depends on that person's social category. If a smile comes from someone similar to you (i.e., a member of your own ethnic group, religious group, etc.) it makes you feel happy to see it. But if the smile is on the face of someone from a social outgroup—especially one in conflict with yours—it makes you feel afraid. After all, if a competitor or enemy is smiling, you may be about to encounter a serious problem.

The upshot of all these arguments is that any attempt to look for cues to trustworthiness without taking into account the configuration of the entire body and situation it's in, is reminiscent of the old parable of the blind men and the elephant. A man feeling its leg thinks the elephant is a pillar. Another feeling its tail thinks it's a rope. A third feeling its tusk thinks the elephant is a pipe. You get the idea. Considering individual parts of any signal is virtually useless for understanding the whole. If we're not looking at cues as sets in a specific context, we're likely to miss the forest for the trees. If we're looking for trust in single micro-expressions or out of context, we won't see it at all.

The Roots of Success

Sometimes the best way to approach a historically vexing problem is to throw out everything you know and start from scratch. When it comes to decoding trustworthiness, this is the strategy I thought best. Of course, starting from scratch is more likely to be productive if you don't go it alone. Whether we like it or not, each of us brings a perspective and set of tools with which to tackle any new challenge that is necessarily informed by our past. I've been trained as a psychologist, and so, try as I might to think like an economist or a computer scientist, I'd never be as successful at it as someone who was trained in one of those fields.

Luckily, I had the good fortune to know several individuals who have an abiding interest in how trust worked. Two of these scholars were friends from Cornell University. The first was David Pizarro, a social psychologist, who, like me, is quite interested in the links between emotional states and ethical decision making. The second was Robert Frank, an economist to whose views I've already introduced you. Together, the three of us brought to the table expertise in nonverbal behavior, emotional biases in decision making, evolutionary models of trust, and behavioral economic methodologies.

It was a good team, but there was still a central ingredient that was missing. We realized early on that if we were truly going to isolate nonverbal signals, we'd need to do it with high precision. That meant we'd need a way to ensure not only that target cues would be emitted in exactly the same way each time they were shown, but also that they could be separated from other cues. For example, we'd need to know that an individual's hands weren't fidgeting at the same time he averted his gaze, as such co-occurrences would make finding the cues that were relevant to reading trustworthiness nearly impossible. How would we know which sets of cues mattered if any single cues could occur randomly? Scientifically, this requirement made great sense; practically, it was a nightmare.

Most of human nonverbal behavior occurs outside of awareness, meaning people are almost constantly emitting cues without knowing it. And if they're not aware they're doing something, how in the world are we going to make them control it? Training them to be aware doesn't really work. Most individuals can pay attention to no more than three or four behaviors at a time, meaning most cues will still emerge spontaneously.

In reality, there was only one way to solve this problem. Since there's no such thing as a completely controllable human being, we needed the next best thing—a robot. Fortunately for me, one of the world's most innovative roboticists works just across town at the MIT Media Lab. Cynthia Breazeal, who directs the Personal Robots Group, stands on the cutting edge of social robotics—a field that, as its name implies, centers on designing robots that are perceived as social entities. For Breazeal, understanding whether and how nonverbal expressions of a robot might influence perceptions of its trustworthiness wasn't only a fascinating theoretical question, it was also one of great practical importance, as one of her principal interests focuses on human-robot teaming. So, with a four-way handshake, the team was born.

Bootstrapping

Now that we had a team, all we needed was a path to follow. In deciding how best to proceed, we embraced the two notions that I described earlier as our guides. First, we expected that any trust-relevant signals—if they indeed existed—would consist of multiple individual cues and be dynamic in nature. That is, we'd need to look for signals that unfolded through different motions as individuals sized up each other within the course of a brief interaction. Second, we decided we'd start from scratch with respect to what cues might matter—we'd need to pull ourselves up by our boot-straps. If we were going to succeed where others had failed, we'd have to be open to any possibilities. This meant we'd have to be willing to follow the data anywhere they led.

With these two principles in mind, we settled on a three-step strategy. Although it was innovative in methodology, it followed the most basic of logical progressions. Step one: Find evidence that viewing others' nonverbal cues truly increases accuracy in predicting trustworthiness. After all, there's no sense looking for a signal if there's no evidence that people can actually be more accurate than chance at predicting others' intentions in the first place. Step two: Look for sets of cues that together reliably predict trust-relevant decisions and behavior. Or, put another way, find the cues that not only influence judgments of trustworthiness, but also presage the actual cooperative or cheating behaviors of others. Step three: Prove these are the cues that really matter by showing that experimental manipulations of them directly alter people's willingness to trust others.

Steps one and two, though distinct, offered the benefit of allowing us to collect data within the same experiment, the heart of which involved a simple discussion between two strangers. From the participants' points of view, the experiment was quite easy. To see why, imagine the following. You arrive at our lab to take part in an experiment titled simply "Judgments of Others." You're told that the session will have two parts. In the first, you'll converse with another person whom you've never seen before; in the second, you'll play an economic game with this person in which your joint decisions will determine how much money you'll walk away with. That's it. It's an analogue to a situation people commonly face—one where you have to quickly get a sense of someone new and then decide if you can trust him or her. The only rule governing the conversations people had was that they couldn't talk about the upcoming game. In truth, they didn't even know what the rules of the game were, so there wasn't much they could have said anyway. But, as we wanted the experiment to focus primarily on detecting trustworthiness in the absence of attempts to extract promises about how one might subsequently behave, we employed this one restriction.

Before we get to the second part of the experimental session—the financial decisions that allowed us to assess trustworthiness objectively—there's one other feature of the conversations you need to know. In order to show that a signal for trustworthiness—or lack thereof—exists, we needed to demonstrate that making it available—whatever form it might take—increases accuracy in guessing how another person will behave. Doing this was rather easily accomplished through the use of social media. For half of our participants, conversations took place face-to-face (FTF), with individuals sitting on either side of a small table. For the other half, conversations occurred via Web-based instant messaging (IM), with individuals sitting in separate rooms. If our hunch about the existence of signals was right, it would point to a simple prediction: people's guesses about a partner's trustworthiness should be more accurate in the FTF condition. Put simply, if accuracy goes up when you can see the person with whom you're conversing, there can be only one reason. Whether or not you realize it, your mind is making use of additional signals beyond the other person's words.

This brings us to the second part of the experimental session. If we were going to prove that trustworthiness could be assessed, we needed some form of ground truth. We couldn't rely on people's reputations or past behaviors to indicate trustworthiness; instead, we had to show that momentary evaluations could predict actual behavior in a given instance. To do this, we utilized the Give Some

Game (GSG) I mentioned in Chapter 1. To refresh your memory, the GSG offers a wonderful analogue for many situations involving trust by pitting options for large asymmetric selfish gain against smaller communal ones. Each person is endowed with four tokens, with each token being worth $1 to its holder but $2 to a partner. The most trustworthy and cooperative way to maximize profits and ensure a potential for long-term collaboration is to give all four of your tokens to your partner. This choice results in $8 for everyone. Of course, if you're interested in immediate, selfish gain, the best decision is quite different. Keep all your tokens and hope your partner gives you all of hers. You'll end up with $12 and she'll end up feeling swindled with $0.

In our experiment, the GSG occurred right after the conversations, with the participants who were conversing face-to-face having been moved to separate rooms. In addition to observing how many tokens people decided to exchange with their partners, we asked them to predict how many tokens their partners would give to them. These two pieces of data were central to our analysis. The more tokens an individual expected a partner to give, the more trustworthy he believed her to be. The more tokens a partner actually gave, the more trustworthy she in fact was. And calculating the difference between these quantities provides an objective measure of accuracy for detecting trustworthiness.

When we examined the results, they were even better than we had hoped. We initially harbored a concern that just being in the presence of a partner might affect trustworthy behavior. That is, even though the nature and extent of the communication in the FTF and IM conditions were the same—something that we checked—the simple act of meeting a partner in person might have reduced a willingness to cheat. Luckily for us, this didn't happen. The levels of trustworthy behavior were the same across conditions. In fact, the average number of tokens exchanged with partners was exactly

2.5 irrespective of whether people were conversing face-to-face or using instant messaging. In some ways, this result may not be too surprising given that texting has become as common a way to chat as picking up the phone or going for coffee. People are used to it and accept it as quite normal.

When it came to accuracy in assessing trustworthiness, however, the picture was entirely different and, to our joy, looked exactly as we had predicted. People who conversed face-to-face showed a sizable advantage in correctly predicting how their partner would behave in comparison with those who conversed using instant messaging; accuracy in judging the number of tokens a partner would ultimately decide to share increased by 37 percent. This fact alone meant that a signal of some type was present. Somehow, our participants were gaining insight into the minds of their partners just by watching them speak.

At this point, the first step in our project was complete. The second step—identifying the nature of the signal—required a bit more work. To find the signal, we needed to make use of an additional source of data: participants' actual nonverbal behaviors. Although I haven't mentioned it yet, the room where the face-to-face interactions took place was equipped with multiple unobtrusive, time-synced video cameras. This setup allowed us to record time-locked video streams that captured each participant from a both head-on and a sideways perspective. As you might imagine, the resulting video data were fairly massive. Over several months, a small army of trained coders translated participants' movements and expressions into numerical entries in a database. And from that database, features of any conversation could be reconstructed. We could, for example, determine that Participant 23 smiled at five minutes and three seconds into the interaction, and that her partner, Participant 24, touched her own face twelve seconds later.

To begin building our model for a trust-relevant signal, we

calculated the frequencies with which each participant displayed individual gestures and expressions, and examined whether these frequencies predicted decisions in the GSG. As we expected, none of the individual cues was significantly associated with behavior. Counting the number of times an individual averted her gaze, fidgeted with her hands, or nodded her head provided no substantial insight into whether she would subsequently behave in a trustworthy manner.

We next began to mix cues into multiple sets, all the while examining the degree to which each set could predict cooperation and selfishness. After much investigation, we identified a set of four individual cues that, when taken together, were strongly predictive of how trustworthy a person would be both in perception and behavior. The four cues were: crossing arms, leaning away, face touching, hand touching. The more frequently any individual engaged in these behaviors, the less trustworthy he or she acted (i.e., the fewer tokens he or she shared with a partner). Of no small importance, this result provided our ground truth; it demonstrated an objective link between the multicue signal and actual behavior. The overarching question of interest, of course, also involved whether observing the signal influenced judgments of trustworthiness. Here, too, the data provided support. The more frequently partners showed these cues, the less trust individuals placed in them (i.e., the fewer tokens they expected the partner to offer in exchange). And since each participant was not only a perceiver, but also someone else's partner, these two findings close the circle of accuracy. Emitting this signal not only meant your partner would have a hunch that you'd be untrustworthy, it also meant that hunch would be correct.

Although identifying what seemed to be a verifiable trust-relevant signal had never been done before, what was perhaps even more interesting was that people had no insight into its nature, or, for that matter, that their minds were using it. None of our participants could describe what led them to guess that a partner was going to be untrustworthy. Nonetheless, our findings confirmed that their minds were attuned to this constellation of cues, leading them to dial back expectations for fairness and loyalty each time the multicomponent signal was repeated.

In many ways, the components of this signal make good sense. Historically, there is evidence indicating that leaning away from someone can at times suggest a motive to avoid, and crossing arms can at times indicate a desire to block intimacy or the forming of a bond. Similarly, face touching or fidgeting can at times suggest anxiety. When combined, these features offer a picture of a partner who doesn't want to engage and is self-conscious or worried about how he or she is likely to act. They mark someone who doesn't want to be your friend and is thinking about acting in a way you wouldn't like.

By this point, we had found evidence that a specific signal exists whose presence/absence directly enables some level of accuracy in predicting the untrustworthiness/trustworthiness of a partner. Although we were certainly encouraged by these findings, our scientific instincts prevented us from declaring victory. There were two issues with which we still had to contend. First, as any scientist will tell you, findings have to be replicable before much faith can be placed in them; the results of any single experiment could be a fluke. Second, and this is the one that worried us a bit more, studying nonverbal behaviors is always a dicey endeavor. People don't emit cues in isolation; they're constantly expressing many, often at the same instant. So while we found that a set of four specific cues predicts untrustworthy behavior, how could we be sure that it was truly those cues—and those cues alone—that mattered? Maybe every time someone touched her face, her left pupil also dilated.

Maybe every time a partner leaned away, he also flared his nostrils. Maybe, just maybe, we still had it wrong. As I mentioned at the outset, here's where the skills of MIT's Personal Robots Group moved front and center.

Can You Trust This Robot?

Asking whether you can trust a robot may seem like a silly question at first. What does it mean to trust a machine? At first you might think I mean whether you can trust it to work properly. But here we're not focused on the reliability of the mechanics; the issue at hand is whether you can trust a robot to deal with you fairly. For your mind even to begin to fathom this question, a robot has to reach a very high bar. It has to be viewed as a social being. It has to seem so alive that your mind can be tricked into believing, at least for a moment, that it's a sentient entity capable of selfish and selfless motivations. That's a tall order for a robot, but one that has begun to be met by the work of Cynthia Breazeal.

As I noted earlier, Breazeal is one of the world's foremost experts on incorporating social design into robots. From animating their faces and gestures to match human expressions, to designing algorithms that allow robots to follow partners' gazes and recognize emotional tones of voice, even to incorporating movements that mimic biological motions like respiration into robots' repertoires, Breazeal's group continues to push the boundaries for what is possible in making robots act as social beings. Although her robots come in many forms, we needed one that approximated a human for our investigation of trust. Breazeal had just the thing: a robot named Nexi.

As you'll see in the following picture, Nexi, at least from the waist up, provides a wonderful analogue for a human. Every part of her (we gave Nexi a female voice, so we'll refer to it as "her")—head, face, neck, hands, and arms—was built to possess an incredible range of biologically appropriate motion. Although these pictures offer some insight into her capabilities, seeing is truly believing, and so I encourage you to check out this book's Web site (www.truthabouttrustbook. com), where you'll be able to see Nexi in action for yourself.

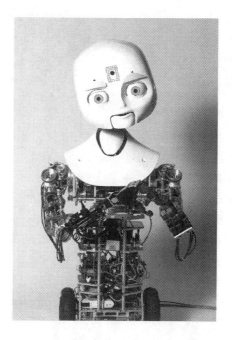

Now that we had our robot, we turned to the third step of our plan. As I noted before, simply finding that a set of cues is associated with believing someone to be untrustworthy doesn't necessarily mean that observing these exact cues in another will *cause* you to view him as untrustworthy. It's like that old example of churches and crimes. While it is true that cities with more churches also have more crimes committed within their boundaries, it is equally true that increased numbers of churches do not cause increased frequencies of crime. The reason for the seemingly surprising association is that the number of churches and the number of crimes in a given city both stem from population. More people means greater numbers of religious types and criminal types. So while one could certainly use the number of churches in a city to predict the number of crimes that will occur, knocking down a few churches won't reduce crime; it will only result in overcrowded worship services. Herein lies the risk with any correlational data, ours included. If we wanted to prove with certainty that the cues we identified were the ones that mattered, we needed to remove any association they might have with other subtle cues that could have been simultaneously expressed.

The best way to accomplish this goal was to use Nexi as a conversation partner in a Wizard of Oz (WOO) design. As its name suggests, a WOO works by having the robot controlled by humans "behind the curtain," or, in this case, in an adjoining room. From participants' points of view, the experiment would unfolded exactly as the previous one did, with the exception that their conversation partner would be Nexi. Behind the curtain, however, an amazing degree of technological wizardry allowed the human puppeteers to bring Nexi to life.

One of my graduate students, Jolie Baumann, was assigned to play the role of Nexi. You might wonder why we needed a human to play Nexi at all. To understand why, stop to consider how natural a conversation with Apple's Siri or similar technology usually is, especially if you try to move from giving commands to having an actual give-and-take. Automatic language processing isn't advanced enough yet to hold its own, and as a consequence we needed Jolie and our other human wizards to pull this off. In the next room,

Jolie sat in front of large screen that provided a video feed from a camera embedded in Nexi, which allowed Jolie to visualize her human interaction partner. A camera on top of the screen was fixed on Jolie as well. Its sole purpose was to track her head motions in three dimensions and to move Nexi's head to match. As a result, Nexi would orient her head and gaze in a way that fluidly followed conversation. Jolie also wore a headset whose mic served two purposes. One was to stream Jolie's voice through Nexi. The other was to code Jolie's phonemes (i.e., discrete speech sounds) and to make Nexi's mouth move to match them in real time. Again, the primary purpose was to allow Nexi to appear as lifelike as possible. And given that human bodies aren't motionless during interactions, Nexi was also programmed to make normal conversational gestures to go along with what Jolie was saying.

This was all well and good, but you might be wondering where the set of four target cues comes into play. Well, before we could have Nexi express them, we had to "teach" her what they were. Teaching a robot means writing computer code to move Nexi's gears in specific ways. Using multiple videos of our human participants from the first experiment as examples, Breazeal's team, headed up by her graduate student Jin Joo Lee, extracted progressions of movements and then translated them into positional information for Nexi's body. The result was a few prototypical examples for each cue that allowed Nexi's gestures to mirror those of humans.

At this point we were almost ready to go. Much of Nexi's motions would be captured in real time from Jolie's movements, and others—like the target cues and related control gestures (i.e., movements of the same size and scope as target cues)—would be triggered by the press of a button. Remember, though, I indicated we needed two "wizards" to operate Nexi. Why the second? We needed to be certain that Jolie didn't know whether any given participant to whom she was speaking was going to see the target cues. She had to be blind to participants' conditions to ensure that she wasn't giving off any other signals that might influence perceptions of trustworthiness. If, for instance, Jolie was the one who hit a button to make Nexi cross her arms, this knowledge, even unconsciously, might have influenced how she moved her head or the tone of her voice. And if that happened, all our attempts to ensure that the cues would occur without an association to any other signals would have been for naught.

Enter Leah, graduate student and second wizard. Leah's sole job was to control whether and when Nexi expressed any target cues of untrustworthiness (i.e., backward leans, crossed arms, face and hand touches) or similar, neutral conversational gestures. Although Leah could hear and see the conversation, neither Jolie nor the participant had any interaction with her. At the start of each experimental session Leah flipped a coin to determine which types of cues—target or neutral—a given participant would see.

These technical issues aside, the experiment with Nexi followed a script similar to the human-human case. Participants arrived and were told that they would be conversing with a robot for ten minutes (the first five minutes were simply Nexi doing an introduction about herself and allowing participants to get used to talking to a robot), following which they'd play a joint economic game. We also informed them that Nexi would be using an artificial intelligence algorithm that would base her subsequent financial decisions on how the interaction went. This illusion was necessary so that people wouldn't assume the robot would just keep or give away all its money. After the conversation, we moved participants to a separate room, where they answered questions about how they viewed Nexi and played the GSG.

Before I tell you what happened, I would be remiss if I let you believe that every session with Nexi unfolded perfectly. Data from some participants had to be dropped. Once in a while, Nexi would malfunction and start gazing off into space. Other times, problems were more "people-centric." One guy, for example, insisted on asking Nexi if she believed in God. Another continuously waved his arms around while talking to Nexi to see if he could mess up the robot's ability to track his face. But aside from these relatively few and far-between aberrations, people found the interactions with Nexi to be quite engaging.

What finally happened? To our satisfaction, it was exactly what we had hoped. Individuals who saw Nexi express the set of target cues during their conversations later indicated that they just didn't trust her. Although they found her as likable as did people to whom she didn't express the cues, those who saw the cues harbored a sense that Nexi was going to cheat them. What's more, seeing the cues not only made people expect Nexi to give them fewer tokens, it also made them less willing to share tokens with her. And of most import, perceptions of trust linked everything together. That is, the extent to which individuals reported trusting Nexi directly predicted both how many tokens they expected the robot to exchange with them and the number they agreed to exchange with her.

In many ways, these findings were quite astounding. For one, they confirmed beyond much doubt that the set of cues we had identified revealed others' intentions to be untrustworthy. Although there were numerous reasons why the use of a robot might not have worked, there was only one reason that could explain why it did—the cues were the correct ones. Even though none of the people in our experiments held any inkling about what truly influenced their judgments, their minds clearly made use of the signal in question. The presence of these cues—and likewise their absence within the context of a potentially cooperative endeavor—offered insight into exactly where a potential partner momentarily stood on the short- versus long-term gain continuum. Those who acted less trustworthily—the ones who gave their partners fewer tokens— were favoring short-term benefits, as knowingly making a selfish choice would provide more money in the moment but likely doom chances for subsequent cooperation with this partner.

A second—and perhaps even more profound—implication of this work is that technology has at last reached a level where it can mirror humanlike social behavior so closely that our minds are willing to ascribe moral intent to artificial entities based on their nonverbal signals. In a world where communication is ever becoming more computer-mediated—a world where we spend more and more time talking to virtual avatars and agents—the extreme precision offered by these virtual entities raises both comforting and disturbing possibilities. Programmers and designers might soon have a powerful method for manipulating our judgments to trust in ways that, before now, did not exist. Such methods are as likely to offer ways to conceal cues from the untrustworthy among us as they are to offer ways to build trust with entities that previously seemed socially barren. These are issues to which we'll turn in the next chapter. Before we do, though, there's another type of trust-relevant signal we need to consider to get the full picture of what influences judgments about whether to rely on others: competency.

Follow the Leader

I've spent a good deal of time arguing that trust isn't one-dimensional. Being trustworthy doesn't just mean intending to be fair and honest in your dealings with others who depend on you; it also involves being competent. Until now I've been focusing on signals that provide insight into whether someone will exploit you. But from an evolutionary perspective, knowing whether others have the ability to help you is as important as knowing whether or not they'll choose to actually do it. As a consequence, nonverbal signals of expertise should exist.

Unlike signals related to fairness and loyalty, however, subtlety isn't quite as important for signals of competence. Although broadcasting a willingness to cooperate might be risky before you know whether a potential partner is similarly inclined, signaling competency poses no similar peril. To the contrary, the only purpose it serves is to demonstrate one's desirability as a partner or leader upon whom others can rely.

Although most of our work has focused on identifying signals related to integrity and a willingness to cooperate, we have begun to document how people respond to signals of expertise as well. Given the lower need for subtlety, the components of these signals are clearer. In fact, cues to expertise are those directly associated with nonverbal expressions of pride and status: expanded posture, head tilted upwards, arms held open and raised or placed akimbo (i.e., hands on waist with elbows tilted outward), and decreased gazing at others during interactions. In many ways, the link of competency to pride makes great sense. Although it is certainly true that at times individuals can cross the line into hubris (i.e., feeling a sense of pride that is undeserved), my own research with the psychologist Lisa Williams has demonstrated that pride can be quite useful—it impels people to push themselves hard to garner valuable skills they otherwise might not seek.

The relevant question here, however, doesn't center on what pride and feelings of competence do for the people experiencing them, but rather on whether these feelings send signals of trustworthiness to others. To find out, Lisa and I concocted an experiment to see whether expressions of competence might determine whom individuals decide to trust to lead a group endeavor. The basic idea was quite simple. When faced with a difficult challenge, people should choose a leader whom they feel they can trust to do a good job. And, in cases where previous knowledge of potential leaders is absent, those individuals expressing signals for competence should be selected to lead, as these signals would be the only information about competence available.

There was one difficulty we had to overcome to test this prediction, though. To confirm that it really was something about expressing confidence that made people attractive leaders, we had to exclude the possibility that those feelings of confidence weren't associated with any other personality traits or abilities. Imagine for a moment that I told you that the person who emerged as leader in a group of strangers that was attempting to solve a complex engineering problem was the one who appeared most confident. Would you believe this fact proved Lisa and me right? I hope not. While selecting a person to lead could stem from his confidence, it could also come from the fact that he might be attractive, that he looks like an engineer (think horn-rimmed glasses), or that he has a dominant personality and bullied his way to dominate the group. To get around this issue—to ensure that feelings of competence didn't overlap with anything else—we needed a way to select the experts, and to do that, we again had to use some subterfuge.

Here's how the experiment worked. We brought participants into the lab under the guise that we were investigating "visuospatial ability." For the first part of the experiment, we had them complete many mental-rotation tasks on the computer. You know, the kind of task where you're presented with what looks like three partially unfolded Rubik's Cubes. In each case, the task is to determine whether Object A, when rotated through three dimensions, would match either Object B or Object C. The task was designed to be difficult enough that participants didn't have an accurate sense of what their scores might be, especially since we told them that the scores were a function of accuracy *and* time. Before moving on to the second part of the experiment—the one where people would work in groups to solve spatial puzzles—we gave some participants surprisingly good information about their performance (more on this in a moment).

The group part of the experiment was equally straightforward. We combined several people who had just been assessed in isolation into groups whose purported sole purpose was to solve a physical mental rotation task. We showed them a Rubik's Cube–type puzzle and then completely unwound it so that what had been a large cube now consisted of a row of connected smaller, individual cubes. Their task was to twist and fold this connected line of cubes to re-form the larger cube in a short period of time. It was not an easy task; hardly any groups finished it in the time allotted. In reality, though, we weren't concerned with whether the groups solved the puzzle. We wanted to know who emerged as the leader—whose advice the others were willing to follow.

Here's where the issue of feedback that I mentioned earlier comes into play. At the end of the mental rotation task, Lisa brought participants individually into a separate room to give them information about their scores. She told some of them that they had performed amazingly well. She gave them an official-looking score sheet showing their results in the ninetieth percentile and gave them a pat on the back while looking impressed. The result was that these participants—and there was only one of these participants in each of the subsequent groups—came to believe that they possessed a high and relatively rare level of ability when it came to mental rotation. And since they were selected randomly, it also meant that they weren't necessarily used to being leaders, habitually dominant, or possessing of any similar characteristic that could have explained what was to come next.

If our suspicions about reading competence were correct—and they were—something rather remarkable was about to happen. The people who were informed of their "greatness"—the ones who were now feeling a good dose of confidence and pride—quickly rose to the top. Time and again, they came to dominate their individual groups. In fact, their leadership status was so clearly evident that both they themselves, as well as the other members of the groups, later reported that these target participants were the ones in charge. Even neutral third-party observers, who later watched videos of the interaction, rated the proud and confident people as group leaders. It's important to remember, though, that the only actual difference among everyone working on the task was whether they secretly believed they possessed expertise, not whether they actually did. Yet this simple belief allowed those who possessed it to emit signals of confidence—more expansive postures, upward head tilts, and the like—that somehow led others to trust their guidance. The followers weren't cowed into following; they reported wanting to follow their confident workmates. They didn't view them in a negative or bossy way; to the contrary, they reported liking the leaders. They were happy to find someone they felt they could trust.

Now, it's true that although our "experts" believed they possessed great skill, they actually didn't. We simply tricked them into believing they did. Signaling is all about intention and belief; it's not always tied to objective facts. In terms of competence, this suggests that as long as a person truly believes she is qualified, she'll emit cues that signal she can be trusted. If her assessment is misguided, however, so, too, will be others' perceptions. In the real world, such misperceptions usually resolve rather quickly. Even if the people in question don't come to realize their own miscalcuations, others who know them will soon learn that they're being hubristic. The same would have occurred in our experiment if we had repeated it with the same people a few times. It would have become apparent quickly that those who thought they possessed expertise actually weren't more competent at solving the puzzle than anyone else. In the short term, though, such misleading signals might allow trust to be misplaced just long enough, either by accident or by design, to allow one to slip into the beneficial role of advisor, valued partner, or leader.

Trust Bugs

At this point, you might be tempted always to trust your intuition when it comes to deciding whether someone is trustworthy. After all, I've just shown you that your mind possesses mechanisms that can give your hunches accuracy. But as I've said before, simple rules tend not to provide optimal results. Deciding always or never to trust your gut will often get you into trouble. Wisdom comes from knowing when and why to rely on reason or intuition—from knowing the strengths and weaknesses of each. The case of trust is no different.

We already know the rationale for why conscious deliberation can be fraught with peril. The cues that people tend to believe offer insights into trustworthiness actually don't. Why not just trust intuition, then? Let's just say it has a few bugs, too. Why haven't millennia of evolution wiped them out? Well, what I'm calling "bugs" aren't really bugs per se, but rather more like crossed signals. They stem not from faulty machinery, but from responses that are, evolutionarily speaking, out of place. Let me give you a couple of examples.

The first has to do with pictures. Admit it, at some point in your life you probably scanned through club directories, Facebook profiles, online dating pages, or the like, not only to see what a potential date or business partner looks like, but also what you might be able to glean about their personality. Do they look like you can trust them? Although it's natural to want to see what someone looks like, photographs have only been in existence for around two hundred years. Before then, you had to go see for yourself. And seeing meant seeing the other person in action; most people don't sit motionless, allowing others to stare at their faces. Checking someone out, then, necessarily provided access to all the dynamic nonverbal cues that matter—the same cues that are completely absent in a photograph. But, as still images are relatively new in terms of the time frame of humanity, our minds don't know enough to make an adjustment for them. As a result, our minds try to extract whatever information they can from what they see, even though it usually ends up being wrong.

Alex Todorov, a social neuroscientist at Princeton, has developed a vast research program demonstrating the human mind's willingness to ascribe all kinds of intentions and characteristics to human faces depicted in static images. By examining responses not only to actual human faces, but also to faces that have had their features manipulated and morphed, Todorov has shown that our minds readily "see" trustworthy and deceitful intentions in still images of others. The only problem is that these judgments provide zero accuracy; they're no better than flipping a coin.

This inaccuracy may seem puzzling at first. After all, why should the mind repeatedly make judgments that are off the mark? Wouldn't it be better not to make any judgments at all in such cases? Yes and no. If the cues our minds are using were always wrong, I'd certainly agree the tendency to make these judgments would have been extinguished long ago. But the cues aren't always wrong; they're only wrong when the mind overgeneralizes them. For example, one of Todorov's central findings is that in the absence of being able to observe real-time emotional expressions in a face, the human mind will overgeneralize static anatomical differences to "find" emotions. As a consequence, people who have more prominent brows or mouths that turn slightly downward will be judged to be angrier, up to no good, and less trustworthy than those whose facial anatomy looks different. Ordinarily, seeing someone furrow their brows would be a cue that they might not be pleased (especially when it co-occurs with other negatively toned cues). But when all you have is a static picture, you're not going to see movement, meaning all the mind has to utilize are anatomical features that can serve as echoes of the components of emotional expressions. And because pictures didn't exist on the ancestral savannah, the mind hasn't learned to avoid using these features of the face.

The second phenomenon that produces crossed signals in judging trustworthiness comes from a different aspect of facial anatomy—features associated with extreme youth. Most babies share certain features in common: round faces, big eyes, and small noses, to name a few. These are the features that our mammalian minds see and make us go, "Awwww, how cute." They're the features that evolution has endowed with an ability to signal innocence and a need for care, and as such, they make us want to nurture their bearer. Most times, these facial signals provide veridical information. Babies do need care; they're not very competent in most domains. But when adults retain features of extreme youth—when they have a "baby face"—these signals can be wildly off the mark. One need look no further than John Dillinger's murderous partner Baby Face Nelson to find an example of just how far off they can be.

In adults, baby-facedness is characterized by a few central features: a large face, round eyes, and a small nose and chin. Much work by the psychologist Leslie Zebrowitz, as well as by Alex Todorov and colleagues, has confirmed that people possessing these features are typically perceived as warm and good-intentioned, but also as fairly low in competence. The end result is that when people form opinions about the baby-faced—assuming of course that they don't know them very well—how trustworthy they judge them to be depends upon the task at hand. If you're looking for a partner who isn't likely to cheat you, a baby-faced person will appear as a good bet to be trusted. But if you're looking for a partner to provide expertise or be a strong leader, a baby-faced person is likely the last one on whom you'll choose to rely. As with the emotional echo situation earlier, it's not that our minds are completely misguided. In most cases, baby-faced features provide useful information; they push our intuitive judgments to evaluate the very young correctly. It's only when some adults retain these features that the benefits of the signals get lost.

While these biases are interesting, you might still be a bit skeptical about the level of impact they can have. After all, once you begin talking with and observing the dynamic cues of a baby-faced partner, the resulting information should trump that which had been based on facial anatomy alone. In fact, we just saw this clearly to be the case with Nexi. In an effort to make Nexi appear a bit more approachable, Breazeal intentionally designed her to be slightly baby-faced—large round eyes, smaller nose, etc. Yet any bump-up the robot enjoyed in seeming honest was quickly overridden by the dynamic cues it expressed.

Perhaps the most compelling evidence for how face-based judgments of trustworthiness can matter, though, comes from Todorov's examinations of their influence on elections. In what has become a highly cited and classic set of studies, Todorov examined voter preferences based solely on candidate faces over five election cycles from 2000 to 2004. In each case, his team simply presented people living in the Princeton, New Jersey, area with head shots of candidates running for office in other parts of the country. No other information about the candidates was provided, and since these candidates were not involved in high-profile national races (e.g., presidential or senatorial campaigns) but rather contests for the House of Representatives, all the research participants really had to go on was the candidates' faces. What happened was as amazing as it was consistent. The candidates judged to be most competent based on facial features alone won their respective elections about 70 percent of the time. They were the ones the populace trusted to lead.

At first these findings might be hard to accept. But if faces didn't matter, the average association between competence features and electoral success should have been 50 percent (or even less if there were more than two candidates in the race). The figure of 70 percent clearly shows that intuitive judgments of competence weren't, thankfully, the sole determining factor. Yet they do appear to carry some weight. And if you stop to consider how little most Americans really know about the policy positions and experience of their congressperson, it suddenly becomes clear why subtle factors like appearance can have a big impact. We're becoming a culture that wants to make fast, effortless decisions. Why look at voting records when you can simply look at a campaign flyer? And that's why, as political analyst Larry Sabato has stated, "You'll find that Congress has been taken over by people who resemble news anchors and game show hosts."

These and related findings are yet other examples of why it's a fool's errand to rely steadfastly on intuition when it comes to trust.

When it's working correctly, intuition can provide the key to identifying who can be trusted in a way conscious reasoning cannot, but
when it goes awry, it can lead one to make potentially disastrous
decisions. Once again, the trick to optimizing your outcomes rests
on understanding when intuition does and does not offer the best
solution.

Key Insights

• **The whole is more than the sum of its parts.** As we've
seen, accuracy in detecting trustworthiness comes from looking
for cues in sets—cues that, taken as a whole, express a more
general representation, or gestalt, of a partner's internal motivations and thoughts. Looking for the clichéd "shifty eyes" or similar "tells" will tell you nothing. So don't fall prey to supposedly
validated tactics that identify the untrustworthy by using single
markers or micro-expressions. Unfortunately, the TSA did just
that, spending more than $400 million on a program that a
2010 report by the Government Accountability Office confirmed to be a failure. Many individuals who were on terrorist
watch lists raised no alarms, and of all the people this program
did identify as possible security threats, only 1 percent were
truly engaged in any nefarious activity (and most of those were
simply illegal aliens trying to escape notice).

• **Context is everything.** Goals matter. Your mind intuitively shifts from using signals of affiliation and integrity to using signals of competence to determine trustworthiness as
needed. It all depends on whether your goal in finding someone
to trust involves needing a partner with honesty or expertise.
This basic fact explains why you might at times feel differently
about trusting the same person. For example, you might not want

to trust a new college roommate with your money but still have a hunch you can rely on her advice when it comes to calculus.

- **Trust your gut, but not blindly.** No one in our experiments possessed insight into the actual cues their minds were using to assess partners. Nevertheless, their minds utilized the four cues we identified to good avail, giving those who were able to see their partners greater accuracy in predicting trustworthiness than to those who had no face-to-face contact. What this means is your intuitive mind possesses some knowledge that your conscious one doesn't (at least until now). It also has much more practice in using this knowledge. The upshot, as I noted earlier, is not to disregard your hunches as some irrational feeling or intuition, but to give them serious consideration. Consideration, however, means just that; it doesn't mean blind allegiance. As we've just seen, intuitions can go awry, especially when psychological mechanisms that were honed in one environment or for one purpose begin to process information of a different type. So when your intuitions tell you something based on a photograph or slightly surprising face (e.g., very baby-faced or one having been altered due to accident or injury), take a moment to think whether your initial gut response may be a bit misguided.

- **Practice works, for humans and machines.** Now that you possess some knowledge about what cues do matter, practicing looking for them should allow your conscious mind to catch up to your unconscious one. And when that happens, your ability to detect dishonesty and expertise should move beyond the baselines we've seen. But looking for patterns (patterns of cues in this case) isn't something that only humans can do. Computers are even better. In fact, Jin Joo Lee of MIT's Personal Robots

Group has shown that automated systems can be trained to classify sets of cues and use the resulting information to predict trustworthy behavior with an accuracy much greater than that shown by humans. Now that we have a new way to identify the correct cues, its incorporation into technology should rapidly follow.

CHAPTER 7

CYBERTRUST

The Risks and Rewards of Trusting Those You Virtually Know

Cybertrust. The term tends to evoke a foreboding feeling, as if the Internet itself were encircling you in its web, just waiting to pounce on any inadvertent error you make in safeguarding a password or Social Security number. We've all seen the failure of corporate software meant to protect our personal information, the magazine cartoons of the questionable-looking older man posing as an attractive teenager in a chat room, and the e-mails from the ubiquitous Nigerian uncle who has left us money to be transferred into our bank accounts if we'll only send the routing numbers. Although examples like these suggest we're entering a perilous new world when it comes to figuring out whom (or what) we can trust, the basic issue of whether to trust technology has in fact been around for thousands of years. What makes it feel new now, however, is that technology is beginning to encroach on what had until recently been a solely human domain—sociality. Concerns about technology are no longer just mechanical; they're not just about whether a widget will malfunction or circuit will short. As we know from our Facebook

pages and saw with Nexi the robot, technology and social communication are becoming ever more intertwined. And it's this fact,
more than anything else, that has opened up vast new ways in which
trust can be manipulated for the better or the worse.

The Allure of the Machine

The first issue to consider when it comes to trust and technology
centers on whether a machine—and I use that word liberally—can
be trusted to work as intended. Picture every space launch you've
ever witnessed. There's always an anxious hush in the crowd during
liftoff as everyone holds their breaths, waiting to see if it will be
successful. Will the technology function as intended? Everyone
hopes so, but as we've unfortunately seen several times, there's always a risk that it won't. But trepidation in trusting technology isn't
reserved only for big events that capture national attention; it also
regularly hits closer to home, as I'm reminded every tax season
when my elderly relatives ask if the software I use to help them file
their taxes is working correctly. Yet whether the issue at hand is big
or small, it's important to recognize that even though the "partner"
is a machine of some sort, the underlying dynamics involving trust
are the same. By relying on technology to ferry us into space or to
calculate our expenses and move our money, we're making ourselves vulnerable to its competence. If the technology works well,
all will be fine. If it doesn't, we'll be broke or worse.

For all its trappings of modernity, this situation, as I've just noted,
isn't a new one. In reality, humankind has relied on technology—and
thereby accepted some level of vulnerability in order to gain its
benefits—for thousands of years. Ever hear of the astrolabe? By 150
BCE, this device was already being used to calculate time, the

position of the stars, and geographical locations with great precision. As a result, those willing to trust an astrolabe's calculations
would have ready access to information that otherwise would have
been much more difficult to obtain. Yet, if their trust was misplaced—
if the astrolabe they were using possessed imperfections—their
calculations might well go awry, leading to potentially disastrous results. Such vulnerability stands as a fundamental challenge with all
technology, ancient or new. One need look no further than Apple's
debacle with the initial release of its mapping software in 2012 to
see this is so. Errors in locating addresses were so pervasive that
Australian police were actively warning citizens not to use Apple's
maps to plan their routes. As just one example of the seriousness of
the mapping software's glitches, Australians attempting to drive to
the city of Mildura were being directed to an arid national park
more than forty miles away, where they often became stranded
without gas in temperatures close to 115 degrees Fahrenheit.

In the face of such failures, it might seem reasonable to ask why
we continue to trust technology. The answer, of course, is quite
straightforward. As it is with trusting other humans, the benefits
tend to outweigh the costs. Technology usually serves us well, and
misfires are quickly corrected through competition. If one product
is found to be unreliable, people quickly turn to a different one.
Moreover, deciding to trust technology, much like deciding to trust
other people, allows us to accomplish much more than we ever
could on our own. The invention of the printing press increased the
production of books in a way that was previously unimaginable.
The development of e-mail allowed for communication at a pace
and volume that was never before possible. In both cases, it was
surely a possibility that the printed text or electronic communica-
tions would contain errors, but the cost of not utilizing such technology eclipsed these concerns.

For all the similarities between trusting technology and trusting humans, there is one fundamental difference, however. Humans have skin in the game. We're always comparing, consciously or not, the benefits of being trustworthy versus the benefits of being selfish in terms of short- and long-term gain. Machines, at least in most cases, don't have desires. They're not looking to maximize their own outcomes; they're made to accomplish a given task. This basic fact means that the domain of integrity is removed from the trust equation. All that matters in trusting a nonsocial machine is its competence, and as a result, trusting technology is becoming more and more seductive.

As technology's presence and usefulness in our lives grows, it seems our minds, unconsciously at least, are becoming increasingly willing to accept markers of scientific sophistication as cues for competence. Cloak information in a more technological "garb" and people are suddenly more likely to believe it. In my field, many of us jokingly refer to this phenomenon as the MRI effect. If you show people an image of brains where certain parts "light up," the validity of claims for why these areas are active—let alone for what they influence—suddenly becomes much more persuasive. Right now, in fact, there are several companies promising to deliver accurate reads of people's trustworthiness, attitudes, and beliefs simply by scanning their brains. And, infatuated by the promise of technology they don't understand, there are myriad other companies dropping big money to use these services. What these corporate consumers don't realize, of course, is that brain imaging is in its infancy. Every day we're finding out that what we thought some anatomical structure did is incorrect. No self-respecting neuroscientist would argue that fMRI images provide any reliable information regarding trustworthiness or the like. Of course, decades from now, as the technology is refined, it will surely offer useful information, but that day is still far off when it comes to understanding human social behavior. Nonetheless, our minds fall prey to the heuristic that technology implies competence and validity.

Evidence for just how deeply use of this heuristic runs comes from work by the psychologists Joseph Lyons and Charlene Stokes of the U.S. Air Force's research arm. Together, they designed an experiment in which they tasked individuals with playing the role of a convoy leader who had to decide which of three routes would be the safest for his or her troops to use. Each participant was given three sources of information about the potential routes. The first source—route parameters—simply consisted of information about the features of the potential paths: number of traffic lights, typical traffic densities, road quality, route length, etc. The second source—an automated tool—provided a dynamic, visual display of the relevant geographical area that highlighted hostile zones where previous attacks had occurred and noted differences in the severity and the use of explosive devices in those zones. The third source of information—a human aide—took the form of a briefing by an intelligence officer who provided updated information regarding threats in the different zones and offered a specific route recommendation.

What Lyons and Stokes found is exactly what you'd expect if technology were acting as a nonconscious cue for competence. When asked how much they thought they'd rely on the human aide and the automated tool to make their decisions, no differences emerged; people believed they were as likely to trust one source of information as the other. Yet when the team examined the decisions the participants actually made, a distinctly different pattern emerged. As risks increased, participants' decisions became more and more consistent with information provided by the automated tool rather than by the human aide. The implications are clear.

When vulnerability was high, people unwittingly used the cue of competence provided by technology to make their decisions, so much so that they were willing to disregard information provided by a seemingly competent human.

Do this and similar findings mean we're hopelessly gullible when it comes to trusting technology? Not exactly. Remember, people's intentions to trust technology weren't significantly greater than their intentions to trust other humans. It's just that when there isn't a good reason to distrust technology, the unconscious bias toward viewing it as more competent plays a decisive role. But when we're actively unsure about the reliability of any technology—when we have some reason to be cautious—the situation can quickly become more complex. And that's the world we as a society are rapidly entering—a world where the perils of technology don't only stem from its incompetence but rather from its users', or even its own, intentions.

Chatting with Proteus

Social Media. Virtual agents. Massive multiplayer online games (MMOGs). Today we're using technology to be social—to talk, to persuade, to negotiate, and to comfort—like never before. We're using it to be *us*, or, perhaps even more astonishingly, to replace us. Not only do services like Facebook and Twitter allow us to share our views with hundreds of others in seconds, but virtual agents—computer-controlled and -animated characters we increasingly see on digital displays—offer us information under the guise of two-dimensional human forms.

Although we may not initially recognize it, when we accept information that arrives electronically, we make ourselves vulnerable to the intentions of the people or systems that sent it. But unlike in the past—when any technology would simply offer information in the form of a readable output—we're now becoming subject to attempts to tweak the "trust machinery" of our minds through the manipulation of social cues. Just like the participants in our experiment with Nexi, we're all entering Oz. But in this version, the wizards behind the technological curtain aren't scientists in pursuit of knowledge. They're our fellow citizens and corporations who possess not only a variety of goals, but also a heightened ability to control every signal they send.

Although still in the relatively early stages, the public's use of avatars and virtual agents is growing exponentially. In 2011, more than half a billion people spent more than twenty hours per week interacting with others as *avatars*—an ancient Hindu term that originally referred to deities that descended to earth in various incarnations, but now refers to the digital representations of individuals that are "given life" through various types of real-time operator interfaces. It sounds technical, but my guess is that many of you have already "avatarized" yourselves. It's as simple as playing with an Xbox Kinect or Wii. These common devices assess your movements in real time and embody them as a digitally created being in any one of numerous virtual worlds. If you jump, your avatar jumps. If you dance, it dances. But avatars aren't just for fun; uses for this technology are moving far beyond gaming. By 2015, corporations like IBM are expecting a majority of their employees to be able to attend meetings or give presentations from remote locations by utilizing avatars.

Your initial response toward such uses of avatars might be a bit skeptical. Although I've shown you evidence that the human mind does respond to the nonverbal cues of a three-dimensional robot, that doesn't necessarily imply that the same will hold true for animated characters on a computer monitor. After all, they're a bit flat, pardon the pun, and somewhat removed from the physical world. Yet it's also true that we spend a lot of time viewing modified versions of the real world on two-dimensional television screens. The question, then, of how our minds interpret and interact with virtual characters is pretty significant, and it's also one on which Jeremy Bailenson, who directs the Virtual Human Interaction Lab at Stanford, is a leading expert. You see, before one can make an argument that human social cues can influence interactions in a virtual realm, he or she must first confirm that interactions in that realm actually follow human social norms. That is, one has to show that the same nonverbal language applies in both worlds, otherwise we're left comparing apples and oranges.

Recognizing this issue, Bailenson and colleagues were among the first to conduct something of a field study using the *Second Life* platform a few years back. For those unfamiliar with it, *Second Life* is a virtual world in which users create their own avatars, and navigate them through real-time interactions in every kind of space you can imagine (e.g. restaurants, clubs, parks, apartments). Into this world, Bailenson set loose a cadre of research assistants whose job it was to be virtual ethnographers of a sort. These observers would enter areas where other people's avatars were interacting and trigger a computer script that immediately recorded a host of relevant social variables—the gender of the avatars, the distance between them, the directions of their gazes, who was speaking to whom, etc. During seven weeks of exploration, the team garnered a massive amount of information that enabled them to assess how closely the norms of virtual interactions mirror those of the real world.

What did they find? Much as they predicted, the normal rules of social interaction—even the nonconscious ones—continued to apply. For example, male avatars—just as men in the real world—maintained a significantly greater distance between themselves when conversing than did female-female or mixed-gender pairs. A similar story emerged for eye-gazing behavior. Mirroring the norms for regular human interaction, the time avatars spent looking directly at each other was negatively correlated with the distance between them, assuming the two weren't carrying on a conversation. If you think about it, it's a familiar pattern. When you're feeling squeezed at rush hour on the bus or train, you'd probably find it quite uncomfortable to have the person next to you staring into your eyes. However, when avatars were conversing, their gazes were focused on each other, though with females exhibiting this behavior more than males (again, just like real life).

These findings, and those like them, confirm that the norms governing our daily interactions automatically extend to the worlds of avatars and agents. In some ways, this fact is a big plus, as it means our minds are willing to accept and interpret the intentionality and humanness of avatars and agents based on a universal nonverbal language. We don't have to train to enter a virtual world; our minds are already primed to interpret what's going on. But with this readiness also comes a greater potential for manipulation. As I noted earlier, the control of nonverbal cues in digital entities far surpasses that of humans. The wizards controlling these beings can add in or filter out trust-relevant cues—behaviors like fidgeting or touching one's face—and thereby deprive us of what normally would be reliable signals of the intentions of others.

Even worse, attempts at manipulation don't end with filtering cues. Avatars and agents possess an additional power. Much like their mythological namesakes, they can assume whatever form their creators desire, meaning that each of us, like the ancient Greek god Proteus, can fashion ourselves an image that suits our purposes in any given moment. If, for instance, you want to increase your dominance, make your avatar physically imposing. If you want others to like you, make your avatar more classically attractive. Such changes are quite easy to do in a virtual world, as they don't require exercise or surgery. Still, modifications such as these are quite rudimentary in nature. Tailoring communication can get much more complex if you know the specific users you're targeting.

As an example, let's say someone wants to increase the odds that another person will trust her avatar. What should she do? Much work, including that from my own lab, has demonstrated that the amount of empathy and responsibility we feel toward others is a function of how similar we believe they are to us. If I can highlight a subtle marker of affiliation between you and someone else—even something as minor as having you put on a wristband that matches the one she is wearing—you'll feel more bonded to her. The underlying logic of this phenomenon is quite simple; it's a fact that people who are similar to you are the ones more likely to support you in the future. As a consequence, it's worth it to accept the risks of supporting similar others in the short term to ensure you'll benefit later when you'll need it.

While my lab has documented the importance played by similarity in trust-relevant real-world interactions, Bailenson and colleagues demonstrated its importance in the virtual realm. Their first stroke of genius was to recognize that the power of similarity could be used in a novel way in the realm of digital images—a way that would make Proteus proud. If you want someone to see a target as similar to herself, all you need do is morph the target's face with that of the observer. And in several experiments, that's just what they did.

In the first such experiment, Bailenson and colleagues constructed political profiles of supposed candidates, but accompanied these profiles with faces of the candidates that had been morphed with those of each individual participant. So, if you had taken part in this experiment, when you viewed two candidates to decide which you favored, one of their faces would have been morphed with your own such that it was 40 percent you. This level of morphing was small enough that individuals' conscious minds wouldn't recognize it, but still large enough that their nonconscious minds, which are more sensitive to patterns, would.

The results of the experiment were quite impressive. A majority of people indicated that they would vote for the candidate that was 40 percent them irrespective of any other information provided about policy positions. Okay, you say, but this might just be because the experiment involved unknown politicians about whom most people do not particularly care. Fair enough. That's why Bailenson conducted a similar study, this time morphing the faces of George W. Bush and John Kerry—the presidential candidates at the time—with those of participants. Amazingly—or frighteningly, depending on your point of view—a similar pattern emerged. As you might expect, the morphing (which this time was 80 percent candidate to 20 percent participant to maintain the candidates' identities) didn't change the voting intentions of those who were strong partisans. Yet among the less committed it significantly altered voting intentions. Once again, people reported being more favorably disposed toward trusting the candidate in whom they literally saw themselves.

What do these findings suggest for avatars? Quite simple. If avatars can be tweaked to incorporate the features of a target person—information readily available from a Facebook page, Twitter account, or Web cam—the user behind that avatar is already one step closer to garnering trust. Research has already confirmed that simply enhancing the realism of avatars significantly improves their power to persuade humans. Taking the additional step of dynamically shaping the countenance of an avatar toward that of a given viewer would require relatively little added computational power. Doing so, however, holds potential to offer a cutting-edge advantage in the microtargeting of messages—an advantage that leverages the innate trust mechanisms of the mind.

As I'm sure you'll agree, efforts to gain a strategic advantage over interaction partners by shaping the appearance of avatars makes great sense from a business or security standpoint. The question I find most fascinating, though, is whether such alterations can actually flow backward and affect an avatar's user. It may seem a far-fetched idea at first, but Darryl Bem's self-perception theory—the idea that people learn about their personalities from observing themselves as another person would—suggests it just might have some validity. In the virtual realm, this view implies that changing your avatar might similarly change *you*.

To examine this possibility—a phenomenon termed the *proteus effect*—the team of Bailenson and colleague Nick Yee decided to use a full-scale virtual reality environment in which participants were wired with sensors that recorded their movements, and fitted with goggles that allowed them to see the digital world. Inside the goggles, small monitors displayed a three-dimensional replica of the room they occupied. They weren't alone in this virtual room, however; they could see another avatar who, unbeknownst to them, was operated by the experimenters. As the goggle-wearing participants moved in the real world, the sensors they wore caused their avatars to do the same. As participants turned their heads or walked around the actual room, so, too, did their avatars in the virtual room.

There was, of course, one fundamental difference that separated groups of participants in this study: the size of their avatar.

Half of the participants saw themselves as a tall avatar, while the other half saw themselves as short. We know from research in the real world that increased height is associated with greater confidence, dominance, and self-esteem when interacting with others—qualities that when combined allow one to feel more independent and thus less inclined to behave in a trustworthy manner. If the proteus effect were true, individuals who used a larger avatar should not only act more selfishly in the virtual world but also carry that behavior back into this one.

To test their prediction, Yee and Bailenson had the true participant and confederate in each interaction play a negotiating game where they could treat each other fairly by dividing money equally or cheat each other by taking more for themselves. Of import, they played this game both in the virtual environment and then again outside of it (though now in separate rooms). Confirming the proteus effect, participants assigned taller avatars kept more money for themselves not only when playing in the virtual realm, but also when playing back in the real one. Without their awareness, the sense of power provided by their dominant avatar spilled over into their understandings of their "normal" selves, and in so doing altered their trust-relevant behavior for the worse.

The implications are difficult to overestimate, especially in a world where many gaming avatars are designed to be big, aggressive, and domineering. As individuals while away the hours playing *World of Warcraft* or similar multiplayer online games, little do they realize that the forms of the avatars they select are subtly rewiring their own views of themselves. The unintended result is that choosing an avatar that offers more power and opportunities for selfish behavior in a fantasy world may in subtle ways evoke those same behaviors in daily life. And if everyone is trying to win and dominate in these games at all costs, as is likely, we as a society may be nudging ourselves toward a downward spiral in our general level of trustworthiness.

Virtual Angels

By now you may be feeling a sense of dread at the thought of turning on your computer, as the picture I've painted emphasizes the dark side of technology's relation to trust. But, as with trust's links to the other domains we've discussed thus far, the notion that its ties to technology must be unequivocally negative is too simplistic. As technology becomes a social medium, the long-term benefits of trust for social support will emerge, just as will its short-term risks from attempts to exploit it. In other words, relax a little; there are people out there working tirelessly to use technology to enhance trust for the greater good. In the same way that vast computational power can be utilized to present information or cues meant to con people, the same power can be used to enhance fairness, safety, and harmony.

To see how, let's first focus on a fundamental challenge posed by the Internet: How do you know if you can trust a person in an online transaction? Whether you're buying something on eBay or reserving a room in a new B&B, you rarely have firsthand experience with the individuals with whom you're dealing. Most times, in fact, you're not even conversing with them face-to-face, meaning that the cues of trustworthiness I presented in the last chapter wouldn't be of much help anyway. In such cases, most of us instinctively head straight for the relevant online ratings or reviews. Although they may seem quite useful at first, it's important to realize that they possess one major shortcoming: people who stand to gain from such ratings can often easily manipulate them. False e-mails and user IDs easily give them opportunities not only to boost their own ratings of trustworthiness, but also to sabotage the ratings of others for spite or competitive advantage.

The only way to begin to address such problems is through the aggregation and verification of big data—amounts of information that would be difficult for lone individuals to fake. It's an idea that several start-ups have begun to tackle. One of the most promising was a company named Legit that recently closed shop when Facebook hired its founders to integrate their ideas into the social media behemoth. In its earlier life, Legit was designing a cross-platform service that could be "plugged in" to other sites to provide reputational information on users. Unlike other common ways to gauge reputation, Legit's information wouldn't be based on simple metrics such as reviews from a single site or fan base (e.g., numbers of Twitter followers or Facebook friends). As noted by its cofounder Jeremy Barton, the simple fact that someone has thousands of fans shouldn't be taken as a sign that he is truly honest and trustworthy; he could still be cheating on business deals or swiping stuff from apartments.

Legit's goal was to solve this problem by aggregating verifiable information about people from their online behavior across a multitude of sites and domains. The result would be an easily interpretable score—a trustworthiness index. And now, by joining with Facebook, the reach of this endeavor will be vastly increased. If you think about it seriously, it's a tool that offers a benefit beyond the economic increase in online commerce; it will also enhance the safety of Facebook users. And this is no small benefit, as a recent survey by the Pew Research Center offered clear evidence that regular users of Facebook not only tend to be more trusting of others compared to non-Internet users, but also more trusting than Internet users who don't regularly use Facebook.

If all this talk of the benefits of reputation sounds somewhat surprising, you're probably remembering correctly that I'm not the biggest fan of using reputation as a solution for trust dilemmas. It's true that reputation alone can't always provide a good answer as to whether or not you can trust someone. In any one instance, a person's decision to cooperate with or exploit another will be determined by the short- versus long-term trade-offs in question, not his or her past behavior. This truism doesn't mean, however, that reputation is completely useless. If it comes from huge quantities of data sampled across many types of situations—situations varying dramatically in the types of long- versus short-term trade-offs they offer—it can provide some insight if used correctly. And using it correctly means using it as *one* piece of information in judging the odds of another's trustworthiness. Mistakes arise when it is relied upon as a magic bullet. Aggregated reputations offer a hint of how people will behave on average, which offers a hint of how they'll behave in any single instance, but it's just that—a hint. Still, when you have nothing else to go on—like intuitions from face-to-face interactions—it's better than nothing.

Luckily, however, attempts to foster trust and harmony online don't end with issues of reputation and commerce. As important as risks from financial vulnerabilities can be, they can pale in comparison to the risks from social ones—bullying, ostracism, or related types of stigmatization. These are the problems that keep people like Arturo Bejar, Facebook's director of engineering, up at night. I met Bejar a few years ago when he invited me to give a lecture at Facebook headquarters. To his credit, I found that he doesn't see his purview as being limited solely to technical elements of Facebook's security and functionality; he rightly recognizes that improving the social media platform means providing ways to help resolve social difficulties as well. And to that end, he has formed working alliances with teams of social scientists, myself included, aimed at adding tweaks and nudges to the system that are designed to facilitate social harmony among users.

Although we've been working on several projects, one theme that continues to emerge centers on helping vulnerable individuals obtain the assistance they need—assistance that requires finding someone they can trust. Let's take the issue of bullying, for example. As you are undoubtedly aware, the frequency of online bullying continues to grow. And for those of you lucky enough not to have witnessed or experienced it yourself, it is unfortunately no exaggeration to say that some of the messages and images people post can be downright vicious. In an effort to respond, Facebook has created special procedures that allow users to report being bullied. Of course, if the words or images themselves don't violate a specific policy—not every nasty or sarcastic statement qualifies as hate speech—Facebook can't easily remove the offending content. Freedom of expression is a closely guarded right. What it can do, however, is encourage individuals who report bullying to seek assistance from others who *can* help—responsible others who are in close proximity to them. The big question, though, is how to do this in a way that actually works.

Consider for a moment if you were being bullied. Yes, you'd want it to stop, and if you couldn't stop it yourself, you'd probably welcome help from others, at least in the abstract. But when the abstract becomes real—when you actually have to consider reaching out to a flesh-and-blood person and not a faceless company for help—the situation can quickly become more complex. Out of many possibilities, whom should you choose to contact? Whom can you trust to understand your feelings? And probably most importantly, whom can you trust to want to help you as opposed to feeling bothered by being asked? Finding good answers to these questions can make all the difference in whether a distressed teen actually opts to contact someone for help or just clicks off the screen.

How Facebook can help users find good answers is a project that my colleague Piercarlo Valdesolo and I are exploring with Jake Brill, a senior member of Bejar's team. One strong suspicion we hold is that feelings of similarity may offer a key. If you think back to the work from my lab that I described earlier, you'll remember that any types of subtle markers of similarity linking two people serve to dramatically increase their willingness to help each other. Simply reminding people that they have something in common makes them not only feel more bonded, but also experience more compassion for each other. As a result, when people are feeling vulnerable— when they want someone to help but are worried no one will care enough to do so—sorting options for whom to trust based on a metric of similarity stands as a great strategy. After all, the basic elements are already hardwired into the mind; we just need to give them a boost.

Here's where the power of computation and big data come into play. When a platform like Facebook needs to find someone who might be willing to help you, it doesn't need to do it blindly. It has more information available at its fingertips than you or I could easily process in a year. It has data on every person with whom you're friends—their likes, their friends, their posts—and can quickly utilize that information to identify the individuals with whom you share the most. The trick, of course, is to sort options wisely. If the person you share the most in common with is also your ex-boyfriend, he may not be the best candidate from whom to seek help in a bullying situation. The goal, then, is to identify people within certain social categories and age groups—individuals who on the numbers could function as responsible and appropriate sources of support—and then to sort them based on profiles to identify the individuals who will appropriately "ping" your mind's similarity sensors.

If the process works as intended, it should offer users reporting bullying a set of people to contact—people whom their minds are already primed to trust. In essence, the system would be nudging users toward getting the assistance they need not only by facilitating identification of potential helpers, but also by increasing confidence that these helpers can and will want to offer assistance. And in the moments of turmoil and despair that often accompany bullying, any aid in helping a frightened or similarly overwhelmed adolescent reach out for assistance can only be a good thing. Of course, we don't yet know how successful this strategy will be, but based on the science that gave rise to the idea, we're very hopeful. Nonetheless, this project and related ones at Facebook stand as evidence that greater technological ability need not only be used to exploit trust; it can just as readily be used to promote it appropriately. Before we leave this topic, then, let me offer one other example to prove the point—one that has already begun to pay dividends.

Think of the times in your life when you've felt the most vulnerable. Although many of the instances you might list are probably rather idiosyncratic, I'd hazard to guess there is at least one type of event that would be fairly ubiquitous across people: the dreaded hospitalization. It's difficult to imagine many other situations where your well-being is so fundamentally dependent on the intentions and competencies of others. Unless you possess medical training yourself, when you're ill or injured you have to trust that other people are acting with your best interests in mind. You have to trust your doctors to be competent in diagnosing ailments and prescribing treatments; you have to trust your nurses to be skilled at monitoring your health and attentive to addressing your needs.

Yet as vulnerable as most of you reading this book might feel in such a situation, it can't hold a candle to the level of vulnerability experienced by those the medical profession labels as low in health literacy—individuals who don't possess the basic reading and math skills necessary for making health-relevant decisions and following medical advice. Although low health literacy can have many causes—poor education, loss of cognitive function due to age, injury, or declining health—its outcomes with respect to hospitalization are the same: significantly poorer health after discharge due to an inability to understand treatment recommendations and to follow prescribed procedures. To make matters worse, low health literacy is not uncommon; 36 percent of American adults show limited literacy, with the prevalence climbing to over 80 percent in some poor, urban populations.

This was a problem that Timothy Bickmore decided to see if he could help fix. Bickmore directs the Relational Agents Group at Northeastern University, which is one of the nation's leaders in the development of virtual agents related to health care. Bickmore correctly surmised that one reason those with low health literacy often have negative outcomes is that they don't devote the effort necessary to comprehend the information in their after-hospital care plan (AHCP) fully. It's not that increased effort would guarantee that low-health-literacy patients would understand their AHCP as well as high-literacy ones, but any increase in learning would certainly benefit their post-hospitalization outcomes.

Fair enough, you might say, but what does this have to do with trust? If you think back to the work of Paul Harris I described in Chapter 3, you'll likely remember that how well people learn information isn't only a function of intelligence; it also depends on the characteristics of the teacher. If the person providing health information is someone patients believe they can trust—trust to be nonjudgmental, to have their best interests in mind, and to provide correct information—not only will they likely be more engaged in the learning process, but also more successful at it. As you might guess, many of those lowest in health literacy are also those who feel most intimidated by and dissimilar to health care providers, meaning they are less likely to trust and engage with these medical professionals before leaving the hospital.

How to solve this problem? Simple—change the nature of the nurse providing medical information at discharge. How to accomplish this efficiently? Create a virtual nurse. And that's just what Bickmore's team did. Through painstaking study of the ways that the most successful nurses interact with patients, the team designed a virtual agent that possessed the appearance, vocal patterns, and nonverbal cues associated with these effective medical professionals. And then, in collaboration with Boston Medical Center, they provided low-health-literacy patients the opportunity to interact with this agent on their day of discharge. Before leaving their rooms, the patients were introduced to the agent who would go through their AHCP with them. Using a touch screen, patients could communicate with the agent in many ways—they could ask her to repeat information, to provide additional details, and the like.

The results were startling, to say the least. Not only did low-literacy patients report very high levels of trust and comfort with the agent, a majority indicated they'd rather interact with the agent than with an actual human nurse. Their behaviors backed up these views; the patients spent more time interacting with the agent and asked for more details about their discharge information from it than they normally would with a human nurse. When asked their views of the virtual nurse, the patients weren't shy about the reasons for their preference; it seemed to boil down to demeanor. For example, one said, "She [the agent] treated me like a real person!

She's not like a computer!" And another, "I prefer Louise [the agent's name], she's better than a doctor, she explains more, and doctors are always in a hurry."

What many of the patients didn't realize, of course, was that their views of the agent—the sense that it was engaged and provided more information—were directly due to changes in their own willingness to seek information from it. Increases in engagement and trust were the phenomena that were specifically being targeted, as they—besides being central to successful learning—are the ones that those low in health literacy tend to shy away from with human nurses and doctors. In this case, the agent's nonverbal behaviors, both through the use of empathic emotional cues and the use of hand gestures to guide patients' attention to the information on the AHCPs, created an interactive relationship where patients felt empowered through working with an individual on whom they felt they could rely. And just to ensure that the patients' increased comfort and success with the agent wasn't solely due to the fact that they were more relaxed interacting with a machine, Bickmore ran the experiment again, but dialed back the agent's social expressivity and interpersonal responsiveness. The result was a "dialing back" of patients' preferences for the agent as well.

Although this and similar uses of virtual agents are in their infancy, I'm certain that continued refinement of the technology will lead to greater opportunities to build trust with them that fosters human well-being. In fact, Bickmore's work offers a tantalizing peek. Yes, the patients who interacted with the virtual nurse liked her more than a human version, but in truth, that's not the most important datum. The major finding—at least from a public health standpoint—is that when the discharge nurse was a virtual agent, the patients also reported greater intentions to follow their medication regimens more closely once they were home.

Although it's certainly true that some of this intent derives from better comprehension of the information, I have a sneaking suspicion that some also comes from the patients wanting to be trustworthy themselves—to prove themselves reliable to the digital nurse. Already in Japan—a nation with a rapidly expanding elderly population—many corporations are hard at work designing robots that can function as caregivers and companions to seniors. While you might protest that a human caretaker would be superior, when the numbers of caretakers simply aren't great enough to meet the need, having technological entities advanced enough to allow them to be perceived as trusted social beings is certainly preferable to loneliness. Our minds and our bodies are meant to trust when appropriate; for better or worse, technology is fast approaching the level at which it can help us do that even when no other humans are around.

Key Insights

- **Don't be seduced by technology.** The tendency to believe what one hears from "experts" is a well-known phenomenon that we psychologists colloquially term the white coat effect. As the name implies, most people's trust for what another says or does goes up if that other is wearing a white lab coat. Why? We usually see scientists and physicians, who are typically assumed to possess high levels of expertise, wear such coats. So when we see someone we don't know wearing a similar white coat, our minds implicitly assume that the person knows what he's talking about. We use the coast as a heuristic, or mental shortcut. As we saw earlier in this chapter, most people do the same with technology. If information comes from a computer, they assume, nonconsciously at least, that it must have more validity than if it comes from a human. That is, they assume they can trust it more. Don't fall prey to this mistake. As we move into a world where communication and the sharing of information between people is rapidly becoming dominated by computer-based platforms, the reliability of any information we may receive online is only as trustworthy as the persons who supplied it. While I'm certain we all know this to be true at a conscious level, that doesn't mean our intuitive minds won't be trying to tip us toward accepting whatever a given Web page might say.

- **Beware becoming what you play.** The result of online and video games becoming ever more sophisticated is that we're spending increased amounts of time in virtual worlds that are ever more enticing to our senses. This deepening engagement holds the potential to blur the lines, again nonconsciously, between what's real and what's not. Remember, our brains didn't evolve in environs where there were "fake" worlds, and thus are less able to resist their influence as they become more visually engaging. As we saw with the proteus effect, the greater feelings of power that come from using an avatar designed to be dominant can seep into one's views of her or his true self and alter trustworthiness accordingly. So while none of us would ever explicitly believe we're influenced by an avatar we use, the characteristics of that avatar—which often may diverge quite strongly from our own—can nonetheless alter the calculations of our intuitive minds so that we, in essence, may become an avatar of the digital persona. At times, we may come to act as it would.

- **There are costs (and benefits) to reading agents and avatars.** The precision that comes with digitally rendering agents and avatars brings with it ample opportunities for the manipulation of trust. We already know from our work with Nexi, and

Timothy Bickmore's work on virtual agents, that the human mind will respond to a technological entity's nonverbal cues. But unlike humans, who often signal their true intentions nonverbally without awareness, agents and avatars only signal what their users or programming intend. Like Nexi, they can express sets of cues that signal trustworthiness or a lack thereof. Like Louise the virtual nurse, they can appear warm and sympathetic in the absence of any true emotion being felt. The implication is that digital entities can be the perfect con artists; they can speak to our intuitive trust mechanisms fluently and thereby gain leverage to guide our decisions. Combatting this influence is fairly easy, but there's also a cost to be kept in mind. You can decide to ignore or consciously react against the nonverbals an agent or avatar expresses. For example, you can interpret a welcoming gesture, an accent that matches yours, or an expanded posture as a signal meant to manipulate your trust. The problem, though, is that manipulation isn't always bad. Sometimes manipulations meant to increase your trust in a digital entity can exist to help you. It all depends on the goals of a given entity's designer. If you blindly assume malice on the designer's part, you'll limit the benefits you can reap as interactions with agents and avatars continue to become more commonplace.

CHAPTER 8

CAN YOU TRUST YOURSELF?

Why You May Not Know Yourself as Well as You Think You Do

For all the risks inherent in trusting someone (or something), it would be nice, just once in a while, to have a break. It would be a welcome change to face a situation where you don't have to worry about what another person will do—a situation where you have perfect insight into his or her reliability. A situation, say, where you know the other person as well as you know yourself. Yet in reality such situations are not rare; you face them almost every day. But the partner in question isn't someone you know as well as yourself; it is yourself. Unfortunately, that doesn't necessarily make it any easier. Think about it. Have you ever wondered if you can trust yourself not to cheat on your taxes or business expense reports? Not to use your debit card at the casino? Or even not to eat that extra piece of chocolate cake?

Each of these situations, and the many others like them, involve trust, plain and simple. You're vulnerable; your future success depends on the decisions of someone at a later time. The only difference is this someone isn't a different person, he or she is a different (i.e., future) you. The success of your financial well-being depends on the future you not giving in to short-term desires for cash at the expense of investing in your retirement account for the long run. The success of your marriage depends on not valuing a short-term fling more than the benefits of a loving and stable relationship. And the success of your long-term health depends on resisting cigarettes, candy, cake, and other treats during repeated moments of temptation. In point of fact, deciding to trust yourself is just like deciding to trust another person—you're placing a bet on what the future you is likely to do.

Given this situation, you might expect that decisions to trust would be easy. You know *you* probably better than you know anyone else, meaning that these situations should be ones where accuracy in assessing trustworthiness is high. But if that's right, why are we sometimes surprised by our own actions? If we had perfect insight into our motives, why are we shocked when we let ourselves down? Why don't we see it coming? The answers lay in a basic fact. Although it's true that we may know ourselves better than we know others, it's also true that we don't know ourselves completely. In fact, we can't. It's not a shortcoming of intelligence, introspection, or character; it's a built-in limitation of the mind. How much we value different possible rewards—and therefore how trustworthy we will be to our earlier intentions—depends not only on where, but also *when*, we are.

Mirror, Mirror, on the Wall, Who's the Fairest One of All?

Are you a fair and honest person? If you believe a principle is morally correct and that you'll follow it, will you? These are the types of questions we regularly ask people who take part in experiments in our lab. Almost everyone answers yes, but time and again the behaviors that follow don't always seem to support it. The experiments that show this disconnect—the ones that reveal individuals' own difficulties in knowing themselves—tend to be the ones people find most fascinating, as they shatter the illusions we hold about our own personalities. And of all the experiments of this type we've conducted, my favorite is one that confirms just how self-serving people can be without their even recognizing it—how they believe they're trustworthy, but then rapidly give in to temptation while still managing to convince themselves they're being fair and honest. If I'm going to convince you that you can't always trust yourself, this is a good place to begin.

Let's start with a thought experiment. If I left you alone with a coin to flip and asked you to write down whether it showed heads or tails, would you do it honestly? Probably so. What about if I now told you that the two outcomes of the flip held very different consequences for you? Heads means you get to play a short, fun video game. Tails means you get stuck completing forty-five minutes of boring, onerous work. And to make matters more interesting, it's also the case that the person in the next room gets whatever outcome you don't. Now what would you? Could you trust yourself to be honest? Would you let your neighbor complete the fun game while you faced drudgery? This was the experiment that Piercarlo Valdesolo and I concocted to see just how poor people's predictions are for how they'll behave when their own interests are on the line.

As a first step, we needed to be sure that the average person viewed breaking the coin-flipping rule to be an untrustworthy act. We did, but that doesn't necessarily mean the general populace was in agreement. So we asked more than one hundred people to tell us if they believed not flipping the coin and simply taking the better task for oneself was wrong. The results were astonishingly clear. In what

has been and will probably be the only time we've ever found una-
nimity on anonymous questionnaires, every single person we asked
indicated that failing to flip the coin or lying about the outcome was
indefensibly wrong. Yet, when we put people in this exact
situation—when we left them alone (watching by hidden camera)
with a coin to flip that would determine whether they or the next
person got stuck with the onerous task—90 percent of them did not
flip the coin. Well, that's not quite true. Some did flip the coin
once, and then again, and then a third time, until they got the outcome they wanted. Others didn't even bother to flip; they just reported they got heads right off the bat.

When 100 percent of people indicate that a given action is
wrong and that they wouldn't do it, but then fully 90 percent of
them do, something just isn't right. It could mean that people actually didn't think breaking the rule was too bad when they saw it
happen in real life (as opposed to answering a hypothetical question). To check on that possibility, we also ran a condition where
individuals watched another person cheat in the same way. That is,
we had them watch someone via concealed video fail to flip the coin
and just assign the good task to himself. When they viewed this
person fall prey to selfish desires, they had no qualms about cruci-
fying him for it. When we asked them how fairly the "nonflipper"
acted, the results were plain; everyone saw his actions as unfair.
They clearly believed that he was being untrustworthy and that
breaking the rule was morally incorrect. But when we asked participants how they themselves acted in the case where they cheated
on the coin flip, they reported something entirely different. Even
though their transgressions were exactly the same as the other person's, they believed that *their* behaviors were acceptable, even fair.
They didn't feel they were letting themselves down by breaking the
rules. They were perfect hypocrites—absolving themselves of guilt

for the same moral failures for which they condemned others and as such were immune to self-reproach.

This tendency to delude ourselves—to rationalize our own untrustworthy behavior away—is a finding that's quite robust, having been replicated both by us and by others many times. But it's also one that, in many ways, exemplifies why trusting ourselves can be perilous. Albeit for different reasons, predicting our own behavior is often no easier than is predicting that of others, even though it certainly feels like it should be.

Be Here Now, Everything Else Is Illusion

Yes, I know "be here now" is a little hippie-sounding, but when it comes to trusting yourself, this sentiment has some truth to it. Let's face it, all the techniques I've discussed in the last two chapters for trying to determine if you can trust someone are pretty useless when it comes to focusing on yourself. Looking in the mirror to see if you're leaning away or touching your face just isn't going to work. The conversation between the two parties—the present you and the future you—is going on inside your head and thus impossible to observe. Based on the experiment I just described, you may grudgingly accept that predicting whether you'll resist temptation and do the right thing—whatever that right thing may be—might be difficult, but you may still wonder why this is so. Why, after all, are future predictions often so incorrect? And why, after a few instances of surprising themselves, wouldn't people learn that they won't always honor commitments they make to themselves?

These are good questions. To find the answers, we have to confront two illusions that our minds often impose on us: a forward-looking myopia and a rearward-looking whitewash. In the moment,

neither of these biases exists. When you're reaching for the chocolate cake, you know you're breaking your New Year's resolution.
When you make a date with an old flame while your spouse is out
of town, you know you're not only breaking a vow you made to your
spouse but also one you made to yourself. But days before you do
such things, you're often sure you'll be able to resist them. And moments after, you convince yourself that you had good reason, that
you're not really untrustworthy, that there were extenuating circumstances. We saw the same illusions influence behavior in the
experiment I just described. People there not only acted selfishly in
ways they wouldn't have predicted, but also convinced themselves
a few minutes afterward that they were still honorable. The scale
was admittedly smaller, but the mechanisms were the same. Let me
unpack the two mechanisms one at a time.

As its name implies, forward-looking myopia means focusing
more on the present than on the future, which subsequently leads
to two related problems. Because the present is closer in time, it is
not only clearer but also matters more. By clearer, I mean that our
accuracy in predicting how something will make us feel decreases
dramatically as a function of how far it is in the future. The psychologist Dan Gilbert has shown time and again that our ability to
forecast our feelings is limited at best. Most of us regularly mispre-
dict how a future event will make us feel, meaning that our predictions for how we'll behave when confronted with said future event
are also poor. After all, how do you know if you can trust yourself
to do something if you don't have a good sense of how doing it or
not doing it will actually make you feel?

As Gilbert's work has shown, our forecasts for future feelings
are hampered by the ways we construct them. Our simulations of
events yet to come are usually decontextualized. We hyperfocus on
the event in question while ignoring both the context of what we're

currently feeling when thinking about it and what we're likely to be feeling just before we actually face it. For example, when you think about whether you can trust yourself not to overeat tomorrow night, you're probably not taking into account whether you feel happy right now or whether you're likely to be feeling stressed tomorrow evening because of a meeting set to happen right before dinner. As you can imagine, the former will leave you feeling quite positive as you look into the future, meaning that you'll overestimate how easy it will be to adhere to your dietary plans. That latter will likely leave you feeling negative and emotionally spent at the moment when you face the temptation at hand. In each case, these feelings have nothing to do with the actual event in question (e.g., overeating) but they nonetheless will shape your responses to it.

Dan Gilbert's work with the psychologist Tim Wilson offers a clear example of the perils forward-looking myopia provides. To see why, think about how much you'd like to eat spaghetti tomorrow. That's a type of question that Gilbert and Wilson often ask their participants. What they find time and again is that hungry people mistakenly believe they like spaghetti so much that they'd enjoy eating it for breakfast. Their sated peers, however, erroneously believe they won't much enjoy eating it for dinner. In actuality, both groups like spaghetti to similar degrees when not famished or full. But if you ask people to imagine how much they like spaghetti when they're hungry, they tend to overestimate it so much that they actually believe they'd like eating it in the morning, although in truth they'd be none too pleased if they found it in their cereal bowls. Same with trust. If you're feeling happy today, you might not appreciate the fact that tomorrow you're likely to feel stressed and cognitively depleted, which will make it much more difficult than you now expect for you to keep your promise to resist that extra slice of pizza.

These emotional forecasting errors constitute the part of looking-forward myopia that makes responses to future events appear fuzzy. Yet, even if we could somehow correct our predictions for bias from extraneous feelings, we'd still face difficulties. This is where the mattering more part of the illusion comes into play. As I mentioned in Chapter 1, the human mind has a built-in bias to skew how it values potential rewards. Most people will prefer to receive $20 today as opposed to $25 three days from now, even though that rate of return would be hard to beat. Unless you need money this instant because you forgot your wallet at home, an option to earn 25 percent more cash in three days' time makes quite rational sense. But the mind is not always rational. Waiting has a risk of its own; there's always a slim chance the payoff might never come. You might drop dead tomorrow or your partner might change his or her mind about paying you your share. As a result, our minds tend to favor the "bird in the hand is worth two in the bush" principle, meaning that any future reward will have to be much, much bigger than an immediate one if we're going to be willing to wait for it.

Trusting yourself, then, involves making a guess about whether your partner will be able to resist short-term rewards for longer-term gains. If you'll remember, the motif I introduced for trust at the start of this book is a scale flanked by Aesop's grasshopper and ant where each symbolizes the desires for short- and long-term gains, respectively. To understand how that scale really works when it comes to trusting yourself, you need to realize that there isn't just one scale that defines what you'll do; there are many arrayed along a line stretching into the future.

The problem posed by myriad scales is that it's difficult to see how they're all balanced. As you move through time, the weights on each side of the scale change. With fewer minutes separating you and a desired reward often comes increased weights on the grasshopper's side of the scale. What seems easy to resist today—the chocolate cake or opportunity to gamble you'll confront two months from now on your vacation—can become much more difficult to resist when you actually face the potential for these rewards in what will become the present. As a consequence, it will take much more effort to tip the scale back toward trustworthy behavior than you might originally have predicted. You'll likely have to use more willpower than anticipated to ensure you behave as you intended.

Kathleen Vohs, a psychologist at the University of Minnesota's Carlson School of Management, whose work on money and trust-worthy behavior we covered earlier, probably knows more about how difficult resisting temptations can be than almost any other scientist. Together with colleagues, she has conducted some of the most clever and compelling work on this topic to date. One of the clearest findings has been that resisting short-term rewards often takes effort, meaning that once your willpower becomes taxed, you're likely to act in ways you'll later regret.

On of my favorite examples of this phenomenon comes from Voh's work with Dartmouth psychologist Todd Heatherton. The idea for their experiment was quite simple. If willpower works like a fixed resource, then once you use it to behave trustworthily in one situation (i.e., to resist immediate selfish reward), behaving trustworthily in the next becomes increasingly difficult. To put this idea to the test, Vohs and Heatherton selected two special types of participants: chronic dieters and nondieters (i.e., those who never diet). Both were recruited for what was billed as a marketing study for flavors of ice cream. Once participants arrived, they were seated in a waiting room where the experimenter had previously placed a bunch of snacks (e.g., M&M's, Doritos, Skittles, salted pea-nuts) either within arm's reach of their chair or more than ten feet away on the opposite side of the room. The differential distance served as an easy way to manipulate how difficult the snacks would be to resist.

Once participants were seated in the waiting room, the experimenter told them that she'd return when the ice cream samples in the next room were ready. In the meantime, the participants were told that they could help themselves to the snacks. Now, remember, the primary differences here are twofold: (a) some participants were actively dieting and thus promising themselves they'd limit their food intake while others were not, and (b) some participants had snacks that were easily accessible (i.e., highly tempting) while others did not. And just to be sure everyone was a bit peckish, the experimenter had told people not to eat in the two hours before they arrived. As a result of this setup, it was the dieters who had the snacks at their fingertips who were facing the greatest temptation. They were hungry, they had snacks close by, and yet they were motivated not to eat them. Fourteen percent of them ultimately gave in to temptation, but the 86 percent of chronic dieters who successfully resisted the snacks at their fingertips likely exerted the most willpower of anyone else in the experiment to do so.

At this point, the experimenter returned to the room to escort participants to the ice-cream tasting part of the session. In this phase, participants (who completed the experiment individually) were seated in front of large tubs of three flavors of ice cream. The experimenter left them alone to sample from the different tubs while noting that she'd return in ten minutes with survey sheets to evaluate the different flavors. As you might by now suspect, the measurements in which Vohs and Heatherton were truly interested didn't involve flavor; they centered on how much ice cream people actually consumed. You don't really need to eat much ice cream to know if whether you like the taste. One of those little plastic spoons they give out at the gelato counter will do. In truth, you don't need to eat any of the ice cream at all. Wine tasters often do not drink the wines they sample. But, okay, most people will eat some ice cream as part of sampling. How much they'll eat, though, is a different question.

What Vohs and Heatherton found is exactly what you'd predict if keeping a promise to one's self takes effort. Among nondieters, the amount of ice cream consumed didn't much differ as a function of whether the previous snacks were readily available. Among dieters, though, the picture was quite different. Those who successfully resisted high temptation—a bowl of snacks at their fingertips—ended up gobbling almost three times more ice cream during the sampling phase than did those who didn't have easy access to the snacks (182 grams on average compared with 72 grams). This gorging didn't occur because people in the high-temptation group were any less motivated to keep to their diets. To the contrary, they were just as motivated as the other dieters. The increased consumption happened precisely because these individuals had just exerted greater effort to resist the tempting snacks in the first part of the experiment. So when it came time to be trustworthy again—this time in front of the ice cream—they failed; they had no willpower left.

Okay, you say, maybe it's just food. Maybe they lost control because they were hungry, and that's a biological need. Not so. Vohs has found similar patterns in another area where many of us promise ourselves we'll be restrained: shopping. In this work, she asked people to engage in a relatively simplistic exercise of self-control before she set them loose to buy things. In the first phase of the study, all they had to do was spend six minutes listing the thoughts that came into their minds. The only catch was that half the participants were told they could think about anything they liked, with the exception of a white bear. In fact, they were explicitly told not to think about a white bear and, if they did, to put a checkmark each time they did so on a sheet of paper. It may sound a little silly, but work by the psychologist Daniel Wegner has shown again and again that trying to suppress thoughts often makes them hyperaccessible; suddenly you can't seem to get them out of your head no matter how hard you try. He's used the white bear technique repeatedly as a way to exhaust people cognitively, and that's what Vohs used it for, too.

After the thought listing part of the experiment, there were now two distinctly different groups of participants—relaxed writers and stressed writers with lots of white bear checkmarks. All were then handed $10 that was theirs to keep. They had the option to leave the experiment being $10 ahead, or they could choose to use it to purchase any of twenty-two items arrayed before them. The items were basic ones—chewing gum, coffee mugs—and ranged in price from less than a dollar to almost five. They weren't the kind of items anyone would truly need; they were the kind that are often impulse buys in checkout lines or tchotchke shops. And as the findings attest, the word *impulse* here turned out to be quite apropos.

When Vohs looked at purchasing patterns, she again found her suspicions were correct. Individuals who had been exerting self-control—the ones trying their hardest not to think of the dreaded white bear—ended up buying a lot more. People who hadn't been trying to monitor and control their minds only spent about $1 on the trinkets, but those who had been trying to regulate themselves spent four times more. And it wasn't just that the impulse buyers selected more expensive items; they bought a greater quantity of items, too.

These examples and the many like them demonstrate the perils of forward-looking myopia. As you peer forward in time to judge what the future you will do, your vision is usually a bit blurry. It's clouded not only by errors in judging how much you'll want something as time draws nearer to it, but also by not being able to see what situational factors might inhibit your ability to control yourself when the specific time arrives. While today it might seem you'd have no trouble resisting a tempting ice-cream sundae, new suit or dress, or other treat, you're setting yourself up for failure—or at least a more difficult fight to remain trustworthy to yourself—if you assume that assessment will remain accurate.

The fact that most of us will fail ourselves at times raises equally perplexing questions: Why don't we learn from our mistakes? Why do most of us continue to believe that we can be unquestionably trustworthy? It seems quite irrational. If a friend or business partner failed to keep a promise several times, we'd certainly label him as untrustworthy and often refrain from relying on him in the future. Yet we tend to believe ourselves when we promise that we won't fall prey to a specific temptation for a fifth time. This unwavering trust doesn't come from an abiding optimism, however; its source is much more insidious. It comes from a universal and deep-seated motivation to see ourselves as virtuous—a motivation that leads to our second problematic illusion: the rearward-looking whitewash.

Yes, But . . .

Ayn Rand had it right when she said, "Rationalization is a process of not perceiving reality, but of attempting to make reality fit one's emotions." We humans possess a strong, innate desire to view ourselves as competent and upstanding, meaning that when we fail ourselves in some way, we tend, consciously or not, to explain it away. In fact, this rationalization bias is so ingrained that we use it for just about everything—from excusing our cheating to even convincing ourselves why it wasn't our fault that we missed a train.

Imagine you're hurrying down a platform to catch the T (that's what we call the subway here in Boston), but as you approach you see it pulling away. How would feel, and would you blame yourself for missing it? These are the questions that Dan Gilbert and colleagues asked commuters at the Harvard Square T stop a few years back. The only difference among the people they approached was that some were asked these questions while they were waiting for their train, while others were asked after they had in fact just missed it (i.e., seen it pulling away), meaning they would now be delayed about another ten minutes. Those who didn't miss the train (i.e., those who were making predictions about how they'd respond if they had missed it) reported not only that they'd feel much regret at missing the train, but also that they'd blame themselves for running late. In their view, actions such as hitting the snooze button too many times or forgetting to pack a needed object would have been the likely causes for the problem. However, those who actually missed their train by a minute offered quite different responses. Not only didn't they feel as much regret as the predictors expected, but they also offered quite different rationales for why they missed the train. Their explanations emphasized situational factors beyond their control: the lines were too long, some of the turnstiles were broken, etc. Put simply, missing the train wasn't their fault, and so they didn't feel nearly as much regret about it.

Now, I know what you're probably thinking: What does missing a train have to do with trust? Not much in a narrow sense, but in a broad view, these findings demonstrate how pervasive the desire to avoid blame is—even blame from ourselves. To borrow a metaphor from Gilbert, humans appear to have a built-in immune system for threats to their own well-being. If we're about to blame ourselves for bad behavior, our minds intervene with a whitewash. A commuter didn't miss the train because she couldn't get out of bed this morning; she missed it because someone else didn't fix the turn-stiles. Or, moving up an order of magnitude: a struggling alcoholic didn't break a two-week dry spell because he wanted to, he did it so as not to offend his host by refusing to sip the champagne. Although everyone will agree that such behaviors can have a negative result, they'll also work hard to avoid personal blame for engaging in them. Something else intervened to cause the behavior; they, too, were victims. See, I told you it was insidious.

We've already seen an example of this phenomenon in the experiment with which I began this chapter. If you'll remember, people unanimously agreed that it would be wrong to assign themselves an onerous task at another's expense rather than to follow directions to flip a coin to see who got stuck with it. But, when given the opportunity to cheat themselves, fully 90 percent didn't flip the coin; they simply took the better option. Perhaps the most interesting part of this finding, however, was that these cheaters didn't view their own actions as untrustworthy or unfair. When judging themselves, they tended to offer rationalizations like, "Well, I'm sure the next person isn't as swamped as I am right now," or "I usually wouldn't do this, but right now I have to get to class." They seemed, in essence, to suggest they had no choice; they believed that any trustworthy person would have done the same in a similar situation.

But how do we really know these excuses stemmed from rationalization aimed at protecting their ability to trust themselves? Simple—we conducted the experiment again, but this time prevented some of the participants from engaging in rationalization. You see, rationalization always takes a bit of extra effort. The mind has to recognize it did something wrong and then engage in some extra thinking to wipe it away. If it doesn't have the time or luxury to convince itself that the immoral or untrustworthy act really wasn't its fault—that it resulted from situational factors as opposed to a dicey disposition—it'll be stuck realizing that what it chose was wrong and, as a consequence, that it can't as readily trust itself.

To prevent participants from rationalizing, we employed a basic technique that psychologists have been using for decades: cognitive load. As its name implies, putting someone under cognitive load means keeping his or her mind busy. If you have ever tried to solve a problem that required a lot of thought but couldn't manage it because you were distracted, you've experienced this phenomenon. In this version of our experiment, the events unfolded exactly as before, but this time, just as people were about to judge how trustworthily they acted, we asked them to remember a string of seven digits. Accomplishing this feat meant that when they turned their attention to evaluating their questionable behavior (i.e., assigning themselves the pleasant task as opposed to flipping the coin), they were simultaneously repeating seven digits under their breath. What we found proved our point. When people's minds were tied up so that they couldn't rationalize their behavior after the fact, there was no whitewash; they condemned themselves as readily as they condemned others for not flipping the coin. In their gut, they knew they were being untrustworthy; when they couldn't rationalize, they had to confront the fact that they were violating a principle they endorsed. But give them ten seconds when their minds weren't occupied and hypocrisy quickly emerged. As I noted before, those who weren't experiencing load excused their actions, believing themselves to be fair.

Now, it is certainly true that these findings involve relatively minor infractions. Thankfully, we can't run experiments where people are allowed to spend hundreds of dollars of their own money on impulse buys or make selfish decisions that potentially ruin the lives of others. Science is important, but not at that level of cost.

Still, these phenomena are scalable. One need look no further than the daily headlines for proof.

One of the best recent examples comes from Eliot Spitzer, the former governor of New York. As you may remember, one of Spitzer's claims to fame in the early part of his career came from his successful crusades against prostitution as a district attorney. Yet, as he rose to power, Spitzer became a regular client of an escort service known as the Emperor's Club. Although he believed being a john was wrong in principle and certainly held risks to the long-term success of his career and marriage, at certain moments the short-term hedonic rewards appeared too great for him to resist.

Many wondered how he ended up in such a predicament. In an interview after being publicly identified and humiliated as Client #9, Spitzer said, "The human mind does, and permits people to do things that they rationally know are wrong, outrageous." But like participants in the experiments I've just described, he goes on to note the role of the situation in his actions, stating, "I'm not going to say anything that . . . should be thought to be an excuse for anything. But there's got to be some element to its [his actions] being a result of tension and release. And that builds up." Herein lies the problem. This view of the reasons for his transgressions links a sense of untrustworthiness to a specific situation, not to personal responsibility. And while it is certainly true that situational influences can alter people's likelihoods of being trustworthy—that's what much of this book is about—it doesn't excuse this behavior; it doesn't make it right. The problem here is that Spitzer—like others in similar situations—didn't recognize in advance how much specific situations can tax self-control when confronted. And that lack of knowledge caused him time and again to be unprepared to avoid the temptations that arose.

Catch-22: What's a Person to Do?

At this point, you might feel as if you're in a bit of a quandary. You want to trust yourself but now realize that doing so is about as risky as trusting anyone else due to the illusions that come from peering forward or backward in time. Two questions naturally arise from this predicament: Why in the world does our mind work this way? And what can we do about it?

In answer to the first question, it's partly flaw but also partly design. The flaw part comes from a fact I've hinted at previously. Mental time travel—the ability to run simulations about the future in our minds—is a relatively new ability on the evolutionary time-line. Our species only obtained this power with the increasing size of our frontal cortices, which themselves constitute the most recent, distinctive part of the human brain. Next time you're at a science museum, you'll notice just how much the skull size for this area of the brain (the part closest to your forehead) has increased over our ancestral lineage. But as any computer user knows, new hardware and software always comes with bugs. In our case, this means that although the ability to run simulations and predictions offers great benefits, some parts of the system do it better than others. And the part that seems the most buggy right now is the part with which we make predictions about how we're likely to feel in the future. The result is that we're saddled with forward-looking myopia. I can run fairly accurate simulations to predict how my health might decline as I age, or about how many resources I'll need to save over the next year to be insulated against losing my job (mostly because these involve manipulating numbers and statistics), but I'm not yet as good at predicting exactly how losing my job will make me feel. Sure, I know I'm likely to feel cruddy, but I have no real accuracy in predicting just how cruddy I'll feel or even in exactly what way. And, as we've seen, degrees of desiring or detesting can make all the difference in how we behave.

The design part of the answer has to do with the rearward-looking whitewash. If we realized how untrustworthy we can be, we might just give up. We might never trust ourselves again, treating the future us as defectors in a tit-for-tat death spiral. But if we can't trust ourselves to do the right thing in the future because we know we've let ourselves down in the past, our motivation to strive toward important long-term goals evaporates. Why should the present you deny itself a new iPad to save money for retirement if the future you is just going to break down next month and spend that saved money on something else? As you can imagine, this is not an optimal way to live, especially as we sometimes do keep our promises to ourselves. Consequently, our minds whitewash our reputations when we go astray in order to make us acceptable partners to ourselves once again.

But is this the best we can do? I think not. To make better decisions about whether to trust ourselves, we have to attack the source of the problem: time distortions. To do that, we have to follow the advice relayed at the start of this chapter—be here (or there) now. You might protest that this is more easily said than done, since humans haven't quite solved the time-travel problem yet. That may be true, if you're talking about projecting your body into the future, but not if you're talking about projecting your thoughts or goals. The smartphone revolution is upon us, and believe it or not, some of the more popular apps are designed to solve just this type of problem. There are the ubiquitous apps to urge you to keep to your diet or to exercise. And then there are the more specialized ones, like *Drunk Dial NO!*, that prevent you from calling certain numbers on your phone during preset periods of time. The one feature all these apps have in common is that they allow the present you to speak to, or even control in the case of phone use, the future you. By so doing, they allow one partner to interact directly with the other across time. As a result, they can get rid of the rearward-looking whitewash, as the past you can remind the future you that he or she sometimes makes mistakes, even after promising not to make them again.

It is true, of course, that humanity has almost always had ways by which it's attempted to solve this problem. From reminders recorded on papyri to warnings scribbled on sticky notes, we've tried to allow the different versions of us to communicate, and thereby increase trustworthiness and reliability, over time. But as technology becomes an ever more facile tool for providing us with information, its integration into our lives will likely aid this endeavor. This fact alone doesn't necessarily mean that the future you will listen to the present you, but at least it will be required to make a more informed decision, and one that will provide subsequent data to the next iteration of itself.

Key Insights

- **Accept that you have an untrustworthy side.** The participants in our experiments weren't morally comprised. They were normal people. And much as we may hate to admit it, the minds of all normal people—ourselves included—possess mechanisms that favor immediate reward and selfish gain. It's not something to lament; it's something to manage. We saw much earlier in this book why a society of pure altruists and cooperators would be unlikely to survive. But we've also seen the benefits that can come from trust when it's correctly placed—including when we correctly place it in ourselves. Correct placement, however, requires recognizing that at times each of us is likely to break promises to ourselves. To the extent that we can predict which situations are likely to tempt us the most and proactively avoid or manage them, we can ensure that our future selves become better partners for our current ones.

- **Willpower is not infinite.** Willpower is a resource that takes effort. Consequently, it can and will fail at times. This fact means we must abandon assumptions that we'll always be able to deal with any temptations to be untrustworthy that may arise in the future. Even if your intentions are noble, your follow-through may be weak. As a result, you'll end up in the same place as if you were being guided by desires for immediate gain all along. Yet as we've also seen, our intuitive systems for trustworthiness don't require direction. So while it's true that our nonconscious minds possess mechanisms that respectively favor immediate and long-term rewards, the latter, when engaged, can push trustworthy behavior rather autonomously. So if you face a moment when you feel too depleted to resist a temptation to break a promise you made to yourself, focus your mind on the long-term outcomes and then pause—not to think, but to feel. Focusing on the long term will ensure that the emotional responses that well up aren't the craven ones (the ones that want you to eat the snacks now) but are rather the more moral ones. As a result, that guilty pang you feel in your gut when thinking about behaving questionably will be magnified, thereby increasing the chances that you'll be true to your goals instead of rationalizing them away.

- **Knowing what you'll do means understanding when you are.** Our minds have built-in biases when it comes to evaluating rewards and our own behaviors. Temptations that won't offer benefits until far in the future are easy to ignore. But as the possibility of a reward become imminent, its value looms larger and it becomes more difficult to resist. Similarly, although we can clearly recognize why breaking a promise to ourselves in the moment means we're being untrustworthy, we're quick to ratio-nalize such behavior away as the result of an aberrant situation after the fact. The end result is that our vision is warped both for predicting what we'll do in the future and for why we acted as we did in the past. One way to remedy these biases is to allow our different selves to communicate across time, a process that can occur through the use of notes, logs, or now even apps.

CHAPTER 9

TRUST OR DUST?

In the End, It's Usually One or the Other

August 29, 2005, is a day that the residents of Gulfport, Mississippi, will unfortunately never forget. It's the day that Hurricane Katrina began battering their city with sixteen hours of damaging winds and ocean surges that at times exceeded twenty-eight feet. It was a storm the likes of which none had ever seen; the level of devastation was almost unimaginable, even to those who had weathered many other hurricanes. So when the winds had calmed and the waters receded, the residents who ventured out saw before them a city in ruins—a place where homes and businesses had been destroyed.

The people of Gulfport—much like the people of any other town in America facing a similar situation—swallowed hard and set their sights on rebuilding. But rebuilding lives and homes in the immediate aftermath of Katrina meant obtaining the necessary materials: building supplies, cleaning products, even food. And in our modern society—a society where most of us don't grow our own food or cut our own lumber—getting needed supplies relies on commerce. And commerce relies on money. Why money? It's a negotiable instrument—it symbolizes resources. When we give someone $20 for a product, our debt to him is over. He doesn't need to trust that we'll do something in the future to pay him back; he already has the fruits of our labor in the form of cash, which he can then use as he wishes.

In Gulfport, though, there was a problem. With electricity unlikely to be restored for days or weeks, access to money was frozen. Banks were closed; ATMs weren't working. Whether you had $100 or $100,000 in the bank didn't much matter; you couldn't get to it. If the citizens of Gulfport were going to begin reclaiming their lives and homes quickly, this situation had to change, and change fast. Recognizing the seriousness of the problem, the CEOs of Hancock Bank—one of Gulfport's local financial institutions—made a surprising decision. They were going to jump-start commerce using a basic strategy: trust. Without electric power, bank employees couldn't identify what funds people had in their accounts, let alone if they were even customers of Hancock. Nonetheless, co-CEOs Carl Chaney and John Hairston decided that they were going to trust that people whom they allowed to withdraw money would pay it back, either through their holdings in Hancock Bank or from accounts at other institutions. The next day, bank employees were instructed to set up folding chairs and tables around the community and give up to $200 to any person who would write their name, address, and Social Security number on a scrap of paper.

One of the first problems, of course, was where to get the physical cash. Much of it was locked in banks that had been flooded and ATMs that had been submerged. As a result, bank employees spent the first few days retrieving money and literally laundering it to remove the sea salt and silt; they actually ran it through washing machines before ironing the bills into shape. In the meantime, the cash that was available was being distributed, and where the cash ran short, yellow sticky notes with scribbled amounts were being used in its place as negotiable instruments.

In all, Hancock Bank released more than $40 million into the hands of those affected by Katrina, and in so doing offered inhabitants of the stricken area a way to purchase the resources they needed. Yet, being the first to extend a hand of cooperation meant that Hancock was opening itself to a good deal of vulnerability; $40 million isn't pocket change for any institution, especially a regional bank. And sticky-note IOUs aren't typically binding in courts of law. But, believing in their mission to serve and trust the members of the community, the bank's leadership accepted the risk. They bet that their trust in people was warranted—that their willingness to extend support would be repaid in the long run. And they were right. People honored the IOUs they had received; even those whose names could not ultimately be linked to existing accounts or phone numbers paid back their debts. In the end, not only had all but $200,000—approximately one-half of 1 percent of the amount originally distributed—been returned to the bank, but Hancock's coffers also bubbled over. The number of customers grew by thousands and the bank's assets increased by over 20 percent.

Now, you might wonder if a story like this one—a story that shows the power of trust to help make us resilient as individuals and societies—is too good to be true, where by *true* I mean an event that constitutes a special case unlikely ever to occur again. Sure, Hancock's willingness to trust strangers worked out well for everyone involved, but maybe the initial decision only happened because the folks who ran the bank were overly trusting types in the first place. Or maybe the executives were willing to trust because they weren't making themselves personally vulnerable; it was the corporation's funds that were on the line. After all, single counterintuitive exemplars can be found to buttress most any claim one wants to make.

To parry this objection, I could retreat back into the world of mathematical models and lab experiments to explain how and why the events in Gulfport make perfect sense. Yet as I write this, the city I love has just experienced its own tragedy—one that in a few seconds replaced the dust from running shoes pounding the pavement with the dust of gunpowder, shrapnel, and bone. On April 15, 2013, a bombing near the finish line of the Boston Marathon tragically altered the lives of many. The moments after the bombs exploded can only be described as surreal—a mixing of pain, bewilderment, and loss, but also of great heroism by those who risked much to aid the injured. With respect to the role of trust, however, it was what unfolded over the next few days that was amazing.

The authorities quickly cordoned off several city blocks in an effort to secure the crime scene. Mass transit was shut down; Amtrak service was stopped; even taxi service was interrupted in an effort to prevent the assailants—who were unknown at the time— from fleeing the city or targeting other areas. The unintended yet unavoidable consequence of these actions was that hundreds if not thousands of people were suddenly left stranded. Families couldn't return to their hotel rooms; runners couldn't pick up their belongings. Issues of personal injury and loss aside, many of the people who had come to Boston were just plain stuck.

Yet in those few days something rather surprising happened. Residents of Greater Boston opened their homes to welcome complete strangers. They offered their couches, their apartments, even their bikes and cars to people they had never met. Altruistic as such acts are, they clearly make one vulnerable to exploitation, so much so that under normal circumstances behaviors like this are relatively rare. But these weren't normal circumstances. This was a situation where everyone felt vulnerable. And from that sense of shared vulnerability—from the need to rely on each other—minds automatically began to trust in ways they usually never would.

As the events of Katrina and the Boston bombings make clear, trust is one of the keys to building resilience. Having faith in each other is what allowed the citizens of both cities to rise from the disaster around them. Had people chosen the opposite strategy—had they retreated into metaphorical caves, hoarding their resources and refusing to share—their ability to bounce back would have been greatly impaired. Trust and, in turn, trustworthiness were the engines that allowed social and economic capital to flow, and with that capital came a level of support and growth that would have otherwise been impossible. It's a point that was driven home again in an Associated Press–NORC Center for Public Affairs poll that surveyed more than a thousand people in the New York metro area who had been affected by Superstorm Sandy. Neighborhoods that were characterized by the highest levels of trust among their citizens were the ones that bounced back from devastation the quickest. This is why we trust, and why our minds push us to trust more when shared vulnerability is high—it's a solution that works.

If that's right—if trusting others tends to work better than refusing to do so—why not stop there? Why not just decide that you'll trust everyone? You could, but there's that one phrase muddying the waters in the sentence that begins this paragraph: "*tends* to work better." *Tends* is just another form of my central argument's bête noire—a phrase I usually refer to as "on average." If you have nothing else to go on, yes, trusting is better than not doing so. But blind trust, useful as it can be, is not the optimal solution. Although many Bostonians exhibited the highest virtue in response to the bombings, others, sadly, were gathering marathon mementos like the number tags the runners wore or the medals they dropped and selling them on eBay. Exhibiting similarly self-interested behaviors, many gas station owners in areas affected by Katrina (as well as other hurricanes) engaged in price-gouging. There are, and always will be, those in whom trust would be misplaced. Although a pervasive sense of vulnerability might increase trusting and trustworthiness on average, it certainly doesn't in every single case, especially for individuals who, due to real or subjective feelings of power, have the luxury of acting in a predatory manner. And when vulnerability due to a tragedy or disaster hasn't occurred—when it's a normal day—everyone, as we've seen throughout this book, is a bit more free to maximize the balance between immediate and delayed reward.

So while it's true that always trusting others will be beneficial on average, it's not the best approach. How could it be? To always give, to always be loyal, would simply be an analogue for wearing an EXPLOIT ME sign on your chest. A smarter system, one optimized for living in this world, needs to be a bit more complex. It needs to want to trust, but to know when to pull back. And as we've seen, both you and I possess just such a system—one that has been honed through millennia to help us navigate our social worlds. Still, perfect it's not, especially as the milieu of our social worlds begins to change rapidly with encroaching technology. Maximizing well-being in this world requires having a clear understanding of your innate "trust machinery." If you're going to operate it correctly, knowing when to let it lead you becomes just as important as knowing when to override it. Toward that end, these are the points I hope you'll take with you.

The Rules of Trust

1. Trust Is Risky but Necessary, Useful, and Even Powerful

In a perfect world—a world where everyone could be trusted—cooperation would bloom, and with it the likes of social and economic capital the world has never seen. In fact, such a world wouldn't even require trust; you can't quite consider anything a bet if you know how it will turn out. But, of course, our world isn't perfect. We're a social species, but also one that values individual rewards, the result being that our minds have to balance opportunities for immediate selfish gains against longer-term communal ones (which, of course, benefit us as well). Evolution didn't sculpt the mechanisms of our minds to make us saints; it did so to make us winners in the sense of successful adaptation. That means our minds come equipped with a calculus to make our trustworthiness malleable in response to the conditions at hand.

Much like the ant and grasshopper motif I introduced at the start suggests, our minds, both above and below our awareness, are regularly engaged in computations to determine whether serving our immediate or long-terms needs offers the best results. As situations change, so, too, will our trustworthiness, or at least our impulses toward it. The important point to remember is that the strategy determined to be the best by biology isn't always the one that our ethical or religious principles would lead us to select. Herein lies what science has to offer when it comes to human morality: it can tell you how your mind works, but not which decision you should ultimately make. Nonetheless, in deciding whether to go with or override your instincts regarding trustworthy behavior, understanding how, where, and why those instincts emerge can be immensely beneficial. If you want to guide your behavior successfully, you need to understand how your mind nudges you toward being trustworthy or deceitful in any given instance.

2. *Remember That Trust Permeates Almost Every Area of Life*

For most people, the thought of trust brings to mind the image of a handshake—a promise that each person will be loyal to the other with respect to some promise or monetary exchange. Although this focus on integrity certainly captures one aspect of trust, it is much too narrow in scope. For one, trust isn't only about integrity. As we've seen, competence matters just as much. The success of depending on someone for assistance isn't only a function of whether he or she intends to provide it; it also depends on whether he or she is capable of providing it. Intent matters little if ability is absent. As a result, deciding whether to trust another can involve assessing both expertise and competence.

The second way the common view is too narrow is that issues of trust pervade almost every aspect of our lives. It's not restricted to the big things, like major financial transactions or marital infidelity. It also plays a role in the seemingly mundane. As we've seen, trust in teachers and parents affects how well children learn their daily lessons, trust in relationship partners affects day-to-day feelings of well-being, and trust in technology determines the quality of information we can access and how secure we can feel in so doing. If we ignore issues of trust—if we're not attentive to cultivating it where warranted and limiting it where not—we're not optimizing the experiences of our daily lives.

3. *Don't Examine Reputation, Examine Motives*

Past behavior is, at best, a decidedly imperfect predictor of future behavior. In a nutshell, that's the problem with relying on reputation to judge another's trustworthiness. Findings from the many experiments I've described, as well as a multitude of others, clearly shows that ethics are often situationally determined. If they weren't, the sentence "I thought I could trust him" would be heard much less frequently than it in fact is. The best assessments of trust, then, rest on attempts to infer a person's motivations in each instant, not on the presence or absence of a long-standing label.

Although on one level you might find this truism disheartening, it does have an upside. You see, it works both ways. While past trustworthiness may not reliably predict future virtue, neither does past untrustworthiness always imply continued vice. Just as supposed saints can become sinners, supposed sinners can become saints. In other words, redemption from habitual deceit is possible if one understands the internal and external forces that inhibit trustworthiness—an important fact to remember both for judging others and for judging ourselves.

4. Pay Attention to Your Intuitions

Once we recognize the limitations of reputation, the import of finding a valid way to assess another's trustworthiness becomes even greater. As I've said, however, we luckily enter this world endowed with psychological mechanisms meant to address this very challenge. It's only because scientists have been looking in the wrong way all along that evidence to support this view has been lacking. As the work from my group has shown, humans have the ability to infer whether a partner will be trustworthy in any given instance. Albeit imperfectly, we can read another's intent and know where on the scale from immediate self-interest to long-term loyalty her or his motivations lie.

The trick in so doing is to consider what our intuitions tell us. Rather than choose to utilize cues stemming from naïve theories about what signals deceit (e.g., averted gazes or twitches of the mouth), we need to let our innate pattern detectors—systems that have been honed to look for sets of co-occurrences of cues—do their work unimpeded. Once we recognize what our intuitions, left to their own devices, tell us, we can adjust based on other information if needed (e.g., noticeable change in the power status of another, looming immediate rewards), but we should do so sparingly and only with clear reason. Every finding available suggests that intuition usually offers better advice. Of course, those findings come from participants who, unlike you after reading this book, don't possess as solid a grasp of the factors that shape trust. As a result, it's my strong suspicion that, armed with a better understanding of the nonverbal cues that are truly meaningful and the situational factors that actually matter, your accuracy in deciding whom to trust will be decidedly improved.

5. *Appreciate the Benefits of Illusion*

In the short term, there's no question that accuracy is good. But what about in the long term? Every one of us has at times acted selfishly, often unintentionally, toward those about whom we care. If our friends, our partners, and our children were to weigh those misdeeds equally, it might harm a relationship that in general is quite positive. As a consequence, a method for the careful burnishing of our views of valued others, or even ourselves, can serve a beneficial purpose. It can correct for the noise that would otherwise inflict difficulties on relationships that we need to work well. A relationship based on trust can lead to illusions of a partner's support and devotion that can, at times, help us smooth the bumps in the road—bumps that would otherwise send the relationship into a tailspin. In short, the biasing effect of trust can help us to forgive even when we don't realize we're doing it; it all occurs behind the curtain of consciousness and will.

So, yes, accuracy can be good, but a slavish devotion to it can be debilitating. Here again, examine but do not regularly override what your intuitions tell you. At times, intuitions may need to be corrected. But when considering the long-term success of relationships that usually have been rewarding, sometimes the illusions that are built into the intuitive system can be your best friend.

6. Cultivate Trust from the Bottom Up

For my last piece of advice, let me return to the issue with which I began this chapter. Deciding to trust someone, more than almost any other decision we make, holds the keys to how resilient we, both as individuals and as a society, will be. Each of the preceding rules is designed to be of aid in optimizing your individual interactions with others. But at a group level—a level where we're talking about enhancing the general level of trust in the world—what can one person do? Social and evolutionary equilibria being what they are, the world will never be occupied solely by trustworthy people. But that doesn't mean we can't work to push the average level of trustworthiness upward. It doesn't mean that attempts at moral education are futile. It's just that I think there's a better way to go about it than what usually occurs.

When we raise our children, we usually tell them to be trustworthy. We teach the importance of honoring one's word and using willpower to do it. That's all well and good, but we also know something else about willpower. It can and will fail. All the participants in all the experiments I've discussed knew how they should act, yet cheat they often did, sometimes even surprising themselves in so doing. These failures in trustworthy behavior arise from that never-ending battle of intertemporal choice—choices favoring short- versus long-term rewards—that is fought on both the conscious and nonconscious levels of our minds. When we teach our kids and remind ourselves that we should be good, and that we should use willpower to do so, we're really only addressing one part of the equation. We're only arming our conscious minds to fight desires for expedience and exploitation. The result is that when the rational mind is biased or fatigued—when it can create a story that justifies less-than-honorable behavior or is too tired to care—what's left to rein in selfish impulses?

To find the answer we need to recognize that trustworthiness cannot be enhanced solely from the top down. What's also needed is a more effortless source of virtue that functions from the bottom up—one that doesn't require willpower but rather automatically flows forth. We've already seen such a force in action. We've seen feelings of gratitude make people willing to trust others they've never even met; we've seen feelings of shame make people condemn their own untrustworthy behavior when the ability to rationalize their actions was inhibited.

These moral emotions—or what Adam Smith termed moral sentiments—constitute an ancient mechanism that guided virtuous behavior by putting a brake on motivations for immediate self-interest. But at present, attention to these emotional phenomena has fallen somewhat out of favor in moral education. Many parents often resist allowing their children to experience feelings of shame and guilt, yet these states, along with similar ones of gratitude and humility, constitute necessary experiences for the building of emotional intelligence. Part of raising the next generation is helping them work through and grow from these experiences, not to avoid them. Learning how to manage and use these feelings will only enhance capacities to understand transgressions and to modify future behavior accordingly. Helicopter parenting to prevent any negative feelings from failures to be honest, competent, or trustworthy will habituate kids to an internal moral scale that is constantly tipped toward favoring their own immediate rewards. Although this strategy may lead our children to be happy in the short term, it will doom them to failure in the long one. The capacity to trust and be trustworthy is innate; its correct usage, however, comes through learning from success and failure.

If we're to better not only our individual welfare but also the greater good, we need to adopt a bifurcated approach to increasing trustworthiness. We need to embrace principles to which we aspire while also augmenting and leveraging the innate, intuitive mechanisms that increase our empathy for others. We need not only to think about trust, we need to feel it. And while this tactic certainly won't make the world a utopia, it will nudge it in that direction. Trust me.

ACKNOWLEDGMENTS

This book was made possible by the insights and support of many people. First and foremost, I will be forever grateful to my family, especially my wife, Amy, who acted as an indispensable editor, debater, and all-around sounding board, and who helped not only hone the logic of my ideas and arguments, but also their clarity. I have also had the good fortune of being able to work with many colleagues who are not only some of the sharpest minds on the planet, but also some of the warmest people you'd ever meet. In particular, my thinking benefited from conversations with Lisa Feldman Barrett, Bob Frank, David Pizarro, Cynthia Breazeal, Margaret Clark, Adam Russell, Piercarlo Valdesolo, Jolie Baumann, Leah Dickens, Jin Joo Lee, Lisa Williams, Monica Bartlett, and Paul Condon.

Many thanks also go to Caroline Sutton, my editor at Hudson Street Press, both for believing in the promise of this project and for helping me to organize, critically analyze, and communicate its content in an engaging way. It's also a project that would never have seen the light of day without the guidance and support of my agent

Jim Levine and the good folks at the Levine Greenberg Literary Agency. And finally, I'd like to thank the institutions and agencies that have financially supported my programs of research and have enabled me to conduct much of the work that I've described herein: Northeastern University, the National Science Foundation, and the National Institute of Mental Health. I hope they've found their trust in me to be well placed.

NOTES

PREFACE

xi **suspected of being the BTK killer:** News coverage of this unfortunate story can be found here: http://www.cbsnews.com/stories/ 2005/09/29/48hours/main890980.shtml.

CHAPTER 1: FUNDAMENTALS, FOIBLES, AND FIXES

2 **hurts more in absolute terms than gaining the same amount of** X **feels pleasurable:** Khaneman, D., and Tversky, A. (2000.) *Choices, Values, and Frames.* New York: Cambridge University Press.

5 **central dilemmas of human life:** Frank, R. H. (1988.) *Passions Within Reason: The Strategic Role of the Emotions.* New York: W. W. Norton.

10 **tit-for-tat:** Axelrod, R. (1984.) *The Evolution of Cooperation.* New York: Basic Books.

11 **first to recognize this problem:** May, R. M. (1976.) "Simple mathematical models with very complicated dynamics." *Nature* 327: 15–17.

12 **overtaking the cheating defectors:** Nowak, M. A., and Sigmund, K. (1989.) "Oscillations in the evolution of reciprocity." *Journal of Theoretical Biology* 137: 21–26.

Nowak, M. A., and Sigmund, K. (1992.) "Tit for tat in heterogeneous populations." *Nature* 355: 250–253.

Nowak, M. A., and Sigmund, K. (1993.) "A strategy of win-stay, lose-shift that outperforms tit-for-tat in the prisoner's dilemma game." *Nature* 364: 56–58.

14 **gains that when aggregated often outweigh a single loss:** Delton, A. W., Krasnow, M. M., Cosmides, L., and Tooby, J. (2011.) "Evolution of direct reciprocity under uncertainty can explain human generosity in one-shot encounters." *Proceedings of the National Academy of Sciences* 108(32): 13335–13340.

17 **latitude of everyone's moral behavior is greater than most expect:** For a review of the malleability of human character, see DeSteno, D., and Valdesolo, P. (2011.) *Out of Character: Surprising Truths About the Liar, Cheat, Sinner (and Saint) in All of Us.* New York: Crown Archetype.

20 **tracked the level of gratitude they were experiencing at the moment:** DeSteno, D., Bartlett, M., Baumann, J., Williams, L., and Dickens, L. (2010.) "Gratitude as moral sentiment: Emotion-guided cooperation in economic exchange." *Emotion* 10: 289–293.

20 **those who were stressed increased their rate of cooperation:** Von Dawans, B., Fischbacher, U., Kirschbaum, C., Fehr, E., and Heinrichs, M. (2012.) "The social dimension of stress reactivity: Acute stress increases prosocial behavior in humans." *Psychological Science* 23: 651–660.

21 **greatly increased the propensity to lie:** Gino, F., Norton, M., and Ariely, D. (2010.) "The counterfeit self: The deceptive costs of faking it." *Psychological Science* 21: 712–720.

22 **beneficiaries of others' resources when we need them:** Trivers, R. L. (1971.) "The evolution of reciprocal altruism." *The Quarterly Review of Biology* 46: 35–57.

26 **agreed to give them less funds to invest:** Righetti, F., and Finkenauer, C. (2011.) "If you are able to control yourself, I will trust you: The role of perceived self-control in interpersonal trust." *Journal of Personality and Social Psychology* 100: 874–886.

28 **shown to be virtually useless:** DePaulo, B. M., Lindsay, J. J., Malone, B. E., Muhlenbruck, L., Charlton, K., and Cooper, H. (2003.) "Cues to deception." *Psychological Bulletin* 129: 74–118. Barrett, L. F. (2012.) "Emotions are real." *Emotion* 12: 413–429.

28   possess no strong empirical validity: News coverage of the GAO
      report can be found here: http://www.homelandsecuritynews-
      wire.com/gao-tsas-behavior-screening-program-has-no-scientific-
      proof-it-works. And the report itself here: http://www.gao.gov/
      products/GAO-12-541T.

30   penchant for assessing status, power, and leadership potential:
      Tracy, J. L., Weidman, A. C., Cheng, J. T., and Martens, J. P. In
      Tugade, Shiota, and Kirby (eds.). (In press.) *Handbook of Positive
      Emotion*. New York: Guilford Press.

31   brain areas integrally involved in social computations: Contreras,
      J. M., Schirmer, J., Banaji, M. R., and Mitchell, J. P. (In press.)
      "Common brain regions with distinct patterns of neural responses
      during mentalizing about groups and individuals." *Journal of Cog-
      nitive Neuroscience*.

CHAPTER 2: BUILT TO TRUST?

41   provide intonations to human speech: Porges, S. W. (2007.) "The
      polyvagal perspective." *Biological Psychology* 74: 116–143.

42   heightened social skills: Calkins, S. D., and Keane, S. P. (2004.)
      "Cardiac vagal regulation across the preschool period: Stability, con-
      tinuity, and implications for childhood adjustment." *Developmental
      Psychobiology* 45: 101–112.

42   greater compassion for the suffering of others: Stellar, J., Manzio,
      V. M., Kraus, M. W., and Keltner, D. (2012.) "Class and compas-
      sion: Socioeconomic factors predict responses to suffering." *Emotion*
      12: 449–459.
      Kok, B. E., and Fredrickson, B. L. (2010.) "Upward spirals of the
      heart: Autonomic flexibility, as indexed by vagal tone, recipro-
      cally and prospectively predicts positive emotions and social con-
      nections." *Biological Psychology* 85: 432–436.
      Oveis, C., Cohen, A. B., Gruber, J., Shiota, M. N., Haidt, J., Keltner,
      D. (2009.) "Resting respiratory sinus arrhythmia is associated with
      tonic positive emotionality." *Emotion* 9: 265–270.

43   correctly identify the feelings of others: Côté, S., Kraus, M. W.,
      Cheng, B. H., Oveis, C., van der Löwe, I., Lian, H., and Keltner,

D. (2011.) "Social power facilitates the effect of prosocial orientation on empathic accuracy." *Journal of Personality and Social Psychology* 101: 217–232.

45   **out the window for these very reasons:** Gruber, J., Johnson, S. L.,
Oveis, C, and Keltner, D. (2008.) "Risk for mania and positive
emotional responding: Too much of a good thing?" *Emotion* 8: 23–33.

45   **than those possessing more moderate levels:** Kogan, A., Oveis,
C., Gruber, J., Mauss, I. B., Shallcross, A., Impett, E. A., van der
Löwe, I., Hui, B., Cheng, C., and Keltner, D. "Cardiac vagal tone
and prosociality: A test of Aristotle's principal of moderation." Manuscript under review.

47   **greater than 80 percent/20 percent:** Henrich, J., Boyd, R., Bowles,
S., Gintis, H., Fehr, E., Camerer, C., McElreath, R., Gurven, M.,
Hill, K., Barr, A. , Ensminger, J., Tracer, D., Marlow, F., Patton, J.,
Alvard, M., Gil-White, F., and Henrich, N. (2005.) "Economic
man in cross-cultural perspective: Ethnography and experiments
from 15 small-scale societies." *Behavioral and Brain Sciences* 28:
795–855.

49   **appear to get quite angry and indignant about it:** Brosnan, S. F.
(2011.) "A hypothesis of coevolution between cooperation and
responses to inequity." *Frontiers in Neuroscience* 5: 43.
Brosnan, S. F., and deWaal, F. B. M. (2003.) "Monkeys reject unequal pay." *Nature* 425: 297–299.

50   **don't reflexively become upset in the face of unequal treatment:**
Ibid.
Russon, A. E. (1998.) "The nature and evolution of intelligence in
orangutans (*Pongo pygmaeus*)." *Primates* 39: 485–503.

51   **trustworthy partners in future endeavors:** Brosnan, S. F., Talbot, C.,
Ahlgren, M., Lambeth, S. P., and Schapiro, S. J. (2010.) "Mechanisms underlying responses to inequitable outcomes in chimpanzees, *Pan troglodytes*." *Animal Behaviour* 79: 1229–1237.
de Waal, F. B. M., Leimgruber, K., and Greenberg, A. (2008.)
"Giving is self-rewarding for monkeys." *Proceedings of the National
Academy of Sciences* 105(36): 13685–13689.

51   **choose partners who have previously proved themselves:** Melis, A.
P., Hare, B., and Tomasello, M. (2006.) "Engineering cooperation

in chimpanzees: Tolerance constraints on cooperation." *Animal Behavior* 72: 275–286.

Melis, A. P., Hare, B., and Tomasello, M. (2006.) "Chimpanzees recruit the best collaborators." *Science* 311: 1297–1300.

54 **played a role in social bonding for both females and males:** Carter, C. S., Lederhendler, I. I., and Kirkpatrick, B. (1997.) *The Integrative Neurobiology of Affiliation, Annals of the New York Academy of Sciences* 807. Rereleased by Cambridge, MA: MIT Press, 1999.

54 **appeared in 2005:** Kosfeld, M., Heinrichs, M., Zak, P. J., Fischbacher, U., and Fehr, E. (2005.) "Oxytocin increases trust in humans." *Nature* 435: 673–676.

55 **even in the face of a betrayal:** Baumgartner, T., Heinrichs, M., Vonlanthen, A, Fischbacher, U, and Fehr, E. (2008.) "Oxytocin shapes the neural circuitry of trust and trust adaptation in humans." *Neuron* 58: 639–650.

56 **bias toward favoring you and yours over the interests of others:** de Dreu, C. K. W., Greer, L. L., Handgraaf, M. J. J., Shalvi, S., van Kleef, G. A., Baas, M., ten Velden, F. S., van Dijk, E., and Feith, S. W. W. (2010.) "The neuropeptide oxytocin regulates parochial altruism in intergroup conflict among humans." *Science* 328: 1408–1411.

56 **lead to greater ethnocentrism and bigotry:** de Dreu, C. K. W., Greer, L. L., Handgraaf, M. J. J., van Kleef, G. A., and Shalvi, S. (2011.) "Oxytocin promotes human ethnocentrism." *Proceedings of the National Academy of sciences* 108(4): 1262–1266.

57 **greater gloating in the face of the partner's misfortune:** Shamay-Tsoory, S. G., Fischer, M., Dvash, J., Harari, H., Perach-Bloom, N., Levkovitz, Y. (2009.) "Intranasal administration of oxytocin increases envy and schadenfreude (gloating)." *Biological Psychiatry* 66: 864–870.

CHAPTER 3: IN THE BEGINNING

65 **a ball should land below where it was dropped:** Hood, B. (1995.) "Gravity rules for 2- to 4-year-olds." *Cognitive Development* 10: 577–598.

66   **ignoring the data at hand:** Bascandziev, I., and Harris, P. L. (2010.) "The role of testimony in young children's solution of a gravity-driven invisible displacement task." *British Journal of Developmental Psychology* 23: 587–607.
Hood, "Gravity rules," 1995.

66   **stopped making errors when an adult told them how it worked:** Bascandziev and Harris, "The role of testimony," 2010.

68   **evaluating schools that was drawing a lot of attention:** Ripley's article can be found here: http://www.theatlantic.com/magazine/archive/2010/01/what-makes-a-great-teacher/307841/.

71   **over those provided by the unfamiliar teacher:** Corriveau, K. H., and Harris, P. L. (2009.) "Choosing your informant: Weighing familiarity and recent accuracy." *Developmental Science* 12: 426–437.

73   **from a stranger as from their own parent:** Corriveau, K. H., Harris, P. L., et al. (2009.) "Young children's trust in their mother's claims: Longitudinal links with attachment security in infancy." *Child Development* 80: 750–761.

74   **they had earlier deemed competent:** Ibid.

74   **as opposed to an untrustworthy one:** Sabbagh, M. A., and Shafman, D. (2009.) "How children block learning from ignorant speakers." *Cognition* 112: 415–422.

75   **turned to the stranger, whose competence they could trust:** Corriveau and Harris, "Choosing your informant," 2009.

76   **share some level of affiliation:** Kinzler, K. D., Corriveau, K. H., and Harris, P. L. (2010.) "Children's selective trust in native-accented speakers." *Developmental Science* 14: 106–111.

79   **instinct to support and cooperate with others is already active:** Warneken, F., and Tomasello, M. (2006.) "Altruistic helping in human infants and young chimpanzees." *Science* 311: 1301–1303.

81   **At five years of age, the same pattern emerges:** Kanngiesser, P., and Warneken, F. (2012) "Young children consider merit when sharing resources with others." *PLoS ONE* 7(8): 1–5.

81   **(and thus aware of the distribution of rewards):** Blake, P. R., and McAuliffe, K. (2011.) "'I had so much it didn't seem fair': Eight-year-olds reject two forms of inequity." *Cognition*, doi:10.1016/j.cognition.2011.04.006.

Shaw, A., and Olson, K. R. (2012.) "Children discard a resource to avoid inequity." *Journal of Experimental Psychology: General* 141: 382–395.

81   **if they believe others won't know about it:** Leimgruber, K. L., Shaw, A., Santos, L. R., and Olson, K. R. (2012) "Young children are more generous when others are aware of their actions." *PLoS ONE* 7(10): e48292.

85   **who proved unsupportive of a friend in need:** Hamlin, J., Wynn, K., and Bloom , P. (2007.) "Social judgment by preverbal infants." *Nature* 450: 557–559.

Chapter 4: The Heart of the Matter

97   **the opposite color ink more than 90 percent of the time:** Clark, M. S. (1984.) "Record keeping in two types of relationships." *Journal of Personality and Social Psychology* 47: 549–557.

101   **the objective amount of accommodations made:** Shallcross, S., and Simpson, J. A. (2012.) "Trust and responsiveness in strain-test situations: A dyadic perspective." *Journal of Personality and Social Psychology* 102: 1031–1044.

102   **as opposed to situational forces:** Jones, E. E., and Harris, V. A. (1967.) "The attribution of attitudes." *Journal of Experimental Social Psychology* 3: 1–24.

103   **into molehills, both in the present and in memory:** Campbell, L., Simpson, J. A., Boldry, J., and Harris, R. (2010.) "Trust, variability in relationship evaluations, and relationship processes." *Journal of Personality and Social Psychology* 99: 14–31.

109   **distanced themselves from partners:** Murray, S., Lupien, S. P, and Seery, M. D. (2012.) "Resilience in the face of romantic rejection: The automatic impulse to trust." *Journal of Experimental Social Psychology* 48: 845–854.

111   **is indicative of pathology:** Freud, S. (1922.) "Some neurotic mechanisms in jealousy, paranoia and homosexuality." Reprinted (1953–1974) in the *Standard Edition of the Complete Psychological Works of Sigmund Freud* (trans. and ed. J. Strachey), vol. XVIII. London: Hogarth Press.

113   **sex outside their primary relationship is just a different form of recreation:** Buunk, B. P. (1991.) "Jealousy in close relationships: An exchange-theoretical perspective." In P. Salovey (ed.), *The Psychology of Jealousy and Envy* (pp. 148–177). New York: Guilford Press.

115   **diminished doubts about their commitment to the relationship:** Murray, S. L., Gomillion, S., Holmes, J. G., Harris, B., and Lamarche, V. (2013.) "The dynamics of relationship promotion: Controlling the automatic inclination to trust." *Journal of Personality and Social Psychology* 104: 305–334.

117   **jealousy was tracking the odds of a future betrayal:** DeSteno, D., and Salovey, P. (1996.) "Jealousy and the characteristics of one's rival: A self-evaluation maintenance perspective." *Personality and Social Psychology Bulletin* 22: 920–932.

119   **more jealousy equaled more hot sauce:** DeSteno, D., Valdesolo, P., and Bartlett, M. Y. (2006.) "Jealousy and the threatened self: Getting to the heart of the green-eyed monster." *Journal of Personality and Social Psychology* 91: 626–641.

CHAPTER 5: POWER AND MONEY

128   **almost 50 percent of drivers broke the law to put their own needs first:** Piff, P. K., Stancato, D. M, Côté, S., Mendoza-Denton, R., and Keltner, D. (2012.) "Higher social class predicts increased unethical behavior." *Proceedings of the National Academy of Sciences* 109: 4086–4091.

129   **the job-seeker placed in them as an honest supervisor:** Ibid.

130   **surreptitiously recorded the totals of the actual rolls:** Ibid.

130   **they would be more likely to engage in these behaviors themselves:** Ibid.

131   **associated with a decreased willingness to trust others:** Piff, P. K., Kraus, M. W., Côté, S., Cheng, B. H., and Keltner, D. (2010.) "Having less, giving more: The influence of social class on prosocial behavior." *Journal of Personality and Social Psychology* 99: 771–784.

135   **than did participants who reported the opposite:** Piff et al., "Higher social class predicts," 2012.

135   **a behavior anathema to trustworthiness:** Lammers, J., Stapel, D. A., and Galinsky, A. D. (2010.) "Power increases hypocrisy,

moralizing in reasoning, immorality in behavior." *Psychological Science* 21: 737–744.

136 **the people who actually were telling the truth:** Carney, D. (2010.) "Powerful people are better liars." *Harvard Business Review* (May 1).

139 **keep more of the money than they deserved:** Gino, F., and Pierce, L. (2009.) "The abundance effect: Unethical behavior in the presence of wealth." *Organizational Behavior and Human Decision Processes* 109: 142–155.

140 **reject others who display a need for help or cooperation:** Vohs, Kathleen D., Nicole L. Mead, and Miranda R. Goode (2006.) "The psychological consequences of money." *Science* 314: 1154–1156.

141 **chose to work on their own significantly more often:** Ibid.

143 **tend to come out ahead in the long run:** Dreber, A., Rand, D. G., Fudenberg, D., and Nowak, M. A. (2008.) "Winners don't punish." *Nature* 452: 348–351.

145 **help you "fake it till you make it":** Amy Cuddy's TED talk summarizing the findings and approach can be found here: http://www.ted.com/talks/amy_cuddy_your_body_language_shapes_who_you_are.html.

CHAPTER 6: CAN I TRUST YOU?

147 **that's not much better than flipping a coin:** DePaulo, B. M., Lindsay, J. J., Malone, B. E., Muhlenbruck, L., Charlton, K., and Cooper, H. (2003.) "Cues to deception." *Psychological Bulletin* 129: 74–118.

153 **accuracy in reading nonverbal cues nosedives:** Aviezer, H., Trope, Y., and Todorov, A. (2012.) "Body cues, not facial expressions, discriminate between intense positive and negative emotions." *Science* 338: 1225–1229.
Barrett, L. F. (2012.) "Emotions are real." *Emotion* 12: 413–429.

155 **it makes you feel afraid:** Weisbuch, M, and Ambady, N. (2008.) "Affective divergence: Automatic responses to others' emotions depend on group membership." *Journal of Personality and Social Psychology* 95: 1063–1079.

161 **increased by 37 percent:** DeSteno, D., Breazeal, C., Frank, R. H., Pizarro, D., Baumann, J., Dickens, L., and Lee, J. (2012.) "Detecting

the trustworthiness of novel partners in economic exchange." *Psychological Science* 23: 1549–1556.

169   **the number they agreed to exchange with her:** Ibid.

171   **decreased gazing at others during interactions:** Carney, D. R., Cuddy, A. J. C., and Yap, A. J. (2010.) "Power posing: Brief nonverbal displays cause changes in neuroendocrine levels and risk tolerance." *Psychological Science* 21: 1363–1368.
Tracy, J. L., and Matsumoto, D. (2008.) "The spontaneous expression of pride and shame: Evidence for biologically innate nonverbal displays." *Proceedings of the National Academy of Sciences* 105: 11655–11660.
Dovidio, J. F., and Ellyson, S. L. (1982.) "Decoding visual dominance behavior: Attributions of power based on the relative percentages of looking while speaking and looking while listening." *Social Psychology Quarterly* 45: 106–113.

171   **skills they otherwise might not seek:** Williams, L. A., and DeSteno, D. (2008.) "Pride and perseverance: The motivational role of pride." *Journal of Personality and Social Psychology* 94: 1007–1017.

174   **they reported liking the leaders:** Williams, L. A., and DeSteno, D. (2009.) "Pride: Adaptive social emotion or seventh sin?" *Psychological Science* 20: 284–288.

176   **"see" trustworthy and deceitful intentions in still images of others:** Todorov, A. (2008.) "Evaluating faces on trustworthiness: An extension of systems for recognition of emotions signaling approach/ avoidance behaviors." In A. Kingstone and M. Miller (eds.), *The Year in Cognitive Neuroscience 2008*, *Annals of the New York Academy of Sciences* 1124: 208–224.

176   **they're no better than flipping a coin:** Rule, N. O., Krendl, A. C., Ivcevic, Z., and Ambady, N. (2013.) "Accuracy and consensus in judgments of trustworthiness from faces: Behavioral and neural correlates." *Journal of Personality and Social Psychology* 104: 409–426.

178   **but also as fairly low in competence:** Todorov, A., Said, C. P., Engell, A. D., and Oosterhof, N. N. (2008.) "Understanding evaluation of faces on social dimensions." *Trends in Cognitive Sciences* 12: 455–460.

Zebrowitz, Leslie A., with McDonald, S. "The impact of litigants' babyfacedness and attractiveness on adjudications in small claims courts." *Law and Human Behavior* 15: 603–623.

179 **won their respective elections about 70 percent of the time:** Todorov, A., Mandisodza, A. N., Goren, A., and Hall, C. C. (2005.) "Inferences of competence from faces predict election outcomes." *Science* 308: 1623–1626.

179 **people who resemble news anchors and game show hosts:** Sabato's quote can be found here: http://news.nationalgeographic.com/news/2005/06/0609_050609_elections_2.html.

180 **confirmed to be a failure: report is here:** http://www.gao.gov/products/GAO-12-541T.

182 **an accuracy much greater than that shown by human participants:** Lee, J. J., Knox, B., Baumann, J., Breazeal, C., and DeSteno, D. (2013.) "Computationally modeling interpersonal trust." Manuscript under review.

CHAPTER 7: CYBERTRUST

187 **rather than by the human aide:** Lyons, J. B., and Stokes, C. K. (2012.) "Human-human reliance in the context of automation." *Human Factors* 54: 112–121.

189 **from remote locations by utilizing avatars:** Bailenson, J. N., and Blascovich, J. (2011.) "Virtual reality and social networks will be a powerful combination: Avatars will make social networks seductive." *IEEE Spectrum* (June).

190 **rules of social interaction—even the nonconscious ones— continued to apply:** Yee, N., Bailenson, J. N., Urbanek, M., Chang, F., and Merget, D. (2007.) "The unbearable likeness of being digital: The persistence of nonverbal social norms in online virtual environments." *Cyberpsychology and Behavior* 10: 115–121.

192 **you'll feel more bonded to her:** Valdesolo, P., and DeSteno, D. (2011.) "Synchrony and the social tuning of compassion." *Emotion* 11: 262–266.

193 **trusting the candidate in whom they literally saw themselves:** Bailenson, J. N., Iyengar, S., Yee, N., and Collins, N. (2008.) "Facial

similarity between voters and candidates causes influence." *Public Opinion Quarterly* 72: 935–961.

194   **the realism of avatars significantly improves their power to persuade humans:** Guadagno, R. E., Blascovich, J., Bailenson, J. N., & McCall, C. (2007.) "Virtual humans and persuasion: The effects of agency and behavioral realism." *Media Psychology* 10: 1–22.

195   **also when playing back in the real one:** Yee, N., Bailenson, J. N., and Ducheneaut, N. (2009.) "The proteus effect: Implications of transformed digital self-representation on online and offline behavior." *Communication Research* 36: 285–312.

197   **than Internet users who don't regularly use Facebook:** Pew report can be found here: http://www.pewinternet.org/Reports/2011/Technology-and-social-networks.aspx.

202   **over 80 percent in some poor, urban populations:** Bickmore, T., Pfeifer, L., and Paasche-Orlow, M. (2009.) "Using computer agents to explain medical documents to patients with low health literacy." *Patient Education and Counseling* 75: 315–320.

203   **it seemed to boil down to demeanor:** Ibid.

Chapter 8: Can You Trust Yourself?

212   **90 percent of them did not flip the coin:** Valdesolo, P., and DeSteno, D. (2008.) "The duality of virtue: Deconstructing the moral hypocrite." *Journal of Experimental Social Psychology* 44: 1334–1338.
Valdesolo, P., and DeSteno, D. (2007.) "Moral hypocrisy: Social groups and the flexibility of virtue." *Psychological Science* 18: 689–690.

212   **believed that *their* behaviors were acceptable, even fair:** Ibid.
Lammers, J., Stapel, D. A., and Galinsky, A. D. (2010.) "Power increases hypocrisy, moralizing in reasoning, immorality in behavior." *Psychological Science* 21: 737–744.

214   **hampered by the ways we construct them:** Gilbert, D. T., and Wilson, T. D. (2007.) "Prospection: Experiencing the future." *Science* 317: 1351–1354.

215   **that they'd enjoy eating it for breakfast:** Gilbert, D. T., Gill, M. J., and Wilson, T. D. (2002.) "The future is now: Temporal correction

in affective forecasting," *Organizational Behavior and Human Decision Processes* 88: 430–444.

219   **(182 grams on average compared with 72 grams):** Vohs, K. D. and Heatherton, T. F. (2000.) "Self-regulation failure: A resource-depletion approach." *Psychological Science* 11: 249–254.

220   **spent four times more:** Vohs, K. D., and Faber, R. J. (2007.) "Spent resources: Self-regulatory resource availability affects impulse buying." *Journal of Consumer Research* 33: 537–547.

221   **to make reality fit one's emotions:** Rand, A. (1982.) *Philosophy: Who Needs It?* Indianapolis, IN: Bobbs-Merrill.

222   **didn't feel nearly as much regret about it:** Gilbert, D. T., More-wedge, C. K., Risen, J. L., and Wilson, T. D. (2004.) "Looking forward to looking backward: The misprediction of regret." *Psychological Science* 15: 346–350.

224   **What we found proved our point:** Valdesolo and DeSteno, "The duality of virtue," 2008.

225   **that they rationally know are wrong, outrageous":** Spitzer's interview can be found here: http://www.thedailybeast.com/news-week/2009/04/17/spitzer-in-exile.html.

CHAPTER 9: TRUST OR DUST?

235   **bounced back from devastation the quickest:** The press release and link to the study can be found here: http://www.apnorc.org/news-media/Pages/News+Media/friends-kin-key-to-sandy-survival.aspx.

INDEX

Printed in the United States
by Baker & Taylor Publisher Services